50% OFF
Online NMLS Prep Course!

By Mometrix

Dear Customer,

We consider it an honor and a privilege that you chose our NMLS Study Guide. As a way of showing our appreciation and to help us better serve you, we are offering **50% off our online NMLS Prep Course**. Many NMLS courses are needlessly expensive and don't deliver enough value. With our course, you get access to the best NMLS prep material, and **you only pay half price**.

We have structured our online course to perfectly complement your printed study guide. The NMLS Prep Course contains **in-depth lessons** that cover all the most important topics, over **950 practice questions** to ensure you feel prepared, and more than **300 digital flashcards**, so you can study while you're on the go.

Online NMLS Prep Course

Topics Included:

- Federal Mortgage-Related Laws
  - Real Estate Settlement Procedures Act (RESPA)
- Uniform State Content
  - Regulatory Agencies
- General Mortgage Knowledge
  - Qualified and Nonqualified Mortgage Programs
- Mortgage Loan Origination Activities
  - Loan Inquiry and Application Process Requirements
- Ethics
  - Ethical Issues

Course Features:

- NMLS Study Guide
  - Get content that complements our best-selling study guide.
- Full-Length Practice Tests
  - With over 950 practice questions, you can test yourself again and again.
- Mobile Friendly
  - If you need to study on the go, the course is easily accessible from your mobile device.
- NMLS Flashcards
  - Our course includes a flashcard mode with over 300 content cards to help you study.

To receive this discount, visit us at mometrix.com/university/nmls or simply scan this QR code with your smartphone. At the checkout page, enter the discount code: **nmls50off**

If you have any questions or concerns, please contact us at support@mometrix.com.

TEST PREPARATION

FREE Study Skills Videos/DVD Offer

Dear Customer,

Thank you for your purchase from Mometrix! We consider it an honor and a privilege that you have purchased our product and we want to ensure your satisfaction.

As part of our ongoing effort to meet the needs of test takers, we have developed a set of Study Skills Videos that we would like to give you for <u>FREE</u>. These videos cover our *best practices* for getting ready for your exam, from how to use our study materials to how to best prepare for the day of the test.

All that we ask is that you email us with feedback that would describe your experience so far with our product. Good, bad, or indifferent, we want to know what you think!

To get your FREE Study Skills Videos, you can use the **QR code** below, or send us an **email** at <u>studyvideos@mometrix.com</u> with *FREE VIDEOS* in the subject line and the following information in the body of the email:

- The name of the product you purchased.
- Your product rating on a scale of 1-5, with 5 being the highest rating.
- Your feedback. It can be long, short, or anything in between. We just want to know your impressions and experience so far with our product. (Good feedback might include how our study material met your needs and ways we might be able to make it even better. You could highlight features that you found helpful or features that you think we should add.)

If you have any questions or concerns, please don't hesitate to contact me directly.

Thanks again!

Sincerely,

Jay Willis
Vice President
<u>jay.willis@mometrix.com</u>
1-800-673-8175

NMLS

Study Guide 2024-2025

5 **Full-Length MLO Practice Exams**

SAFE Mortgage Loan Originator
Test Prep Secrets Book
with Detailed Answer
Explanations

3rd Edition

Written and edited by Mometrix Test Prep

Printed in the United States of America

This paper meets the requirements of ANSI/NISO Z39.48-1992 (Permanence of Paper).

Mometrix offers volume discount pricing to institutions. For more information or a price quote, please contact our sales department at sales@mometrix.com or 888-248-1219.

Mometrix Media LLC is not affiliated with or endorsed by any official testing organization. All organizational and test names are trademarks of their respective owners.

Paperback
ISBN 13: 978-1-5167-2569-4

DEAR FUTURE EXAM SUCCESS STORY

First of all, **THANK YOU** for purchasing Mometrix study materials!

Second, congratulations! You are one of the few determined test-takers who are committed to doing whatever it takes to excel on your exam. **You have come to the right place.** We developed these study materials with one goal in mind: to deliver you the information you need in a format that's concise and easy to use.

In addition to optimizing your guide for the content of the test, we've outlined our recommended steps for breaking down the preparation process into small, attainable goals so you can make sure you stay on track.

We've also analyzed the entire test-taking process, identifying the most common pitfalls and showing how you can overcome them and be ready for any curveball the test throws you.

Standardized testing is one of the biggest obstacles on your road to success, which only increases the importance of doing well in the high-pressure, high-stakes environment of test day. Your results on this test could have a significant impact on your future, and this guide provides the information and practical advice to help you achieve your full potential on test day.

Your success is our success

We would love to hear from you! If you would like to share the story of your exam success or if you have any questions or comments in regard to our products, please contact us at **800-673-8175** or **support@mometrix.com**.

Thanks again for your business and we wish you continued success!

Sincerely,
The Mometrix Test Preparation Team

> **Need more help? Check out our flashcards at:**
> **http://mometrixflashcards.com/NMLS**

TABLE OF CONTENTS

Introduction

Thank you for purchasing this resource! You have made the choice to prepare yourself for a test that could have a huge impact on your future, and this guide is designed to help you be fully ready for test day. Obviously, it's important to have a solid understanding of the test material, but you also need to be prepared for the unique environment and stressors of the test, so that you can perform to the best of your abilities.

For this purpose, the first section that appears in this guide is the **Secret Keys**. We've devoted countless hours to meticulously researching what works and what doesn't, and we've boiled down our findings to the five most impactful steps you can take to improve your performance on the test. We start at the beginning with study planning and move through the preparation process, all the way to the testing strategies that will help you get the most out of what you know when you're finally sitting in front of the test.

We recommend that you start preparing for your test as far in advance as possible. However, if you've bought this guide as a last-minute study resource and only have a few days before your test, we recommend that you skip over the first two Secret Keys since they address a long-term study plan.

If you struggle with **test anxiety**, we strongly encourage you to check out our recommendations for how you can overcome it. Test anxiety is a formidable foe, but it can be beaten, and we want to make sure you have the tools you need to defeat it.

1

Secret Key #1 – Plan Big, Study Small

There's a lot riding on your performance. If you want to ace this test, you're going to need to keep your skills sharp and the material fresh in your mind. You need a plan that lets you review everything you need to know while still fitting in your schedule. We'll break this strategy down into three categories.

Information Organization

Start with the information you already have: the official test outline. From this, you can make a complete list of all the concepts you need to cover before the test. Organize these concepts into groups that can be studied together, and create a list of any related vocabulary you need to learn so you can brush up on any difficult terms. You'll want to keep this vocabulary list handy once you actually start studying since you may need to add to it along the way.

Time Management

Once you have your set of study concepts, decide how to spread them out over the time you have left before the test. Break your study plan into small, clear goals so you have a manageable task for each day and know exactly what you're doing. Then just focus on one small step at a time. When you manage your time this way, you don't need to spend hours at a time studying. Studying a small block of content for a short period each day helps you retain information better and avoid stressing over how much you have left to do. You can relax knowing that you have a plan to cover everything in time. In order for this strategy to be effective though, you have to start studying early and stick to your schedule. Avoid the exhaustion and futility that comes from last-minute cramming!

Study Environment

The environment you study in has a big impact on your learning. Studying in a coffee shop, while probably more enjoyable, is not likely to be as fruitful as studying in a quiet room. It's important to keep distractions to a minimum. You're only planning to study for a short block of time, so make the most of it. Don't pause to check your phone or get up to find a snack. It's also important to **avoid multitasking**. Research has consistently shown that multitasking will make your studying dramatically less effective. Your study area should also be comfortable and well-lit so you don't have the distraction of straining your eyes or sitting on an uncomfortable chair.

 The time of day you study is also important. You want to be rested and alert. Don't wait until just before bedtime. Study when you'll be most likely to comprehend and remember. Even better, if you know what time of day your test will be, set that time aside for study. That way your brain will be used to working on that subject at that specific time and you'll have a better chance of recalling information.

Finally, it can be helpful to team up with others who are studying for the same test. Your actual studying should be done in as isolated an environment as possible, but the work of organizing the information and setting up the study plan can be divided up. In between study sessions, you can discuss with your teammates the concepts that you're all studying and quiz each other on the details. Just be sure that your teammates are as serious about the test as you are. If you find that your study time is being replaced with social time, you might need to find a new team.

Secret Key #2 – Make Your Studying Count

You're devoting a lot of time and effort to preparing for this test, so you want to be absolutely certain it will pay off. This means doing more than just reading the content and hoping you can remember it on test day. It's important to make every minute of study count. There are two main areas you can focus on to make your studying count.

Retention

It doesn't matter how much time you study if you can't remember the material. You need to make sure you are retaining the concepts. To check your retention of the information you're learning, try recalling it at later times with minimal prompting. Try carrying around flashcards and glance at one or two from time to time or ask a friend who's also studying for the test to quiz you.

To enhance your retention, look for ways to put the information into practice so that you can apply it rather than simply recalling it. If you're using the information in practical ways, it will be much easier to remember. Similarly, it helps to solidify a concept in your mind if you're not only reading it to yourself but also explaining it to someone else. Ask a friend to let you teach them about a concept you're a little shaky on (or speak aloud to an imaginary audience if necessary). As you try to summarize, define, give examples, and answer your friend's questions, you'll understand the concepts better and they will stay with you longer. Finally, step back for a big picture view and ask yourself how each piece of information fits with the whole subject. When you link the different concepts together and see them working together as a whole, it's easier to remember the individual components.

Finally, practice showing your work on any multi-step problems, even if you're just studying. Writing out each step you take to solve a problem will help solidify the process in your mind, and you'll be more likely to remember it during the test.

Modality

Modality simply refers to the means or method by which you study. Choosing a study modality that fits your own individual learning style is crucial. No two people learn best in exactly the same way, so it's important to know your strengths and use them to your advantage.

For example, if you learn best by visualization, focus on visualizing a concept in your mind and draw an image or a diagram. Try color-coding your notes, illustrating them, or creating symbols that will trigger your mind to recall a learned concept. If you learn best by hearing or discussing information, find a study partner who learns the same way or read aloud to yourself. Think about how to put the information in your own words. Imagine that you are giving a lecture on the topic and record yourself so you can listen to it later.

For any learning style, flashcards can be helpful. Organize the information so you can take advantage of spare moments to review. Underline key words or phrases. Use different colors for different categories. Mnemonic devices (such as creating a short list in which every item starts with the same letter) can also help with retention. Find what works best for you and use it to store the information in your mind most effectively and easily.

3

Secret Key #3 – Practice the Right Way

Your success on test day depends not only on how many hours you put into preparing, but also on whether you prepared the right way. It's good to check along the way to see if your studying is paying off. One of the most effective ways to do this is by taking practice tests to evaluate your progress. Practice tests are useful because they show exactly where you need to improve. Every time you take a practice test, pay special attention to these three groups of questions:

- The questions you got wrong
- The questions you had to guess on, even if you guessed right
- The questions you found difficult or slow to work through

This will show you exactly what your weak areas are, and where you need to devote more study time. Ask yourself why each of these questions gave you trouble. Was it because you didn't understand the material? Was it because you didn't remember the vocabulary? Do you need more repetitions on this type of question to build speed and confidence? Dig into those questions and figure out how you can strengthen your weak areas as you go back to review the material.

 Additionally, many practice tests have a section explaining the answer choices. It can be tempting to read the explanation and think that you now have a good understanding of the concept. However, an explanation likely only covers part of the question's broader context. Even if the explanation makes perfect sense, **go back and investigate** every concept related to the question until you're positive you have a thorough understanding.

As you go along, keep in mind that the practice test is just that: practice. Memorizing these questions and answers will not be very helpful on the actual test because it is unlikely to have any of the same exact questions. If you only know the right answers to the sample questions, you won't be prepared for the real thing. **Study the concepts** until you understand them fully, and then you'll be able to answer any question that shows up on the test.

It's important to wait on the practice tests until you're ready. If you take a test on your first day of study, you may be overwhelmed by the amount of material covered and how much you need to learn. Work up to it gradually.

On test day, you'll need to be prepared for answering questions, managing your time, and using the test-taking strategies you've learned. It's a lot to balance, like a mental marathon that will have a big impact on your future. Like training for a marathon, you'll need to start slowly and work your way up. When test day arrives, you'll be ready.

Start with the strategies you've read in the first two Secret Keys—plan your course and study in the way that works best for you. If you have time, consider using multiple study resources to get different approaches to the same concepts. It can be helpful to see difficult concepts from more than one angle. Then find a good source for practice tests. Many times, the test website will suggest potential study resources or provide sample tests.

Practice Test Strategy

If you're able to find at least three practice tests, we recommend this strategy:

UNTIMED AND OPEN-BOOK PRACTICE

Take the first test with no time constraints and with your notes and study guide handy. Take your time and focus on applying the strategies you've learned.

TIMED AND OPEN-BOOK PRACTICE

Take the second practice test open-book as well, but set a timer and practice pacing yourself to finish in time.

TIMED AND CLOSED-BOOK PRACTICE

Take any other practice tests as if it were test day. Set a timer and put away your study materials. Sit at a table or desk in a quiet room, imagine yourself at the testing center, and answer questions as quickly and accurately as possible.

Keep repeating timed and closed-book tests on a regular basis until you run out of practice tests or it's time for the actual test. Your mind will be ready for the schedule and stress of test day, and you'll be able to focus on recalling the material you've learned.

Secret Key #4 – Pace Yourself

Once you're fully prepared for the material on the test, your biggest challenge on test day will be managing your time. Just knowing that the clock is ticking can make you panic even if you have plenty of time left. Work on pacing yourself so you can build confidence against the time constraints of the exam. Pacing is a difficult skill to master, especially in a high-pressure environment, so **practice is vital**.

Set time expectations for your pace based on how much time is available. For example, if a section has 60 questions and the time limit is 30 minutes, you know you have to average 30 seconds or less per question in order to answer them all. Although 30 seconds is the hard limit, set 25 seconds per question as your goal, so you reserve extra time to spend on harder questions. When you budget extra time for the harder questions, you no longer have any reason to stress when those questions take longer to answer.

Don't let this time expectation distract you from working through the test at a calm, steady pace, but keep it in mind so you don't spend too much time on any one question. Recognize that taking extra time on one question you don't understand may keep you from answering two that you do understand later in the test. If your time limit for a question is up and you're still not sure of the answer, mark it and move on, and come back to it later if the time and the test format allow. If the testing format doesn't allow you to return to earlier questions, just make an educated guess; then put it out of your mind and move on.

On the easier questions, be careful not to rush. It may seem wise to hurry through them so you have more time for the challenging ones, but it's not worth missing one if you know the concept and just didn't take the time to read the question fully. Work efficiently but make sure you understand the question and have looked at all of the answer choices, since more than one may seem right at first.

Even if you're paying attention to the time, you may find yourself a little behind at some point. You should speed up to get back on track, but do so wisely. Don't panic; just take a few seconds less on each question until you're caught up. Don't guess without thinking, but do look through the answer choices and eliminate any you know are wrong. If you can get down to two choices, it is often worthwhile to guess from those. Once you've chosen an answer, move on and don't dwell on any that you skipped or had to hurry through. If a question was taking too long, chances are it was one of the harder ones, so you weren't as likely to get it right anyway.

On the other hand, if you find yourself getting ahead of schedule, it may be beneficial to slow down a little. The more quickly you work, the more likely you are to make a careless mistake that will affect your score. You've budgeted time for each question, so don't be afraid to spend that time. Practice an efficient but careful pace to get the most out of the time you have.

Secret Key #5 – Have a Plan for Guessing

When you're taking the test, you may find yourself stuck on a question. Some of the answer choices seem better than others, but you don't see the one answer choice that is obviously correct. What do you do?

The scenario described above is very common, yet most test takers have not effectively prepared for it. Developing and practicing a plan for guessing may be one of the single most effective uses of your time as you get ready for the exam.

In developing your plan for guessing, there are three questions to address:

- When should you start the guessing process?
- How should you narrow down the choices?
- Which answer should you choose?

When to Start the Guessing Process

Unless your plan for guessing is to select C every time (which, despite its merits, is not what we recommend), you need to leave yourself enough time to apply your answer elimination strategies. Since you have a limited amount of time for each question, that means that if you're going to give yourself the best shot at guessing correctly, you have to decide quickly whether or not you will guess.

Of course, the best-case scenario is that you don't have to guess at all, so first, see if you can answer the question based on your knowledge of the subject and basic reasoning skills. Focus on the key words in the question and try to jog your memory of related topics. Give yourself a chance to bring the knowledge to mind, but once you realize that you don't have (or you can't access) the knowledge you need to answer the question, it's time to start the guessing process.

It's almost always better to start the guessing process too early than too late. It only takes a few seconds to remember something and answer the question from knowledge. Carefully eliminating wrong answer choices takes longer. Plus, going through the process of eliminating answer choices can actually help jog your memory.

Summary: Start the guessing process as soon as you decide that you can't answer the question based on your knowledge.

7

How to Narrow Down the Choices

The next chapter in this book (**Test-Taking Strategies**) includes a wide range of strategies for how to approach questions and how to look for answer choices to eliminate. You will definitely want to read those carefully, practice them, and figure out which ones work best for you. Here though, we're going to address a mindset rather than a particular strategy.

Your odds of guessing an answer correctly depend on how many options you are choosing from.

Number of options left	5	4	3	2	1
Odds of guessing correctly	20%	25%	33%	50%	100%

You can see from this chart just how valuable it is to be able to eliminate incorrect answers and make an educated guess, but there are two things that many test takers do that cause them to miss out on the benefits of guessing:

- Accidentally eliminating the correct answer
- Selecting an answer based on an impression

We'll look at the first one here, and the second one in the next section.

To avoid accidentally eliminating the correct answer, we recommend a thought exercise called **the $5 challenge**. In this challenge, you only eliminate an answer choice from contention if you are willing to bet $5 on it being wrong. Why $5? Five dollars is a small but not insignificant amount of money. It's an amount you could afford to lose but wouldn't want to throw away. And while losing $5 once might not hurt too much, doing it twenty times will set you back $100. In the same way, each small decision you make—eliminating a choice here, guessing on a question there—won't by itself impact your score very much, but when you put them all together, they can make a big difference. By holding each answer choice elimination decision to a higher standard, you can reduce the risk of accidentally eliminating the correct answer.

The $5 challenge can also be applied in a positive sense: If you are willing to bet $5 that an answer choice *is* correct, go ahead and mark it as correct.

Summary: Only eliminate an answer choice if you are willing to bet $5 that it is wrong.

Which Answer to Choose

You're taking the test. You've run into a hard question and decided you'll have to guess. You've eliminated all the answer choices you're willing to bet $5 on. Now you have to pick an answer. Why do we even need to talk about this? Why can't you just pick whichever one you feel like when the time comes?

The answer to these questions is that if you don't come into the test with a plan, you'll rely on your impression to select an answer choice, and if you do that, you risk falling into a trap. The test writers know that everyone who takes their test will be guessing on some of the questions, so they intentionally write wrong answer choices to seem plausible. You still have to pick an answer though, and if the wrong answer choices are designed to look right, how can you ever be sure that you're not falling for their trap? The best solution we've found to this dilemma is to take the decision out of your hands entirely. Here is the process we recommend:

Once you've eliminated any choices that you are confident (willing to bet $5) are wrong, select the first remaining choice as your answer.

Whether you choose to select the first remaining choice, the second, or the last, the important thing is that you use some preselected standard. Using this approach guarantees that you will not be enticed into selecting an answer choice that looks right, because you are not basing your decision on how the answer choices look.

This is not meant to make you question your knowledge. Instead, it is to help you recognize the difference between your knowledge and your impressions. There's a huge difference between thinking an answer is right because of what you know, and thinking an answer is right because it looks or sounds like it should be right.

Summary: To ensure that your selection is appropriately random, make a predetermined selection from among all answer choices you have not eliminated.

Test-Taking Strategies

This section contains a list of test-taking strategies that you may find helpful as you work through the test. By taking what you know and applying logical thought, you can maximize your chances of answering any question correctly!

It is very important to realize that every question is different and every person is different: no single strategy will work on every question, and no single strategy will work for every person. That's why we've included all of them here, so you can try them out and determine which ones work best for different types of questions and which ones work best for you.

Question Strategies

✓ READ CAREFULLY

Read the question and the answer choices carefully. Don't miss the question because you misread the terms. You have plenty of time to read each question thoroughly and make sure you understand what is being asked. Yet a happy medium must be attained, so don't waste too much time. You must read carefully and efficiently.

✓ CONTEXTUAL CLUES

Look for contextual clues. If the question includes a word you are not familiar with, look at the immediate context for some indication of what the word might mean. Contextual clues can often give you all the information you need to decipher the meaning of an unfamiliar word. Even if you can't determine the meaning, you may be able to narrow down the possibilities enough to make a solid guess at the answer to the question.

✓ PREFIXES

If you're having trouble with a word in the question or answer choices, try dissecting it. Take advantage of every clue that the word might include. Prefixes can be a huge help. Usually, they allow you to determine a basic meaning. *Pre-* means before, *post-* means after, *pro-* is positive, *de-* is negative. From prefixes, you can get an idea of the general meaning of the word and try to put it into context.

✓ HEDGE WORDS

Watch out for critical hedge words, such as *likely, may, can, sometimes, often, almost, mostly, usually, generally, rarely,* and *sometimes.* Question writers insert these hedge phrases to cover every possibility. Often an answer choice will be wrong simply because it leaves no room for exception. Be on guard for answer choices that have definitive words such as *exactly* and *always.*

✓ SWITCHBACK WORDS

Stay alert for *switchbacks.* These are the words and phrases frequently used to alert you to shifts in thought. The most common switchback words are *but, although,* and *however.* Others include *nevertheless, on the other hand, even though, while, in spite of, despite,* and *regardless of.* Switchback words are important to catch because they can change the direction of the question or an answer choice.

10

⊘ Face Value

When in doubt, use common sense. Accept the situation in the problem at face value. Don't read too much into it. These problems will not require you to make wild assumptions. If you have to go beyond creativity and warp time or space in order to have an answer choice fit the question, then you should move on and consider the other answer choices. These are normal problems rooted in reality. The applicable relationship or explanation may not be readily apparent, but it is there for you to figure out. Use your common sense to interpret anything that isn't clear.

Answer Choice Strategies

⊘ Answer Selection

The most thorough way to pick an answer choice is to identify and eliminate wrong answers until only one is left, then confirm it is the correct answer. Sometimes an answer choice may immediately seem right, but be careful. The test writers will usually put more than one reasonable answer choice on each question, so take a second to read all of them and make sure that the other choices are not equally obvious. As long as you have time left, it is better to read every answer choice than to pick the first one that looks right without checking the others.

⊘ Answer Choice Families

An answer choice family consists of two (in rare cases, three) answer choices that are very similar in construction and cannot all be true at the same time. If you see two answer choices that are direct opposites or parallels, one of them is usually the correct answer. For instance, if one answer choice says that quantity x increases and another either says that quantity x decreases (opposite) or says that quantity y increases (parallel), then those answer choices would fall into the same family. An answer choice that doesn't match the construction of the answer choice family is more likely to be incorrect. Most questions will not have answer choice families, but when they do appear, you should be prepared to recognize them.

⊘ Eliminate Answers

Eliminate answer choices as soon as you realize they are wrong, but make sure you consider all possibilities. If you are eliminating answer choices and realize that the last one you are left with is also wrong, don't panic. Start over and consider each choice again. There may be something you missed the first time that you will realize on the second pass.

⊘ Avoid Fact Traps

Don't be distracted by an answer choice that is factually true but doesn't answer the question. You are looking for the choice that answers the question. Stay focused on what the question is asking for so you don't accidentally pick an answer that is true but incorrect. Always go back to the question and make sure the answer choice you've selected actually answers the question and is not merely a true statement.

⊘ Extreme Statements

In general, you should avoid answers that put forth extreme actions as standard practice or proclaim controversial ideas as established fact. An answer choice that states the "process should be used in certain situations, if…" is much more likely to be correct than one that states the "process should be discontinued completely." The first is a calm rational statement and doesn't even make a definitive, uncompromising stance, using a hedge word *if* to provide wiggle room, whereas the second choice is far more extreme.

☑ Benchmark

As you read through the answer choices and you come across one that seems to answer the question well, mentally select that answer choice. This is not your final answer, but it's the one that will help you evaluate the other answer choices. The one that you selected is your benchmark or standard for judging each of the other answer choices. Every other answer choice must be compared to your benchmark. That choice is correct until proven otherwise by another answer choice beating it. If you find a better answer, then that one becomes your new benchmark. Once you've decided that no other choice answers the question as well as your benchmark, you have your final answer.

☑ Predict the Answer

Before you even start looking at the answer choices, it is often best to try to predict the answer. When you come up with the answer on your own, it is easier to avoid distractions and traps because you will know exactly what to look for. The right answer choice is unlikely to be word-for-word what you came up with, but it should be a close match. Even if you are confident that you have the right answer, you should still take the time to read each option before moving on.

General Strategies

☑ Tough Questions

If you are stumped on a problem or it appears too hard or too difficult, don't waste time. Move on! Remember though, if you can quickly check for obviously incorrect answer choices, your chances of guessing correctly are greatly improved. Before you completely give up, at least try to knock out a couple of possible answers. Eliminate what you can and then guess at the remaining answer choices before moving on.

☑ Check Your Work

Since you will probably not know every term listed and the answer to every question, it is important that you get credit for the ones that you do know. Don't miss any questions through careless mistakes. If at all possible, try to take a second to look back over your answer selection and make sure you've selected the correct answer choice and haven't made a costly careless mistake (such as marking an answer choice that you didn't mean to mark). This quick double check should more than pay for itself in caught mistakes for the time it costs.

☑ Pace Yourself

It's easy to be overwhelmed when you're looking at a page full of questions; your mind is confused and full of random thoughts, and the clock is ticking down faster than you would like. Calm down and maintain the pace that you have set for yourself. Especially as you get down to the last few minutes of the test, don't let the small numbers on the clock make you panic. As long as you are on track by monitoring your pace, you are guaranteed to have time for each question.

☑ Don't Rush

It is very easy to make errors when you are in a hurry. Maintaining a fast pace in answering questions is pointless if it makes you miss questions that you would have gotten right otherwise. Test writers like to include distracting information and wrong answers that seem right. Taking a little extra time to avoid careless mistakes can make all the difference in your test score. Find a pace that allows you to be confident in the answers that you select.

⊘ Keep Moving

Panicking will not help you pass the test, so do your best to stay calm and keep moving. Taking deep breaths and going through the answer elimination steps you practiced can help to break through a stress barrier and keep your pace.

Final Notes

The combination of a solid foundation of content knowledge and the confidence that comes from practicing your plan for applying that knowledge is the key to maximizing your performance on test day. As your foundation of content knowledge is built up and strengthened, you'll find that the strategies included in this chapter become more and more effective in helping you quickly sift through the distractions and traps of the test to isolate the correct answer.

Now that you're preparing to move forward into the test content chapters of this book, be sure to keep your goal in mind. As you read, think about how you will be able to apply this information on the test. If you've already seen sample questions for the test and you have an idea of the question format and style, try to come up with questions of your own that you can answer based on what you're reading. This will give you valuable practice applying your knowledge in the same ways you can expect to on test day.

Good luck and good studying!

Federal Mortgage-Related Laws

Real Estate Settlement Procedures Act (RESPA)

RESPA ORIGINS AND PURPOSE

Real estate transactions have many moving parts. Their complexity makes these transactions susceptible to hidden fees, kickbacks, and inflated costs. To protect consumers from abusive practices, the federal government enacted the **Real Estate Settlement Procedures Act (RESPA)** in 1974. RESPA was designed to protect consumers by making real estate transactions transparent and fair. The law requires lenders to clearly disclose to buyers and sellers all of the costs involved in a real estate transaction.

RESPA also attempts to educate home buyers. The law requires lenders to educate consumers about their consumer protection rights. It also gives consumers recourse in the event they believe a lender has treated them unfairly.

RESPA pertains to real estate transactions involving one- to four-family residences and covers most home loans, including mortgages used to purchase or refinance debt and home equity loans. The laws also cover the establishment and maintenance of escrow accounts, forbidding lenders from requiring excessive or inflated escrows.

MORTGAGE BROKER

A mortgage broker is like a matchmaker, connecting borrowers to lenders. **Mortgage brokers** get paid a fee after matching borrowers with lenders, and funds are fully disbursed for the purchase of a residence. The funds used to make the home purchase come from a third party and not directly from the mortgage broker. Unlike a loan officer of a bank who can lend only his or her bank's funds, a broker utilizes a variety of banks and other lenders to secure funds for borrowers.

Brokers are bound by all the same RESPA requirements as mortgage lenders. This is especially true regarding a borrower's right to understand the relationship between the broker and the institution supplying the funds for the mortgage. Brokers must clearly state to borrowers all fees and costs associated with closing the mortgage.

A mortgage broker is required to gather all the documents needed for banks to decide whether to make a loan. This includes the borrower's income and asset statements, employment history, credit scores, bank statements, and any other documentation a lender needs to make an informed lending decision.

PROHIBITIONS, LIMITATIONS, AND EXEMPTIONS SET BY RESPA

RESPA prohibits kickbacks, unearned fees or payments, and excessive escrow requirements. It also prohibits sellers from requiring buyers to use certain settlement service providers as a stipulation to the sales agreement.

Certain real estate transactions are also exempt from RESPA: loans on properties of 25 acres or more; business, commercial, or agricultural loans; temporary loans (that is, construction loans); loans secured by vacant or **unimproved property** (land that does not have basic services like electricity, sewers, road access, phone lines, or water service); assumptions (unless the lender approves the assumption); **bridge** or **swing** loans (a short-term loan used to buy a house and then pay off the loan with the proceeds from the sale of another home); **modification** (when a lender

15

agrees to modify the terms of an existing mortgage in order to lower the payment); and loans that are transferred in the secondary market.

TYPES OF LOANS TO WHICH RESPA IS APPLICABLE

Any mortgage loan regulated by federal law, including purchase loans, home **equity loans** (when a lender extends credit to a homeowner based on the home's equity, which is the value of the home minus the home's outstanding loans), loans secured by a lien on a residential property, assumed loans or **assumptions** (a mortgage on a residential property whose terms and remaining balance are transferred from the seller to the new buyer when a home is sold), refinances, and **reverse mortgages** (when an elderly person uses the equity in his or her home to secure a monthly stipend from the lender), is covered by RESPA. These types of loans are usually done by people who have limited means of generating income.

Essentially, any loan guaranteed by a federal agency is subject to RESPA. These federal agencies include Freddie Mac, Fannie Mae, the Federal Housing Administration (FHA), and the Department of Veterans Affairs (VA), among others. The agencies help improve liquidity in the housing market and also guarantee that loans will be repaid, even if borrowers default. Freddie Mac and Fannie Mae buy mortgages from lenders and package those loans into securities that are sold on the open market. Buying the loans frees up additional funds for lenders to use to help more people become homeowners.

SETTLEMENT SERVICES

Settlement services are akin to a preflight checklist. A pilot must inspect his or her aircraft and deem it ready before flight. The same is true of originating a mortgage. Before funds are disbursed to the buyer, a host of requirements must be met. First, many inspections are required: inspections for damage, pests, and contaminants like radon gas; appraisals that ensure the home is worth the sale price; and land surveys.

All parties to the transaction must also be sure no other person or entity has a claim to the house. Lenders hire title services to examine county records and make sure the sellers are the sole owners. Title services also make sure there are no liens against the house for unpaid taxes, legal fees, or other items. Also, many types of insurance must be placed or offered before a home changes hands: homeowner's insurance, flood insurance, and life and disability insurance.

There are other services, such as printing documents, paying attorneys, taking the actual loan application, and obtaining credit reports, that are also considered settlement services.

BONA FIDE DISCOUNT POINTS AND APPLICATION DURING A MORTGAGE LOAN ORIGINATION

Selling points is a way for a lender to offer a mortgage applicant a lower interest rate in exchange for charging the applicant higher up-front costs. Paying for points can be attractive to buyers because it lowers their monthly payments. Generally, points are calculated as a percentage of the loan amount. For example, for a $100,000 loan, one point would cost $1,000, or one percent. Two points would be $2,000, or two percent.

The exact amount that one point lowers an interest rate depends on many factors, including the market, the lender, the loan type, and pricing structures. For example, lenders with good reputations are able to charge more; on the other hand, a fiercely competitive market may provide less incentive for lenders to offer discounts.

Points must be negotiated up front and clearly listed in closing documents.

FORECLOSURE PROCESS

It is incumbent on the lender to ensure that the borrower knows the consequences of falling behind on mortgage payments. Further, the lender is required to inform the borrower that he or she has certain rights during the foreclosure process—for example, when it begins and the fact that there is an appeals process.

Foreclosure is the lender's remedy for recouping losses when a borrower defaults on a mortgage. When a borrower cannot pay, the lender takes the home and sells it, keeping the proceeds from the sale of the home. Lenders can begin the foreclosure process after a borrower falls behind on payments by 120 days.

INITIAL ESCROW STATEMENTS

According to RESPA, the initial escrow statement must be provided to the borrower at settlement or within 45 days of settlement. When **escrow** is a condition of a loan, it requires the lender to collect certain sums on a monthly basis and hold those sums in a separate account to be paid out later for property taxes and homeowner's insurance on behalf of the borrower. The initial statement must disclose the monthly amounts allocated to the mortgage payment, taxes, insurance, and other charges. The statement must also disclose the anticipated dates of the disbursements for items like property taxes and homeowner's insurance, the cushion maintained in escrow, and a trial running balance.

The thinking behind requiring escrow accounts is that it's often the best way to protect the lender and the borrower against failure to pay for crucial items like property taxes and homeowner's insurance. The failure to pay either could have devasting impacts on lenders and homeowners. For example, if homeowner's insurance was not escrowed, the borrower did not pay the premiums, and a fire destroys the home, then everyone loses. There are no funds to rebuild the home, and the bank loses the collateral securing the loan. This kind of nightmare scenario is avoided by using escrow to pay for crucial items like insurance.

Equal Credit Opportunity Act (ECOA)

FACTORS THAT CANNOT BE USED TO DISCRIMINATE

Lenders cannot use a borrower's age, race, sex, nationality, religion, marital status, or the fact that a borrower receives public assistance to discriminate. Lenders also cannot discriminate against someone for exercising his or her rights under the Consumer Credit Protection Act. The Uniform Residential Loan Application does gather most of this information. However, a creditor must make all loan decisions based on creditworthiness alone. The purpose of **the Equal Credit Opportunity Act (ECOA)** is to give all applicants a fair chance of obtaining credit. Lenders do gather information about applicants' race and personal characteristics to show that they are complying with anti-discrimination laws.

Lenders must provide all borrowers the same information and services, cannot discourage applicants from applying for credit, must use the same lending standards for all applicants, and cannot vary loan terms, rates, loan amounts, or other loan features based on a prohibited factor. Lenders must use the same standards to evaluate collateral for all applicants and cannot treat borrowers differently when servicing loans or use different standards when selling loans on the secondary market. Lenders cannot discriminate against borrowers based on the neighborhood borrowers live in.

Lenders can ask about marital status on joint applications and also in some community property states. Lenders are also prohibited from charging higher rates based on age, race, sex, nationality, religion, marital status, or the fact that a borrower receives public assistance. Lenders can only consider age when making a decision for someone under 18.

INSTANCES IN WHICH LENDERS CAN CONSIDER PERSONAL CHARACTERISTICS WHEN MAKING A LOAN DECISION

A lender can consider things like marital status, age, and permanent residency in some circumstances but only when these factors have a direct bearing on a borrower's ability to repay or to be eligible for certain loans. For example, lenders can inquire about marital status on joint applications or when a spouse will be required to sign off on the loan at closing. A borrower might apply for a loan individually using a home that is also owned by his or her spouse. In this situation, the lender can inquire about marital status and require the spouse to sign at closing before issuing the loan.

Someone's immigration or permanent residency status can be considered in a credit application. Because that person may be deemed a risk to leave the country before repaying a loan, that person can be denied credit.

Some mortgages, like reverse mortgages, can only be extended to persons who are 62 or older. Therefore, age is a consideration in those cases.

CIRCUMSTANCES WHEN IT IS ACCEPTABLE TO DENY CREDIT OR A LOAN

Essentially, anything that affects a borrower's creditworthiness to the extent that it is unlikely the borrower can repay the loan is an acceptable reason to deny credit. For example, if the borrower's credit report shows excessive late payments, high current credit obligations, or little to no credit history, these are all acceptable reasons to deny credit. If a borrower has insufficient income or has not been employed long enough to demonstrate that he or she is an acceptable risk, a lender can deny credit. Lenders can deny credit if the property being purchased is considered to be inadequate in terms of condition. Lenders can also deny credit based on someone's permanent residency status or if critical information is missing from an application. For example, a foreign resident might be considered a bad risk because that person may not reside here long enough to repay the loan.

GENERAL PROVISIONS OF REGULATION B

A lender may not discriminate against a borrower on a prohibited basis (age, race, sex, nationality, religion, marital status, or the fact that a borrower receives public assistance) over any aspect of a credit application. **Regulation B** also prohibits lenders from discouraging an applicant from applying for credit. If a lender denies credit, a written response must be provided to the borrower explaining the specific reasons for the denial. The lender must take a written application when residences are involved in the loan request, that is, a mortgage or home equity loan. All disclosure forms provided by the lender must be clear, concise, and given to the borrower to maintain in his or her records. Disclosures can be given electronically following federal guidelines for electronic disclosure. Disclosures can be provided in other languages provided they are also available in English by request.

ACCEPTABLE TERMS USED TO DESCRIBE MARITAL STATUS

"Married," "unmarried," and "separated" are the accepted terms to describe marital status. For example, "Are you married, unmarried, or separated?" Use of unacceptable terms would include asking an applicant if he or she is divorced or widowed. A lender can ask about a spouse only if the spouse is involved in the application (a joint application) or involved somehow in the transaction.

An applicant does not have to reveal whether any portion of his or her income is derived from alimony, child support, or separate maintenance, unless he or she wants it to be considered in the application. The lender can only request that the applicant reveal this information after explaining the conditions under which it would be used and the applicant's right to decline.

Also, a lender cannot ask an applicant about intentions to bear children, use of birth control, capability of having children, or the rearing of children. A lender can ask an applicant about the number of dependents but only in relation to financial obligations and expenditures, provided that such information is requested without regard to any of the prohibited factors.

ELDERLY

Elderly means 62 or older. Remember, age is a prohibited factor and cannot be used to discriminate against an applicant. However, a lender can consider age for an elderly applicant if the lender's scoring system favors elderly applicants. A lender may consider the adequacy of collateral offered if the terms of the loan exceed the life expectancy of the applicant and the costs of the loan exceed the home's equity at the time of the applicant's death. For example, an elderly applicant might not qualify for five percent down on a 30-year mortgage but might qualify with a larger down payment on a shorter loan term.

DISPARATE TREATMENT SCENARIOS

Disparate treatment is when a lender treats an applicant differently based on one of the prohibited factors. An example would be offering loan choices to applicants based on the applicant's race—for example, offering **subprime** loans to African Americans and conventional loans to all other similarly situated applicants. A subprime loan refers to the creditworthiness of the borrower. Subprime borrowers usually have lower credit scores and are a greater risk to default. A lender might also be practicing disparate treatment if it provides more information to men than women. Lenders are also prohibited from practices that have **disparate impact**. Disparate impact is when a lender establishes a practice that does not directly discriminate but impacts different groups disproportionately. For example, a lender may have a policy of offering mortgages for a minimum amount of $100,000. The policy is not overtly discriminatory; however, it categorically excludes anyone seeking to purchase a home in a neighborhood with low property values.

RECORD RETENTION TIMELINES

ECOA requires lenders to retain all records pertaining to credit applications for 25 months after action is taken on the application or notice of incompleteness is given. The lender must retain the application and any documents it received from applicants, as well as any notifications sent to the applicant, including adverse actions and statements of specific reasons for an adverse action. The lender must retain any written statements submitted by the applicant alleging lender violations of ECOA.

The lender must also retain the texts of any prescreened solicitations for 25 months after the date the offer is first made to potential customers. The criteria used for selecting customers to receive the solicitation must also be retained for 25 months, as well as any complaints from customers who received the solicitation.

REQUIREMENT FOR A COSIGNER

A lender cannot refuse to grant credit to an individual applicant who is creditworthy. However, a lender can request a **cosigner**, co-applicant, endorser, or guarantor, if—under the lender's standards—an individual's creditworthiness is insufficient to support the requested loan. The lender cannot require that an applicant's spouse join an application as a cosigner. Lenders must treat co-applicants the same as applicants. A lender cannot impose different standards of creditworthiness on co-applicants. A lender can impose restrictions on who can be a cosigner on a loan, but the restriction must not be applied on a prohibited basis—that is, based on sex, age, race, and so on. For example, a lender may deny a cosigner that does not live in the United States.

A **joint applicant** is someone who applies for credit simultaneously with the applicant. It does not refer to someone who is required to join the application as a condition of the loan. A person's willingness to apply jointly must be evident from the outset of the application. Signing a joint application would be sufficient to approve a joint applicant's intent.

FACTORS CONSIDERED WHEN DETERMINING CREDITWORTHINESS

Generally speaking, lenders can use any information gathered to determine an applicant's creditworthiness, as long as the information is not used to discriminate against the applicant on any prohibited basis. Realistically, a lender primarily uses three elements to evaluate an applicant's loan application: the applicant's credit history, the applicant's **debt-to-income ratio (DTI)**, and the property being used to secure the loan. Depending on the creditor, tangible factors such as net worth and assets can be used to evaluate an application. In addition, the lender might consider intangibles like the applicant's character. DTI refers to an applicant's means to repay the loan taken as a ratio of debt to income. For example, if an applicant has monthly debt payments totaling $1,000 and income of $2,000, the DTI would be 50 percent.

TYPES OF ACCEPTABLE INCOME CONSIDERED IN A LOAN REVIEW

A lender may consider the amount and continuity of any income on a credit application. Typical sources of income include but are not limited to: employment, Social Security, pensions, investments, interest, annuities, rental income, disability income, public assistance, alimony, and child support. A lender must not discount or exclude from income on any prohibited basis, nor shall a lender nullify a source of income because it is derived from part-time work, annuities, pensions, or a retirement benefit. However, a lender may consider the likelihood that any source of income will continue long enough to repay the debt. For example, regarding public assistance, a lender may consider the length of time an applicant will remain eligible for such income. A lender must evaluate income from part-time work, employment, alimony, child support, separate maintenance, retirement plans, and public assistance on an individual basis. A lender cannot evaluate sources of income using statistics or probabilities derived from a group.

REQUESTS FOR MISSING APPLICATION INFORMATION

Within 30 days of receiving an incomplete application, a lender must notify the applicant of action taken or request the missing information from the applicant. A lender can request the missing information orally. If the applicant does not respond, the lender must send a written request for missing information and give the applicant a reasonable amount of time to submit the missing information. The notice must also state that failure to provide the information will force the lender to terminate the application. The lender has no further obligation after sending a missing information notice. If the borrower responds, the lender must proceed toward rendering a decision.

Lenders also have the right to deny an application for incompleteness. Appropriate notices of adverse action must be supplied. Also, if an application is missing some information but the borrower supplied sufficient data for a decision, the lender can evaluate the application and decide accordingly. However, if the lender declines, the lender cannot give as the specific reason that the application was missing information.

ADVERSE ACTION SCENARIOS

Remember, an **adverse action** is a denial of credit. There are as many reasons to deny credit as there are factors in considering an application. Also recall that there are essentially three elements to consider in a credit application for a mortgage: the applicant's means to repay, including current debt obligations; credit history; and the residence that the applicant seeks to purchase. Within each of these elements, there are myriad factors that could lead to an adverse action or denial. Think of each element as the hub of a wheel, with the spokes representing all the many factors or data that the lender must consider. Common reasons for denial are poor or insufficient credit history; having too much debt, which makes taking on an additional mortgage too risky for the lender; and a lower-than-expected home appraisal.

INFORMATION REQUIRED ON A LOAN APPLICATION

In addition to the basic information (borrower's name, Social Security number, monthly income, the loan amount, the address of the home being purchased, and its estimated value), the lender is also required to gather demographic information about borrowers in some cases to show that the lender is compliant with federal lending regulations. When loans involve the use of a primary residence as collateral, the lender shall gather demographic information concerning ethnicity, race, sex, marital status (using the categories of married, unmarried, and separated), and age. For ethnicity, the lender shall use the aggregate categories of:

- Hispanic or Latino
- Not Hispanic or Latino

For race, the categories would be:

- American Indian or Alaska Native
- Asian
- Black or African American
- Native Hawaiian or other Pacific Islander
- White

Applicants supply this information on a voluntary basis. If the applicants do not offer the information, the lender must note this on the application and furnish this information based on surnames and face-to-face interactions with the applicants. The lender shall also gather the same information for co-applicants.

Truth in Lending Act (TILA)

NOTICE OF RIGHT TO RESCIND

Rescission refers to the borrower's right to cancel a loan application that uses his or her primary residence as collateral. The right to rescind does not apply to mortgage applications. Rescission clauses apply to home equity loan applications to either establish a new loan or increase an existing **home equity line of credit** (a revolving credit line using a residence as collateral). A borrower may exercise his or her rescission rights up to midnight on the third **business day** after closing the loan. Business days are all days except Sundays and federal holidays. On a joint application, a single applicant can exercise his or her right to rescind, thus nullifying the loan for all parties. At the time of loan closing, the lender must provide each applicant two copies of the rescission notice. The notice must clearly explain the borrower's rescission rights, and it must indicate when the rescission period expires, how to exercise this right, and the lender's business address for delivery of the notice should the borrower choose to rescind. The notice must be made in writing and is considered given when the form is mailed, telegrammed, or delivered to the lender's place of business.

PERMISSIBLE FEES AND FINANCE CHARGES

Finance charges are costs to the consumer measured in dollars (not percentages) paid directly or indirectly to a lender in conjunction with a loan application. Finance charges include amounts charged by third parties if the lender requires these services as a condition of the loan, even if the borrower can choose the third-party service provider. Some examples of finance charges are interest, service and transaction fees, points, assumption fees, premiums for insurance that protects the lender, and premiums for life and disability insurance that protects borrowers. Examples of charges that are excluded from the definition of finance charge are application fees, seller's points, title examination fees, property survey fees, and fees for preparing loan documents.

Regulations also set a **total points and fee threshold** to protect borrowers from excessive costs. The thresholds are adjusted annually for inflation. For 2024, the thresholds included the following:

- Three percent of the total loan amount for loans greater than $130,461
- $3,914 for loans between $78,277 and $130,461
- Five percent of the total loan amount for loans between $26,092 and $78,277
- $1,305 for loans between $16,308 and $26,092
- Eight percent of the total loan amount for loans of less than $16,308

CORE CONCEPTS OF TILA

Federal law established the **Truth in Lending Act (TILA)** in 1968 to promote the informed use of consumer credit. The act seeks to make borrowing fairer and more consumer friendly by requiring lenders to clearly state and explain all terms and costs associated with borrowing. Furthermore, the act seeks to make borrowing more uniform across lenders so that borrowers can easily compare the costs and terms offered. The act requires lenders to make advance disclosures so that borrowers have ample time to digest the information needed to make an informed decision. The act also affords consumers ample protections, such as the right to cancel an application. TILA covers all lenders and persons who regularly offer loans to consumers for personal, family, or household purposes.

APR

As a rule of thumb, the **annual percentage rate (APR)** is the cost of credit measured on a yearly basis for the term of the loan. APR includes any additional fees and costs associated with the loan but does not include compounding. In keeping with the spirit of the Truth in Lending Act (TILA), lenders are required to clearly state APR (on a yearly basis) to make it easy for consumers to understand the costs of borrowing and compare offers made by multiple lenders. If a lender says it charges one percent per month, the cost must also be stated for an annual basis, which would be 12 percent.

The difference between APR and interest rate is that interest rate refers only to the interest charged on a loan without taking into account all other applicable fees. APR is essentially the full cost of borrowing, taking into account the interest rate and all fees.

If a lender erroneously quotes APR by 1/8 of a percent above or below the actual rate, the quote is within federal **annual percentage rate tolerances** and is still considered accurate.

LOANS COVERED BY TILA

The Truth in Lending Act (TILA) covers most types of loans, from **closed-end loans** to credit cards. A closed-end loan, sometimes referred to as an installment loan, occurs when the lender disburses all of the funds at once with the requirement that the borrower pay it back over a set time period by means of monthly payments. An example is a mortgage. Credit cards are an example of an **open-end loan** or a revolving loan. In an open-end loan, the lender makes a certain amount of credit available to the borrower, and the borrower uses as much of the loan as he or she wishes, up to the credit limit. A home equity line of credit is also an open-end loan. A monthly payment is due only when the borrower draws on the loan. Finance charges apply to unpaid, outstanding balances.

DWELLING

A **dwelling** is a residential building consisting of a single unit for one family or up to four family units. The term "dwelling" also applies to condominiums, mobile homes, and trailers. The Truth in Lending Act (TILA) defines a **residential mortgage loan** as one in which a lender retains an interest in a borrower's home until the borrower pays back the loan over a specified number of installments. After the mortgage is repaid, the borrower owns the home free and clear. A **mortgage** is basically an installment loan made to purchase a home in which the lender uses the home as collateral. If the borrower fails to repay, the lender can take the home. Mortgages can also be used to refinance existing mortgages when a borrower seeks to redefine or improve the terms of a loan. There are many different types of mortgages. The most common is a mortgage in which the rate is fixed for the life of the loan, usually 15 or 30 years. In a variable-rate mortgage, the rate is usually fixed for a certain length of time in the beginning—for example, the first three, five, or seven years—and then the rate fluctuates for the remainder of the term.

RECORD RETENTION TIMEFRAMES

Section 1026.25 of the Truth in Lending Act (TILA) describes general guidelines for retaining records, and some lenders also have their own more stringent standards. TILA says that as a rule of thumb, lenders must retain records for two years showing that they complied with all disclosures and action notices. Compliance does not require paper records; proof of compliance can be stored electronically.

Records related to requirements for a loan in which a residence is used for collateral must be retained for three years. In a deal involving a residence, closing documents and disclosures must be retained for five years. If a lender sells a loan during this five-year period, the closing documents must be transferred to the loan buyer and retained for the time remaining in the five-year window.

Records related to lender compensation must be retained for three years.

CLASSIFYING SELLER CONTRIBUTIONS

As we have discussed, there are myriad fees and costs associated with a mortgage. The majority of the costs are the borrower's burden. However, many aspects are negotiable in a real estate transaction. As part of an offer, a borrower might request that the seller pay for some of the closing costs. The portion that a seller contributes toward the closing costs is called a seller contribution. Some loans specify limits on how much a seller can contribute toward closing costs. For example, a Federal Housing Administration (FHA) loan limits a seller's contribution to six percent of the sale price.

HOME OWNERSHIP AND EQUITY PROTECTION ACT (HOEPA), HIGH-COST MORTGAGES

MINIMUM TERM FOR A BALLOON PAYMENT

Balloon payments are generally prohibited for high-cost mortgages except for certain circumstances:

- A loan has a payment schedule adjusted for the borrower's seasonal or irregular income.
- The loan is a short-term bridge loan (12 months or less) to finance a new home purchase for a consumer selling an existing home.
- The creditor meets criteria for serving a predominantly rural or underserved area and the loan satisfies the Consumer Financial Protection Bureau's Ability-to-Repay/Qualified Mortgage Rule.

The Home Ownership and Equity Protection Act (HOEPA) also bans other risky features for high-cost mortgages, such as prepayment penalties and due-on-demand features. Due-on-demand clauses are allowed when the consumer commits fraud or makes misrepresentations in connection with the mortgage, when the borrower defaults, or when the consumer's action or inaction adversely affects the collateral.

EXAMPLES OF COVERED LOANS

The Home Ownership and Equity Protection Act (HOEPA) was enacted in 1994 as an amendment to the Truth in Lending Act (TILA) in an effort to curb abusive practices surrounding closed-end mortgages and home equity lines of credit with high interest rates and high closing costs. Consumer loans secured by a borrower's primary residence are covered by this provision. Covered loans are purchase-money mortgages, refinances, and closed-end and open-end home equity loans. The act does not cover reverse mortgages, bridge loans used to finance initial construction, loans originated by the US Department of Agriculture (USDA Rural Housing Service loans), or loans financed by a **housing finance agency** (HFA), which promote affordable housing for low- to moderate-income residents. Mortgages secured by manufactured housing (mobile homes and trailers), recreational vehicles (RVs), and houseboats are also subject to the act if one of these style of homes is a borrower's primary residence.

HOEPA allows high-cost mortgages but forces lenders to follow certain guidelines and restrictions when making these loans, such as giving additional disclosures, avoiding certain loan terms, and ensuring that the borrower receives additional protections, including homeownership counseling. The Consumer Financial Protection Bureau (CFPB) enforces HOEPA.

HIGHER-PRICED MORTGAGE LOANS

If a loan secured by the borrower's principal dwelling meets one of three tests, it is considered a high-cost loan:

- The annual percentage rate (APR) test states that a mortgage is high-cost if the loan's APR exceeds the **average prime offer rate (APOR)** (a rate that is based on average interest rates, fees, and other terms on mortgages available to highly qualified borrowers) by more the 6.5 percentage points for first-lien transactions; by 8.5 percentage points for first-lien transactions that are for less than $50,000; and by 8.5 percent for subordinate-lien transactions.
- For 2024, mortgage is high-cost if the loan is $26,092 or more and the points and fees exceed five percent of the loan amount, or the loan amount is $26,092 or more and points and fees exceed the lesser of $1,305 or eight percent of the loan amount. These thresholds are adjusted annually for inflation.

- A mortgage is high-cost if the lender charges a prepayment penalty more than 36 months after consummation or account opening or charges a penalty that is greater than two percent of the amount prepaid.

If a loan secured by the borrower's principal dwelling exceeds the APOR by a given amount, it is a higher-priced mortgage. A loan is a higher-priced mortgage if it meets any of the following conditions:

- It is a first-lien mortgage that is *not* a jumbo mortgage, and the APR exceeds the APOR by 1.5 percentage points or more.
- It is first-lien mortgage that *is* jumbo with an APR more than 2.5 percentage points higher than the APOR.
- It is a subordinate lien with an APR 3.5 percentage points higher than the APOR.

Lenders who make higher-priced mortgages under Regulation Z face three main restrictions:

- They must verify the borrower's ability to repay.
- No prepayment penalty is allowed.
- Taxes and insurance must be escrowed along with principal and interest payments.

All of the prohibitions found in the Truth in Lending Act (TILA) apply to higher-priced mortgages. Lenders also may not charge fees for second appraisals nor for copying or mailing appraisals. Finally, lenders are prohibited from refinancing a loan when the new loan causes the principal to increase, allows for deferring principal payments, or causes a balloon payment.

LOAN ORIGINATOR COMPENSATION

MLO COMPENSATION BASIS

After the 2008 mortgage crisis, lawmakers began scrutinizing how **mortgage loan originators (MLOs)** and bank officers had helped consumers choose loans. It was discovered that sometimes MLOs steered consumers to higher-priced mortgages because these loans provided MLOs higher compensation. As a result, the Dodd-Frank Act restricted some compensation practices and set standards for MLO qualifications. The new rules prohibit MLOs' compensation from being based on the terms of a loan and prohibits MLOs from being compensated by both their employer and the borrower. The new rules do allow for retirement plan compensation under designated tax-advantaged plans, as well as certain bonuses under non-deferred, profits-based compensation plans based on mortgage business profits.

Permissible compensation includes: salaries, commissions, and any financial incentive such as merchandise, trips, or any similar incentive. An MLO may be compensated by a borrower or a lender but cannot be compensated by both on the same transaction.

TILA-RESPA Integrated Disclosure Rule (TRID)

OVERVIEW OF THE TILA-RESPA INTEGRATED DISCLOSURE RULE

The **TILA-RESPA Integrated Disclosure Rule (TRID)** builds off of all of the previous regulations discussed up to this point, including the Equal Credit Opportunity Act (ECOA). The biggest change under the new integrated disclosure rule is the reduction in disclosure forms from four to two: the Loan Estimate and the Closing Disclosure. The Loan Estimate replaces the Good Faith Estimate and the initial Truth in Lending form, combining them into one disclosure. The Closing Disclosure also combines the HUD-1 and the final Truth in Lending disclosure into one form. Therefore, all of the rules laid out under ECOA regarding discrimination apply under TRID. Remember, lenders cannot discriminate against an applicant based on the applicant's age, race, sex, nationality, color, religion, marital status, or the fact that a borrower receives public assistance. Lenders also cannot discriminate based on the fact that a borrower has exercised his or her rights under the Consumer Credit Protection Act.

SECTION ON DISCLOSURE WHERE ORIGINATION CHARGES ARE REFLECTED

Origination charges are tallied in section A, page 2 of the Loan Estimate under the heading Closing Cost Details and subheading Loan Costs. Originator charges are any charges the consumer pays to the lender for obtaining the loan. The first item specified in this section is the amount the borrower paid in points to lower the interest rate. This charge is expressed both as a dollar amount and as a percentage of the loan amount. This section is left blank if the borrower did not pay points. Only items paid directly to the lender by the borrower are origination charges.

Section B, page 2 of the Loan Estimate details origination Services You Cannot Shop For, and Section C, page 2 is for origination Services You Can Shop For. Section B includes things like appraisal fees, the credit report fee, the flood determination fee, and attorney fees. Section C includes services such as pest inspections, surveys, and title agent fees.

AFFILIATED BUSINESS DISCLOSURE SPECIAL INFORMATION BOOKLET

The lender is required to provide to borrowers the Affiliated Business Disclosure Special Information Booklet in mortgage deals involving the purchase of a principal residence. The Affiliated Business Disclosure Special Information Booklet is referred to by different names, including "the booklet," the Special Information Booklet, the Cost Settlement Booklet, and its official title, "Your Home Loan Toolkit: A Step-By-Step Guide." As described earlier, the booklet is designed to educate borrowers on the process of buying a home, from applying for a mortgage to the ongoing costs of homeownership. If a borrower is applying for a home equity loan, the lender can substitute the booklet titled "When Your Home Is on the Line: What You Should Know about Home Equity Lines of Credit." Lenders must deliver or mail the Special Information Booklet no later than three business days after receiving a mortgage application.

RECORD RETENTION

The lender must retain copies of the Closing Disclosure for five years after the loan closing or consummation, and he or she must retain the Post-Consumption Escrow Cancellation Notice and Post-Consumption Partial Payment Policy disclosure for two years. All other evidence of compliance with all components of TRID and Regulation Z, including the Loan Estimate, must be retained by the lender for three years. If the lender originating the mortgage sells it, and therefore no longer services the loan, then the lender must also transfer the Closing Disclosure to the loan buyer. The Closing Disclosure must be retained by both parties for the remainder of the five-year retention period. Records can be retained in paper form or electronically.

REQUIRED DISCLOSURES

The TILA-RESPA Integrated Disclosure Rule (TRID) requires lenders to give applicants the Loan Estimate within three business days of receiving an application for a mortgage. The Loan Estimate replaces the Good Faith Estimate and the initial Truth in Lending disclosure. The Closing Document is the second required disclosure. This document replaces the HUD-1 and the final Truth in Lending disclosure and must be provided to the borrower at least three business days before closing. Finally, in scenarios that involve the purchase of a primary residence, the lender is also required to supply the Affiliated Business Disclosure Special Information Booklet. All three documents were designed with the consumer in mind to help educate and inform consumers.

TIMING OF DISCLOSURES PROVIDED TO AN APPLICANT

The Loan Estimate must be provided to the borrower or placed in the mail no later than three business days after receiving the borrower's application. The TILA-RESPA Integrated Disclosure Rule (TRID) states that the Closing Disclosure must be provided to the borrower no more than three business days before **consummation**. Consummation is not the same thing as settlement or closing. Consummation is when the borrower becomes contractually obligated to the lender for the loan. For the purpose of delivering the Loan Estimate, a **business day** is defined as a day in which the lender is open and carrying out substantially all of its business functions. "Business day" is defined differently for purposes of the Closing Disclosure. There it is defined as all calendar days except Sundays and legal public holidays.

TYPES OF PERMISSIBLE FEES AND FINANCE CHARGES

There are myriad fees involved in originating a mortgage, also known as a closed-end loan, secured by a primary residence. Permissible fees include costs incurred by the lender in making the loan, origination fees, points, processing fees, and services that can and cannot be shopped for. Other costs that happen in a real estate transaction include government fees such as recording fees, initial escrow, transfer fees, and private mortgage insurance (PMI). PMI protects lenders in the event that a borrower defaults on a mortgage. This type of insurance guarantees that the lender will recoup some predetermined amount in the event of default.

CIRCUMSTANCES UNDER WHICH A LOAN ESTIMATE MAY BE AMENDED

A lender may revise and reissue a Loan Estimate when changed circumstances cause the estimated charge to increase or—in some instances—when charges increase by more than the 10 percent tolerance. Charges for third-party services and recording fees paid by the consumer are subject to a 10 percent tolerance or **10 percent cumulative tolerance.** This means the lender may charge more for these services than what is listed on the original Loan Estimate as long as the total for all such charges does not increase by more than 10 percent of what was disclosed on the Loan Estimate. However, when a lender allows a borrower to shop for third-party service providers and the borrower chooses one that is not on the lender's approved list, this charge is not subject to the 10 percent cumulative tolerance rule. A lender can also amend the Loan Estimate if the lender charges for a service but does not actually perform the service.

GENERAL INFORMATION ABOUT THE TILA-RESPA INTEGRATED DISCLOSURE RULE

TILA-RESPA was an outgrowth of the Dodd-Frank Wall Street reforms, enacted after the 2008 mortgage crisis. During this reform movement, lawmakers—urged by lenders and borrowers—sought to simplify complex mortgage disclosures, making them more accessible and transparent. The biggest change simplified the required disclosures at application. The primary forms are now the Loan Estimate and the Closing Disclosure. The Loan Estimate must be given within three days of submitting an application. This new form is designed to clearly state estimated costs, loan features, and consumer risks assumed when taking a mortgage. The Closing Disclosure was redesigned to make it easy for consumers to understand the closing costs associated with a mortgage. It must be provided three business days before closing. These new disclosures apply to most closed-end loans involving a primary residence. They do not pertain to home equity lines of credit, reverse mortgages, mortgages secured by a mobile home, or homes that are not attached to real property (that is, land). These rules also do not apply to creditors who originate five or fewer mortgages per year.

BORROWER INFORMATION THAT IS INCLUDED ON AN APPLICATION

An **application** is defined as the submission of the consumer's personal financial information with the goal of obtaining a loan secured by the borrower's primary residence. The lender needs six pieces of information for a complete application: the borrower's name, income, Social Security number (to obtain a credit report), the property address, the property value, and the amount of the loan the borrower is requesting. The TILA-RESPA Integrated Disclosure Rule (TRID) slightly alters the minimum information required under Regulation X, which also stipulated that a complete application included the six pieces of information listed above plus "any other information deemed necessary by the loan originator." TRID leaves out this seventh requirement. An application may be submitted electronically, on paper, or orally when there is a written record of the conversation. This definition of an application does not prevent the lender from collecting whatever information it deems necessary to complete an application.

INFORMATION THAT MUST BE DISCLOSED TO CONSUMERS UPON REQUEST

A creditor may use a revised estimate of charges when a consumer requests changes that cause charges to increase from the original Loan Estimate. Providing a revised Loan Estimate protects the lender and allows the borrower to compare the charges in both scenarios. Under these circumstances, a new Loan Estimate may be required. If the revised charges increase or decrease but are still within an acceptable range of tolerance, the original Loan Estimate may still be considered to be in good faith. Redisclosure is permissible but will not reset the tolerances. Tolerances must still be measured using the original Loan Estimate.

APR

Although the Congress considered changing the definition of annual percentage rate (APR) with TILA-RESPA Integrated Disclosure Rule (TRID), in the end, the definition remains the same as discussed in Regulation Z. APR is the cost of credit measured on a yearly basis for the term of the loan. APR includes any additional fees and costs associated with the loan but does not include compounding. If a previously quoted APR becomes inaccurate, the lender must provide a new closing disclosure with the corrected rate along with any other changes. Regulation Z provides two acceptable methods for computing APR: the actuarial method and the United States Rule method. See Appendix J of Regulation Z for further explanation.

PARTY REQUIRED TO PROVIDE THE LOAN ESTIMATE

All lenders originating closed-end loans to borrowers secured by the borrower's home must provide the Loan Estimate. A broker may also provide a Loan Estimate on a lender's behalf. A broker receiving the borrower's loan application can provide the Loan Estimate. This satisfies the lender's obligation to provide the Loan Estimate. However, it is still the lender that is legally liable for any errors, defects, or omissions. If the mortgage broker provides the Loan Estimate, the broker must retain a copy in its records to comply with the three-year record retention rule. The lender must also communicate with the broker to ensure timely delivery and to ensure that the Loan Estimate meets all federal requirements.

TYPES OF LOANS COVERED UNDER TILA

Most consumer closed-end loans secured by real property are covered under the Truth in Lending Act (TILA), including purchases and refinances. Also, credit extended to trusts for tax or estate planning purposes is not exempt from TILA. TILA does not apply to home equity lines of credit, reverse mortgages, mortgages for mobile homes, or homes not secured to real property (that is, land). TILA also does not apply to entities that make five or fewer mortgage loans in a given year and are not creditors. TILA does not apply to commercial, business, or agricultural loans in which the loan proceeds are being acquired for nonpersonal use and no personal residence is included in the transaction.

ACTIONS AN MLO MUST TAKE WHEN THERE IS INCOMPLETE INFORMATION ON A TRID DISCLOSURE

Creditors must act in **good faith**. Good faith is acting sincerely and honestly without malice, with no intention to deceive or defraud. Creditors must sincerely and with due diligence try to obtain the information needed to complete the Loan Estimate. Creditors can rely on the representations of other parties for the required information. It is understood that in a real estate transaction, some information may be unknown at the time the Loan Estimate needs to be delivered. In such cases, the creditor is allowed to estimate some costs or charges. When using estimates, this must be disclosed on the Loan Estimate, and the lender must inform the borrower that new disclosures may be required.

SCENARIO VIOLATIONS OF THE TILA-RESPA INTEGRATED DISCLOSURE RULE (TRID)

Four common violations of the TILA-RESPA Integrated Disclosure Rule (TRID) that happen often in the marketplace are: 1) lenders providing Loan Estimates and Closing Disclosures that have the same issue date, a clear violation of TRID timelines; 2) lenders neglecting to provide a Closing Disclosure to the seller—lenders are reporting that many settlement agents are failing to meet this requirement and that some settlement agents continue to use the old HUD-1 instead of the required Closing Disclosure; 3) fee names on the Loan Estimate that have different names on the Closing Disclosure—regulations require the fee names to be consistent on both disclosures; and 4) omissions and incorrect information provided regarding contact information that have resulted in TRID violations.

BORROWER'S RIGHTS TO RESCISSION

Remember, TRID primarily deals with the introduction of the Loan Estimate and Closing Disclosure, which incorporate some of the previously required disclosures used for mortgages when purchasing a primary residence. There is no right of rescission on a mortgage made for the purpose of purchasing a home. The borrower has the right to rescind or cancel a loan when the loan is made to refinance an existing mortgage, for a reverse mortgage, or for a home equity loan. The borrower has three business days after signing the closing documents to cancel the transaction. The rescission period can extend to three years if it is discovered that the lender made an error, such as overstating finance charges or not providing proper disclosures.

LOAN CONSUMMATION

Consummation often occurs at the time of a loan closing, but legally it is a more distinct event. **Consummation** occurs when a borrower becomes contractually obligated to a lender and to the terms of the loan. This should not be confused with the point at which a buyer becomes contractually obligated to a seller on a real estate transaction. The point at which a borrower becomes contractually committed to a lender depends on state law. It is up to the lender and settlement agent to clarify applicable state laws and to explain when consummation occurs. The lender is required to make sure the Closing Disclosure is delivered three business days prior to consummation.

INFORMATION THAT MUST BE DISCLOSED ON A LOAN ESTIMATE

Page 1 of the **Loan Estimate** contains general information about the loan, the name of the lender, projected payments, and estimated closing costs. The top of page 1 has the date the disclosure is issued, the applicant's name, property address, name of the lender, and the loan term and type—for example, Federal Housing Administration (FHA) or conventional. The next section, Loan Terms, details the loan amount, rate, and projected monthly payment and whether there will be a prepayment penalty or balloon payment. The next section breaks down the monthly payment by principal, interest, and insurance, and it details the estimated escrow required. The last section on page 1 details the estimated closing costs and cash the borrower will need to bring to closing.

Page 2 has four main categories: a good-faith itemization of the Loan Costs and Other Costs, more details about the cash needed at closing, a section for disclosing details about adjustable monthly payments (if required), and a section for disclosing adjustable interest rates (if this is a feature of the loan).

The last page of the Loan Estimate, page 3, contains lender contact information, a Comparisons table, and an Other Considerations table, as well as space for the borrower to sign, acknowledging receipt.

FACTS ABOUT LOAN ESTIMATE

The Loan Estimate is a good faith estimate of credit costs that must be delivered to a borrower within three business days of the lender receiving an application. The Loan Estimate must be in writing and must contain the information prescribed in section 1026.37 of Regulation Z, the Truth in Lending Act (TILA), which includes (among other facts) all of the following:

- The lender's name and contact information
- The loan type, amount, terms, interest rate (fixed or adjustable), costs, and how much cash the borrower will need at closing
- Details about the payment, including whether there might be a balloon payment or prepayment penalty
- Information about escrow
- Costs associated with services one can and cannot shop for
- Taxes and fees
- Origination charges

A Loan Estimate can be revised in the event of a changed circumstance. The revised Loan Estimate must be given to the borrower within seven business days before consummation.

INFORMING A BORROWER OF OTHER LOAN CONSIDERATIONS

As set forth by TILA-RESPA, page 3 of the Loan Estimate provides a table of information lenders are required to disclose to consumers in real estate transactions. The section is labeled Other Considerations and includes information about appraisals, assumptions, homeowner's insurance, late payments, refinancing, and servicing. The section notifies the borrower that he or she will have to pay for an appraisal and will receive a copy, and it details the borrower's right to request a second appraisal. The section clearly states whether the lender will allow an assumption in the event the borrower sells or transfers the home. Other Considerations also informs the borrower about the lender's requirement that the borrower purchase homeowner's insurance and how it will handle late payments. The section also informs the borrower of his or her right to refinance the loan in the future and that under some circumstances refinancing might be impossible. It also informs the lender whether the loan will be serviced by the lender or transferred.

CHARGES AND FEES DISCLOSED

Loan costs include:

- Origination charges (as a percentage of the loan amount, sometimes referred to as points)
- Services You Cannot Shop For:
    - Appraisal fee
    - Appraisal management company fee
    - Credit report fee
    - Flood determination fee
    - Government funding fee
    - Homeowners association certification fee
    - Lender's attorney fee
    - Tax status search fee
    - Third-party subordination fee
    - Title fees
    - Up-front mortgage insurance fee
- Services You Can Shop For:
    - Pest inspection fee
    - Survey fee
    - Title—closing agent fee
    - Title—closing protection letter fee

Other costs include:

- Recording fees and other taxes
- Transfer taxes
- Prepaids, including mortgage insurance premium, property taxes, and prepaid interest
- Initial escrow payments, including homeowner's insurance, mortgage insurance, and property taxes

INFORMATION INCLUDED ON A CLOSING DISCLOSURE

Page 1 on the **Closing Disclosure** is almost identical to page 1 on the Loan Estimate, listing general information, including the date of issue, names of lenders, borrower and seller, loan terms and type, disbursement date, sale price, and the property address. Section 1, Loan Terms, gives the loan amount, interest rate, and monthly principal and interest payment and confirms whether there will be a prepayment penalty or a balloon payment. Section 2, Projected Payments, breaks down the payment by principal, interest, and escrow amounts. The last section on page 1, Costs at Closing, details the total closing costs plus cash required by the borrower to bring to closing.

Page 2 contains an itemization of the closing costs. It is laid out like a grid with lines for each cost and columns detailing who pays the costs: the seller, buyer, or other payer. There are two sections: Loan Costs and Other Costs.

Page 3 calculates cash required at closing. The first section, Calculating Cash to Close, helps the borrower compare how costs may have changed from the Loan Estimate. The second section, Summaries of Transactions, is a line-by-line breakdown of things such as sale price, taxes, assessments, deposits, and more.

ACCELERATION DEFINITION

Acceleration pertains to the practice of paying off a loan faster than the term set by the lender when the loan was originated. For example, a borrower can accelerate the payoff of a 30-year mortgage by paying more than the minimum monthly payment. Any amount paid above the minimum is credited to the principal of the loan, which decreases the compounding of interest. A common practice is to pay one's minimum monthly payment in biweekly installments instead of one monthly payment. This practice results in at least one full extra payment per year and can significantly reduce the time needed to pay off a 30-year mortgage. Acceleration is sometimes referred to as prepayment. The vast majority of mortgages allow for prepayment without penalty. If there is a prepayment penalty, this must be disclosed to the borrower during origination.

THE RIGHT TO RECEIVE AN APPRAISAL REPORT

Lenders are required to provide a copy of the property appraisal to borrowers for first-lien loans in connection with a mortgage application, at no additional cost, promptly upon completion and no later than three days prior to closing. The copy must be provided whether or not the borrower requests it. The lender must notify the borrower of any appraisal or valuation and that there may be a cost for the service. If the loan is not consummated, the lender has 30 days to provide an appraisal copy to borrowers. Lenders cannot charge borrowers for appraisal or other valuation copies, but the lender may charge the borrower for the appraisal or valuation services. A borrower has the right to request and pay for a second appraisal.

Other Federal Laws and Guidelines

HOME MORTGAGE DISCLOSURE ACT (HMDA)
MORTGAGES IN REPORTABLE DATA

The **Home Mortgage Disclosure Act (HMDA)** requires lenders to collect data about their lending activities to ensure that the lenders are complying with federal regulations serving the lending needs of their communities, to ensure public and private investment is distributed where it is needed most, and to ensure that lenders are not discriminating against borrowers. The act pertains to mortgages used to purchase a home or refinance an existing mortgage or home loans used to improve, repair, rehab, or remodel a home. The data collected and reported is available to the public and includes a variety of statistics, including the types of loans made and their purpose, demographic information about borrowers, neighborhoods where loans were made, approval rates, loan amounts, and more.

HOME MORTGAGE DISCLOSURE ACT (HMDA) DEFINITION OF "DWELLING"

A dwelling is a residential structure and does not have to be attached to real property. This includes a detached home, condos or co-ops, manufactured homes, and multifamily homes or communities.

Institutions covered by the Home Mortgage Disclosure Act (HMDA) are banks, savings associations, and credit unions that had assets of less than $56 million as of 2024. This number is adjusted annually based on inflation. The act pertains to banks, savings associations, and credit unions with offices in a metropolitan statistical area that originated at least one home purchase mortgage or refinance that is federally insured or regulated. It also pertains if the loan was guaranteed by a federal agency and meets at least one of the following two criteria: in each of the last two calendar years originated at least 25 closed-end mortgages or 500 open-end lines of credit.

INFORMATION INCLUDED IN BORROWER DATA

The information included in borrower data is comprehensive. It includes extensive borrower demographics, loan details, the loan decision, and more. Because the data is used by the federal government to monitor banks and ensure they comply with federal regulations, the data set needs to be comprehensive. Also, this same data is available to the public. Uses for the data and reasons to access it are quite varied, so the government does its best to be as comprehensive as possible. Some of the basic information collected includes borrower demographics like sex, age, ethnicity, race, and income. Details about the loan include the type of loan (closed-end, open-end, or reverse); the purpose of the loan (purchase, home improvement, or refinance); whether the loan is federally guaranteed (Federal Housing Administration [FHA] or Veterans Administration [VA]); fees and costs; the location of the property (metropolitan statistical area); whether the application is approved, denied, or incomplete; the action date; whether there is a balloon payment or prepayment penalties; and much more.

INFORMATION THAT A BORROWER MUST INCLUDE ON AN APPLICATION

The lender needs to know some basic information about the borrower and the home when taking a mortgage application, including but not limited to the borrower's name, Social Security number, monthly income, the loan amount, the address of the home being purchased, and the estimated value of the home. The consumer will be asked about his or her ethnicity, race, and sex so that the lender can show it has complied with federal regulations; however, the borrower does not have to provide this information. Lenders cannot use a borrower's age, race, sex, nationality, color, religion, marital status, or the fact that a borrower receives public assistance to discriminate.

INFORMATION PROVIDED BY THE BORROWER REGARDING THE RIGHT OF REFUSAL

The lender is required to ask for the borrower or applicant's ethnicity, race, and sex whether the application is taken in person or by phone, mail, or the internet. The lender should state that federal regulations require collecting this information to ensure that banks and lending institutions are complying with federal laws that prohibit discrimination and that promote fair lending. A borrower or applicant can refuse to provide this information. If applicable, the lender must note in the application that the applicant refused to provide the information. When an application is taken in person, the lender must inform the applicant that if he or she refuses to provide his or her ethnicity, race, and sex, the bank will note these demographics by means of visual observation or surname.

FAIR CREDIT REPORTING ACT (FCRA)/FAIR AND ACCURATE CREDIT TRANSACTIONS ACT (FACTA)

FRAUD ALERT

A **fraud alert** is a notice placed with a credit reporting agency that alerts lenders of possible identity theft and requires lenders to follow procedures to protect consumers. Fraud alerts make it more difficult for thieves to obtain credit in another consumer's name. They can also make it more difficult for a consumer to obtain credit. An individual can place a fraud alert in his or her credit file by calling any one of the three credit reporting agencies: Experian, TransUnion, or Equifax. Consumers can place these alerts even if they merely suspect they are identity theft victims; no proof is required. However, if a consumer wishes to place an extended alert, which stays on file for seven years, the consumer must submit an identity theft report filed with a local, state, or federal law enforcement agency.

INFORMATION INCLUDED IN A CONSUMER REPORT

A **consumer report** is any oral or written communication that relays information about a consumer's creditworthiness, character, personal characteristics, or lifestyle to measure an applicant's eligibility to receive credit or insurance or to discern whether the applicant is a suitable employment prospect. An **investigative consumer report** is a written or oral communication that conveys information about a consumer's character, personal characteristics, lifestyle, or reputation through interviews, either in person or by other verbal communication, with the consumer's friends, acquaintances, neighbors, associates, coworkers, or any other person who might have knowledge of the consumer.

REQUIREMENT TO DEVELOP POLICIES AND PROCEDURES REGARDING IDENTITY THEFT

The **Fair and Accurate Credit Transactions Act (FACTA)** was passed in 2003 with an emphasis on protecting consumers from identity theft. The act established the **Red Flags Rule**, requiring all entities in the business of extending credit to create written policies and procedures for detecting red flags they see in their day-to-day operations that could indicate a consumer may become an identity theft victim and to take steps to prevent and/or minimize the damage to a consumer. There are four basic elements the business must create to deal with identity theft: 1) a program must have procedures for identifying red flags, such as fake IDs or suspicious account activity; 2) the business must then have procedures for detecting red flags (e.g., maintaining a file of driver's licenses for each state so employees can compare licenses to it when they think an applicant has presented them with a fake); 3) the program must spell out actions to take in the event of detecting a red flag; and 4) the program must have a plan to keep current with new threats.

DEFINITION OF CREDITOR

A creditor is someone who regularly participates in credit decisions, including setting the terms of credit. A creditor can also be someone who, in the normal course of business, refers applicants to creditors, selects creditors, or offers to select creditors to whom offers of credit can be made. A person is not considered a creditor in regard to any violation of FACTA unless the person had knowledge of the violation before becoming involved in the transaction. Someone who accepts a credit card is not considered a creditor.

INFORMATION INCLUDED IN A FACTA DISCLOSURE

All information in a creditor's files is available to the consumer upon request. The disclosure must identify the sources of all information (with some exceptions for names included in an investigative consumer report); names of entities requesting a report on the consumer (the last two years for employment or one year for all other purposes); a record of all inquiries for the last year in relation to an application for credit or insurance, dates, amounts, and entities involving adverse characterizations of the consumer; the consumer's right to obtain and dispute credit scores and credit history; how to obtain one's credit report; and the frequency that a credit report can be obtained without charge (annually).

LENGTH OF TIME A BANKRUPTCY WILL SHOW ON A CREDIT HISTORY

Chapter 7 and chapter 11 bankruptcies show for 10 years, whereas chapter 13 bankruptcies show for seven years. Chapter 7 bankruptcies are known as liquidations, in which all assets are sold and debts are prioritized and paid. A chapter 11 bankruptcy allows businesses protection from creditors while they reorganize. A chapter 13 bankruptcy allows an individual a chance to create a repayment plan to repay all of his or her creditors under the supervision of the courts. Chapter 7 bankruptcies are allowed only if a debtor has not filed bankruptcy in the last eight years. Credit counseling and a means test are required prior to filing chapter 7.

CREDIT SCORE EVALUATION METHODS

Creating credit scores for individual consumers is complex and varies among creditors and insurance companies. Typically, a creditor takes a random sample of consumers and identifies

34

characteristics related to risk. Each characteristic is assigned a weight based on how good the characteristic is in predicting risk. The system may not use ethnicity, sex, race, national origin, religion, or any other discriminating factor in developing a scoring system. One of the most popular scoring methods is FICO, developed by the Fair Isaac Corporation. Their methods are a closely guarded secret, but it is known that their scores are based on 35 percent payment history, 30 percent amount owed, 15 percent length of credit history, 10 percent new credit, and 10 percent types of credit used. FICO creates a score for borrowers based on its assessments. A FICO score is a measure of a borrower's creditworthiness and ranges from 300 to 850, with 850 being the best.

FTC RED FLAG RULES
PARTIES SUBJECT TO RED FLAG RULES

All financial institutions and creditors are subject to red flag rules. Red flag rules are designed to help institutions spot possible identity theft to protect consumers and their personal financial data. The red flag rules are all about detection, prevention, and mitigation of identity theft. Red flag rules define a financial institution as a state or national bank, a state or federal savings and loan association, a mutual savings bank, a state or federal credit union, or a person who directly or indirectly holds a transaction account belonging to a consumer. A creditor is defined as someone who regularly participates in credit decisions, including setting the terms of credit. The Federal Trade Commission enforces the red flag rules.

BANK SECRECY ACT/ANTI-MONEY LAUNDERING (BSA/AML)
REQUIREMENT THAT COMPANIES PROTECT CONSUMER INFORMATION

The Bank Secrecy Act was established in the 1970s to prevent money laundering. At the time, illegal drug activity was on the rise, bringing large amounts of cash into the United States from abroad. **Money laundering** is concealing the origins of ill-gotten funds and introducing the funds into the banking system to make the money appear legitimate. Generally speaking, the law requires US banks to report suspicious cash deposits. The law was put into effect to fight the drug trade, stop terrorism funding, and catch tax cheats. The law requires banks to establish procedures to report money laundering activities and to establish programs to train their employees to recognize suspicious activity and understand how to report it.

Criminals conceal their money by integrating it in stages into the financial system to make it appear "clean." The first stage is **placement**: placing the cash into the banking system to begin the cleansing process.

The next stage is **layering**: moving the money around and manipulating it or converting the funds into other assets such as traveler's checks, money orders, or postal orders to make the funds appear legitimate. Once the money is in the banks, it can be wired through accounts (including offshore bank accounts), moved through trust accounts, used to buy securities, converted to letters of credit, or used to purchase valuable items like art, jewelry, or real estate. All of these transactions disguise the origins of the cash.

The final state is **integration**: funds being reintroduced into the legitimate economy, appearing to be from a legitimate source. An example would be routing funds through an offshore corporation and returning the money to the United States as foreign direct investment. Another example would be using cash to buy casino chips, gambling in the casino, and cashing out to make the funds appear to be from gambling winnings.

FACTS ABOUT SUSPICIOUS ACTIVITY REPORTS (SARs)

A **suspicious activity report (SAR)** is when banks detect known or suspected criminal activity and report the transaction(s) to federal authorities. The Financial Crimes Enforcement Network (FinCEN) is the federal agency that collects and investigates SARs. SARs must be filed within 30 days of the suspected activity and retained by the financial institution for five years. The reports include detailed information about suspicious transactions to help identify potential criminals or organizations, terrorist financing, money laundering, or other crimes. In many instances, SARs have been instrumental in helping authorities catch and prosecute terrorists, drug lords, and other criminals. The reports are also invaluable in helping authorities understand emerging criminal trends and patterns associated with crime.

CIRCUMSTANCES THAT REQUIRE FILING A SAR

The following circumstances require filing a SAR:

- Any incidence of suspected criminal abuse by a bank employee of any dollar amount
- Criminal activity involving $5,000 or more when a suspect can be identified
- Suspicious activity of $25,000 or more regardless of a potential suspect
- Any other suspicious activity involving $5,000 or more when any kind of criminal activity is suspected, that is, money laundering or terrorist financing
- Activity that appears to be designed to evade Bank Secrecy Act regulations
- Transaction activity that appears to have no genuine business purpose or is unusual for a customer or business and cannot be explained

Examples of transactions are deposits, withdrawals, transfers, currency exchange, stock or bond purchases, opening new accounts (including credit accounts), and payments.

SAR PRIVACY REQUIREMENTS

Banks and their employees are prohibited from notifying people or businesses involved in an SAR that a report has been filed related to one of their transactions. An SAR and all information contained in it are confidential. Even the existence or nonexistence of an SAR is confidential. FinCEN advises banks that even the process of filing an SAR should be done in a way to minimize detection by the suspect of the filing. Banks are allowed to share SARs with other financial institutions when the financial institutions are filing joint SARs or in connection with employment-related inquiries or terminations as long as the suspect of the SAR remains anonymous. Banks are allowed to reveal SARs by order of subpoena in most circumstances.

GRAMM-LEACH-BLILEY ACT—PRIVACY, FTC SAFEGUARD RULES, AND DO NOT CALL
NONPUBLIC INFORMATION REGARDING A CUSTOMER

Nonpublic information is personally identifiable financial information that a consumer provides to an organization during the regular course of business with that organization. The **Gramm-Leach-Bliley Act** states that companies must ensure the security and confidentiality of nonpublic customer information, protect against anticipated hazards threatening the security of such information, and protect against unauthorized access that could result in substantial harm to consumers. The act requires companies to notify customers about any possible situations in which their personal information might be shared. The act also requires companies to give notice to customers that they have the right to opt out of having their information shared with a company's **affiliates** or **third parties**. Affiliates are any companies controlled by or under common control of another company. Third parties would be unaffiliated companies that maintain a sharing arrangement.

PERMISSIBLE USE OF NONPUBLIC INFORMATION REGARDING A CUSTOMER

It is permissible to share nonpublic information regarding a customer only after the customer has been apprised of this possibility in writing and has had a chance to opt out of sharing. The consumer must be given sufficient time to opt out before sharing occurs, and companies must clearly explain to customers how they can opt out. If a company does not provide nonpublic customer information to affiliated or third parties, then the company is not obligated to inform the customer about sharing. Also, if a company does not have a relationship with a customer, the company is under no obligation to disclose its sharing arrangements. A customer relationship exists when a company and a customer enter into a continuing relationship, for example, when a customer opens a credit card or deposit account or buys an insurance product, buys an investment product or agrees to buy investment advice, or becomes a client for the purpose of receiving tax services or debt counseling.

PURPOSE OF THE GRAMM-LEACH-BLILEY ACT

Gramm-Leach-Bliley introduced sweeping new changes to the banking and financial industry, allowing financial institutions to offer more services. One purpose of the Gramm-Leach-Bliley Act was to safeguard consumers' private information by requiring institutions to explain how their personal information is shared and to give consumers the opportunity to opt out of sharing arrangements. Before the act, banks were not allowed to offer insurance or brokerage services. This prohibition arose out of the Great Depression of 1929 when the US stock market collapsed. After the collapse, lawmakers passed legislation that walled off banks from stock brokerages to protect depositors from stock market volatility. In 1993, when mergers between banks, insurance companies, and brokerages began to happen, customers' personal information became vulnerable to sharing among the newly merged entities. An example is the merger of Travelers Group, an insurance company, and Citibank, which ultimately included the brokerage services of Smith Barney and Primerica. This newly formed conglomerate brought many separate businesses under one roof. Now each separate business could potentially market its services to all of the customers under the new umbrella. Lawmakers reacted by making these conglomerates reveal their intent to share information for marketing purposes and to allow consumers to say they wanted their personal information to remain confidential.

REQUIREMENT FOR WRITTEN PRIVACY POLICY DISCLOSURES

All companies sharing nonpublic customer information are required to inform their customers of their policies in writing (or in electronic form) at least annually. The written notice must be clear and conspicuous, meaning the notice is reasonably understandable to anyone with a sixth-grade education and is designed to state the nature and significance of the company's policies. The written notices shall disclose the policies and practices of the company with regard to sharing information; who the information will be shared with; what happens with customers' information after they are no longer customers of the company; what information will be shared; and the company's strategy and policy for maintaining confidentiality and security of the customers' nonpublic information.

PERMISSIBLE HOURS FOR TELEPHONE CALLS

It is permissible for sellers to call consumers to solicit the sale of goods or services or charitable contributions between the hours of 8 a.m. and 9 p.m. This rule aims to protect consumers from aggressive and abusive telemarketing. Telemarketing rules and the Do Not Call Registry were created with the elderly in mind. The elderly are the fastest-growing segment of the American population and are frequent targets of telemarketing fraud and abuse. Overall, telemarketers bilked more than $9 billion from all consumers in 2017. Congress has identified a long list of abusive telemarketing practices that are prohibited by telemarketing sales rules, including using profane language, threats, or intimidation; engaging prospects in repeated telephone calls with the intent to annoy, abuse, or harass; denying requests to be put on the Do Not Call Registry; initiating calls to people who have expressed a desire not to be called; calling people who are on the Do Not Call Registry; callers failing to promptly identify themselves and the reason for the call; and many more.

WRITTEN POLICIES FOR MAINTAINING DO-NOT-CALL LISTS

Businesses are required to implement written procedures that prescribe how the business will honor consumers' requests that they not be called and/or that they be added to the Do Not Call Registry. The written policies must include training procedures to help their personnel understand how to deal with do-not-call requests. Businesses must document the process and procedures for avoiding calls to individuals who are on the Do Not Call Registry. The business must also designate someone in the company who is responsible for monitoring activity and enforcing do-not-call and federal telemarketing regulations and standards. If it is found that sellers (or hired telemarketers) did not have written do-not-call procedures in place, both are liable. Fines per call can be as high as $40,000. If a seller has written procedures in place, but the hired telemarketer ignored them, then only the telemarketer is liable.

PRECAUTIONS TO PROTECT CUSTOMER INFORMATION

Telemarketing rules and a Do Not Call Registry were established with the intention of protecting consumers' right to privacy. The following actions are a direct violation of consumer privacy: calling consumers who have placed their phone numbers on a registry, misusing a do-not-call list, denying or interfering with a consumer's do-not-call rights, calling outside of permissible hours, abandoning an outbound call (abandoning is when a consumer answers a telemarketing call and is not connected to a salesperson within two seconds of the caller's completed greeting), placing robocalls to a consumer without the consumer's express written consent to accept such calls, failure to transmit caller ID information to a consumer, using obscene language, and calling repeatedly. Businesses using robocalls are required to have a voice-activated opt-out mechanism and also provide a number in the beginning of the prerecorded call that tells the consumer where to call to opt out of future robocalls.

PURPOSE OF THE NATIONAL DO NOT CALL REGISTRY

The Do Not Call Registry was created to allow consumers to choose whether they wanted to receive telemarketing calls. The rules pertain to all plans or campaigns that sell goods or services through interstate phone calls. Federal telemarketing rules prohibit robocalls for the purpose of selling goods and services without obtaining prior written consent from consumers. Political and charitable organizations are allowed to call consumers—even those on the Do Not Call Registry. In addition, the do-not-call list does not pertain to surveyors nor to businesses that have an existing relationship with a consumer. In the early 1990s, an increasing number of consumers began to complain about unsolicited telephone calls. In response, federal and state lawmakers began to pass laws regulating telemarketing calls. By 2002, 27 states had their own do-not-call lists. After the Federal Trade Commission began enforcing a federal list in 2002, most states deferred to the Do Not Call Registry, which today maintains a list of more than 230 million numbers.

PERMISSIBLE SOLICITATION SCENARIOS

The do-not-call provisions exempt charitable and political organizations and businesses that already have an existing business relationship with a customer. An **existing business relationship** is defined as when a consumer purchases, leases, or rents a business's good or service or there has been a financial transaction between the business and consumer in the previous 18 months preceding a telemarketing call. A business relationship also exists if a consumer inquires about a business's goods or services in the previous three months prior to a marketing call. Promoting a

38

political party or candidate is permissible as long as the calls are not part of a plan to induce the consumer to buy goods or services. Business-to-business calls are also permissible solicitations. Calls to consumers who have given their written permission to receive telemarketing calls are also permissible solicitations and exempt from do-not-call regulations, even if the consumer is on the do-not-call list. Informational messaging and surveys are also permissible calls and exempt from do-not-call regulations.

DO-NOT-CALL REQUEST

Sellers and telemarketers must honor and have procedures in place to comply with all do-not-call requests, according to federal regulations. A seller or telemarketer who ignores a consumer's do-not-call request is considered to be committing an abusive practice under federal regulations. It is illegal for a seller or telemarketer to deny or interfere with a consumer's request to be placed on any do-not-call registry. Further, companies are not allowed to harass or hang up on a consumer who makes a request to be placed on a do-not-call list. Companies also are not allowed to force a consumer to listen to a sales pitch or charge a fee before accepting a do-not-call request. All requests must be handled by the caller immediately. Sellers cannot tell a consumer to call another number to be placed on a do-not-call list.

RETENTION OF INFORMATION AFTER A SOLICITATION

Sellers are required to keep the following information for 24 months from the date the record is created:

- Advertising, brochures, telemarketing scripts, and promotional materials
- Name and address of prize recipients who won $25 or more
- Name and address of customers who purchased something, goods or services purchased, amount paid, and date of sale

Sellers and telemarketers must keep a list of all employees who make solicitation calls; their job titles, home addresses, and telephone numbers; and all verifiable records of express informed consent or agreement. A **telemarketer** is defined as someone employed by a telemarketing company making phone calls to solicit donations or purchases of goods and services. **Telemarketing** means a campaign conducted to sell goods and services or to obtain charitable donations by the use of more than one telephone involving more than one interstate telephone call.

MORTGAGE ACTS AND PRACTICES—ADVERTISING

ADVERTISEMENTS REFERRING TO SPECIFIC CREDIT TERMS

An advertiser can state specific credit terms only if those terms are actually available to borrowers and will be offered by the lender. A lender cannot advertise a low rate unless it is actually available and the creditor is prepared to offer that rate to borrowers. A lender can offer credit terms that are available for only a short time period or terms that will be available to a borrower in the near future. Specific credit terms refer to any component of a credit plan, for example, periodic payments, points, or term.

For a home equity loan, if the lender uses a triggering term, the advertisement must also clearly disclose any fee that is a percentage of the loan or a fixed fee that will be charged; any periodic rate expressed as an annual percentage rate (APR); and the maximum annual percentage rate that the lender may impose.

LENGTH OF TIME REQUIRED TO RETAIN ADVERTISEMENTS

Mortgage advertisements must be retained by the company or person making the advertisement for 24 months from the last date the advertisement was disseminated. Copies of the advertisement, sales scripts, training materials, and marketing materials must be retained. In addition, the lender must keep records of all mortgage products offered during the time of the advertisement. The lender must also maintain a record of all ancillary products offered in addition to the mortgage products—for example, credit insurance and credit disability insurance—that may be offered along with mortgages during the time of the advertisement. Any lender must keep these records in any legible form, manner, or format that they keep such records in the ordinary course of business. Retention of advertisement copies refers to all forms of advertisements: printed, electronic, radio, television, billboards, the sides of buses or cars, infomercials, and any other format deemed to be advertising.

INFORMATION REQUIRED TO BE INCLUDED IN AN ADVERTISEMENT

Mortgage Acts and Practices—Advertising (Regulation N) does not specifically outline information that is required to be included in an advertisement. Rather, it focuses primarily on prohibited representations. Regulation Z deals specifically with information that must be included as the information relates to triggering terms. Remember from Regulation Z, mortgage advertising must be clear and conspicuous. It must not mislead. The spirit of regulations in mortgage advertising is about promoting honesty and forthrightness with consumers. If a lender cannot deliver on its promises, it should not make the promises. Lenders should especially avoid misusing the term "fixed" and should be careful not to **bait and switch**, the practice of luring customers with an appealing offer with the plan to substitute a less-desirable alternative.

The act prohibits lenders from misrepresenting any term of a mortgage loan in advertising, whether the misrepresentation was implied or a statement was blatantly false. This prohibition includes mispresenting or making false promises about any of the following:

- The amount of interest owed, annual percentage rate (APR), fees, and costs
- The costs of products sold in conjunction with mortgages (e.g., life and disability insurance)
- Taxes and insurance, especially their costs and whether or not these items are included in a borrower's monthly payment
- Prepayment penalties
- Variable interest rates
- Comparisons between actual or hypothetical rates or payments
- The type of mortgage offered
- Credits or rebates
- The number of required payments
- Resolving default
- Government affiliation
- The source of commercial communication
- The consumer's right to reside in the dwelling associated with a mortgage
- The consumer's ability to obtain a mortgage
- The availability and nature of counseling services

TRIGGERING TERMS THAT REQUIRE ADDITIONAL DISCLOSURE

A **triggering term** is a closed-end loan feature that requires further disclosure when mentioned in an advertisement. The following are triggering terms: the amount and percentage of any down payment; the number of payments required to pay off the loan or the period of repayment; the amount of any payment; and the amount of any finance charge.

If any of these terms appear in an advertisement, the following further disclosure is required: the exact amount or percentage of down payment must be stated clearly, for example, "3% down payment required" with the terms of repayment reflecting the full obligation over the term of the loan, including any balloon payment; the rate must be stated as annual percentage rate (APR) and the advertisement must disclose whether this is a fixed rate or if it can increase. The best way to meet the disclosure requirements is to give an example in the ad: "For a $100,000, 30-year loan with an APR of 5%, the payment would be $537 per month."

ELECTRONIC SIGNATURES IN GLOBAL AND NATIONAL COMMERCE ACT (ESIGN ACT)
REQUIRED ESIGN DISCLOSURES

Signing electronically is commonplace in real estate transactions today and has the same legal standing and legitimacy as signing on paper. Since the 1970s and the advent of automated teller machines (ATMs), more and more financial transactions have been converting to electronic formats, from online banking to opening accounts electronically. It was logical that signing and storing contracts would also begin to happen electronically. To encourage electronic commerce, Congress passed the Electronic Signatures in Global and National Commerce Act (ESIGN Act) in 2000. The act states that a lender can use electronic contracts as long as the borrower consents and has not withdrawn consent. The lender must clearly and conspicuously inform the consumer about the use of electronic contracts and the consumer's right to choose paper instead. The lender must clearly state the process the consumer can use to withdraw consent to electronic contracts. The act expressly states that a contract or agreement cannot be invalidated solely because the document exists in electronic format. ESIGN regulations cannot be used to require consumers to accept and use electronic formats. The consumer also has the right to know if any fees or conditions will be imposed for electing to sign on paper.

BORROWER'S CONSENT REGARDING ACCESS TO INFORMATION IN ELECTRONIC FORMAT

Consumers must be told how they are able to obtain paper copies of the documents they sign electronically and if a fee will be charged for paper copies. Businesses must disclose to consumers all hardware requirements needed to access and store electronic records. Also, consumers must demonstrate that they are able to use a computer well enough to sign and access electronic documents before a business can use electronic documents in a transaction. Businesses must also apprise consumers of changes in hardware needed to access electronic documents. Businesses must disclose whether signing electronically applies to a specific transaction or will be used in conjunction with other types of transactions as well. There is an exemption regarding storage of electronic records if an electronic version of a record was created solely for the purpose of sending, transmitting, or delivering the record.

REQUIREMENTS FOR MAINTAINING RECORDS IN ELECTRONIC FORMAT

Existing laws requiring records to be maintained are satisfied if a business decides to store the records electronically. The electronic version must accurately reflect the information in a contract or any other type of record. Records stored electronically must remain accessible to all persons who legally have a right to retrieve and view such records. The electronic version of records must be easily reproduced for later reference in any format, whether by transmission, paper, or otherwise. Electronic record storage is permissible in instances where laws require records to be kept in their original form. Laws requiring checks to be stored in the original format are satisfied by storing check copies electronically. It is permissible to store notarized documents and all other documents related to the transaction in electronic form.

WAYS TO VERIFY A BORROWER'S IDENTITY

It may sound simple, but a key component of ensuring the validity of electronic contracts is to authenticate that the identity of the person signing is indeed the person identified in the contract. The signer must present documents maintained by an independent source that prove his or her identity. The document can be a driver's license or any other document issued by a state government. At a minimum, the lender must verify the borrower's name and date of birth and either the signer's Social Security number or driver's license number. Lenders must maintain sufficient evidence that the signature on loan documents can be attributed to the person named in the contract. The lender must then ensure that electronic records cannot be altered. Industry standard encryption must be used to protect the signer's signature and the integrity of the documents. If changes are required, the lender must show an audit trail of the date and time that changes were made and must identify who made them.

USA PATRIOT ACT

PRIMARY PURPOSE

The **USA PATRIOT Act** was passed in 2001 in response to the 9/11 terrorist attacks. ("USA PATRIOT" officially stands for "Uniting and Strengthening America by Providing Appropriate Tools Required to Intercept and Obstruct Terrorism.") The 9/11 attacks signaled that the United States needed to vastly improve its ability to thwart, catch, and prosecute terrorists. The act seeks to bolster American law enforcement's terrorist-fighting ability by establishing new crimes, penalties, procedures, and investigative techniques against domestic and international terrorism. The act focuses on strengthening measures to detect and prosecute money laundering and the financing of terrorism; scrutinizing foreign financial institutions and international transactions that are susceptible to criminal abuse; preventing foreign officials from using American financial institutions for their own personal gain; and facilitating the repatriation of stolen assets to rightful owners around the world.

MAJOR FUNCTIONS

The majority of the USA PATRIOT Act deals with improving US law enforcement's ability to thwart terrorism. Investigations into 9/11 found that terrorists freely used US and international financial institutions to facilitate their operations without detection by using existing laws and regulations. The USA PATRIOT Act forced major changes, including the following:

- Improved law enforcement's tools to detect organized crime and drug trafficking
- Better facilitated information sharing and cooperation among government agencies so that the agencies could more easily "connect the dots"
- Updated laws to reflect changes in technology and new threats, giving investigators more and improved tools for investigating suspected terrorists through surveillance and broader search warrants
- Increased penalties for those convicted of terrorist crimes

For the financial industry, the emphasis was on thwarting money laundering, properly identifying customers, establishing regulations requiring financial institutions to identify and report suspicious activity, and increasing the security of financial networks.

CONFIDENTIAL NATURE OF FILING REPORTS

The main goal of confidentiality in filing suspicious activity reports (SARs) under the USA PATRIOT Act is to do it in a way that does not tip off the suspect that a report has been filed. The act expressly prohibits an employee of a financial institution from disclosing to a suspect involved in a transaction that an SAR has been filed. Further, the act prohibits disclosing any information that might reveal the existence of a report. Confidentiality of SARs is so sensitive that banks do not have to respond to subpoenas (other than those issued by FinCEN or a regulatory or law enforcement agency) seeking information about these reports. The act protects employees of financial institutions who file a report from civil liability with respect to any statement or information included in the report. Sharing of reports among financial institutions is protected in certain instances. Secrecy helps law enforcement maintain the element of surprise when pursuing criminals and terrorists. It also reassures employees of financial institutions who file reports that they are protected. Essentially, confidentiality allows for more robust reporting and increases the likelihood that criminals and terrorists will be caught.

WAYS TO VERIFY A BORROWER'S IDENTITY

The USA PATRIOT Act requires lenders to obtain two forms of identification from borrowers in a credit transaction. The identity documents must contain a photo of the borrower, name, date of birth, and address. Not all of this information is required to be on one document. A lender can use a combination of documents to confirm identity. In the event that the borrower has no address, the lender must collect a military PO box or address of next of kin. For non-US citizens, the identification must contain a taxpayer ID number, passport number with country of issuance, alien ID card number, or other foreign-issued picture ID. The USA PATRIOT Act prescribes that one form of ID must be primary and another secondary. Two secondary IDs are unacceptable to prove identity. Primary IDs are a valid US driver's license, valid state ID, military ID, passport, and Social Security card. Secondary forms of ID are a birth certificate, utility bill, Medicare card, student ID, voter registration, tax bill receipt, vehicle registration, and credit card.

PARTIES SUBJECT TO USA PATRIOT ACT

There are a wide range of entities subject to the USA PATRIOT Act, with the most obvious being financial institutions. Some of the less obvious businesses subject to the act are boat and airplane dealers. Buying and selling these kinds of high-priced items is a popular way criminals launder money. These kinds of vehicles are also good ways for criminals to move contraband and travel without passing through border patrols and checkpoints. Any type of bank is subject to the act, including thrifts, credit unions, trust companies, and branches of foreign banks. Broker dealers and sellers of securities are also prime targets for criminals seeking to launder money, and thus they are subject to the act. The act pertains to businesses that move money, like Western Union, as well as businesses that convert currency; commodities brokers and merchants who sell commodities futures; insurance companies; dealers of precious metals and gems; businesses that deal in real estate transactions, including closing and settlement agents; casinos; travel agencies; and car dealers.

CUSTOMER IDENTIFICATION PROGRAM

The USA PATRIOT Act prescribes that all financial institutions have a program for identifying individuals and that the program must do three things: verify the identity of a borrower or any person opening an account, maintain records of the documents used to identify persons, and determine whether borrowers or account holders are on any government lists of suspected terrorists. The customer identification program rules state that each financial institution's procedures must be written and that they must designate someone to implement and oversee the program. At a minimum, financial institutions must verify a person's name, address, date of birth, and an identification number such as a Social Security number (US individuals) or passport number (non-US individuals). The bank should collect the customer's address and mailing address if the mailing address is different. To verify identity, lenders must rely on unexpired, government-issued identification bearing a photo and nationality for non-US citizens.

HOMEOWNERS PROTECTION ACT (PRIVATE MORTGAGE INSURANCE CANCELLATION ACT)
DOCUMENTS THAT MUST BE PROVIDED TO A BORROWER AT LOAN CONSUMMATION

To protect buyers from paying for private mortgage insurance (PMI) when it is no longer needed, lenders now must disclose the exact timing and conditions for eliminating PMI. For fixed-rate mortgages, the lender must provide a written amortization schedule and a written notice stating, based on the amortization schedule, the exact date on which the buyer may request cancellation of the PMI (when obtaining 20 percent equity). The disclosure must also state that the buyer can cancel the insurance sooner than the date prescribed by the amortization schedule if the buyer makes sufficient payments to cancel sooner. The disclosures must also state that PMI will automatically terminate when 20 percent equity is reached. To cancel the PMI, the homeowner must submit a written cancellation request, be in good standing and current on mortgage payments, and satisfy the lender's request to show that the value of the home has not decreased and that there are no other liens against the home that would decrease the equity to under 20 percent. The same disclosures hold true for adjustable-rate mortgages, except for the amortization schedule.

Regulatory Authority

CONSUMER FINANCIAL PROTECTION BUREAU (CFPB)
FEDERAL OVERSIGHT OF THE CFPB

The Consumer Financial Protection Bureau (CFPB) was created by the Dodd-Frank Wall Street Reform Act in 2010. Looking back on the 2008 subprime mortgage crisis, lawmakers found that many lenders took advantage of borrowers, lending them loans they could not afford or did not understand. Although most lenders acted responsibly, they were forced to compete with their less scrupulous competitors. In the end, the recession harmed everyone in the economy by crushing home prices, boosting credit card rates, and practically drying up credit and home lending altogether. To better protect consumers and financial markets, lawmakers created the CFPB, whose mission is to protect consumers by regulating providers of consumer financial products and services. The CFPB was designed to centralize consumer protection under one agency, whereas before, this oversight stretched across seven federal agencies. The CFPB was created to be an independent agency. It falls under the executive branch of the US government, and its director is appointed by the president. The bureau has many functions, including overseeing mortgages, credit cards, student loans, and payday lenders. It also monitors and reports on markets and collects consumer complaints.

FUNCTIONS PERFORMED BY THE CFPB

The Consumer Financial Protection Bureau (CFPB) has three major functions: educating consumers, enforcing financial regulations, and researching financial markets to stay informed and better protect consumers.

Educate: The CFPB promotes the free flow of financial information, emphasizing clarity and ease of understanding. The CFPB believes that an informed and educated consumer is a protected consumer. It also believes that the fairest economic markets are transparent, where consumers can easily compare products, companies, costs, and benefits to make the best choices for themselves and their families. The CFPB opposes fine print, overly long and jargon-filled disclosures, and account agreements that mislead and confuse consumers.

Enforce: The CFPB is the only government agency that deals directly with consumer rights and protections. Its job is to pull together all of the acts have been previously discussed, such as the Real

Estate Settlement Procedures Act (RESPA), Truth in Lending Act (TILA), Home Mortgage Disclosure Act (HMDA), and Equal Credit Opportunity Act (ECOA), and enforce regulations that protect consumers.

Research: By fielding thousands of complaints and monitoring consumer behavior and financial markets, the bureau is able to identify new risks and trends that can harm consumers. Before, no single agency had the authority or ability to make consumers' financial protection their top priority. Consolidating all of the government's consumer financial regulations under one roof allows for more focus on protecting consumers.

CFPB OVERSIGHT AUTHORITY

The Consumer Financial Protection Bureau (CFPB) oversees banks, thrifts, and credit unions with more than $10 billion in assets. It also oversees mortgage originators and service providers and payday and student lenders of all sizes. The CFPB also oversees credit reporting agencies, consumer debt collectors, international money transferrers, and automobile lenders. Before the CFPB, so-called non-bank financial institutions like **payday lenders** (companies that loan small amounts of money to people at high interest rates on the promise that the money will be repaid with their next paycheck) virtually escaped federal oversight. Abuse in the industry was rampant, an especially egregious problem since most of the consumers using these services were already financially vulnerable. Nearly 20 million Americans use payday lenders. A typical $100 loan might cost $16, which equates to an annual percentage rate (APR) of 400 percent. But if customers miss payments or take too long to pay, huge penalties and more interest can greatly increase the amount owed, often to levels that are financially impossible for borrowers to repay.

FILING COMPLAINTS WITH THE CFPB

The Consumer Financial Protection Bureau (CFPB) handles a variety of complaints, with the most popular concerning mortgages, student loans, vehicle loans, banking services, and credit reporting. Complaints can be filed online at consumerfinance.gov/complaint or by calling 855-411-CFPB. The phone center offers help in more than 180 languages and for those with hearing or speech impairments. The bureau advises that the best complaints clearly state the situation, provide supporting documents, ask for a specific resolution, and state what the consumer has done so far to remedy the situation. The bureau has returned more than $12 billion to consumers through refunds and canceled debts. Each week the bureau sends thousands of complaints to companies to get their side of the story. This dialogue helps the bureau maintain the pulse of the economy and trends in consumer finance. The bureau has the power to levy fines against companies and enforce numerous financial regulations.

DEPARTMENT OF HOUSING AND URBAN DEVELOPMENT (HUD)
PRIMARY FUNCTION OF HUD

The **Department of Housing and Urban Development (HUD)** is a federal agency whose primary aim is to create affordable housing and enforce America's housing laws. The agency was created in 1965 as part of President Lyndon B. Johnson's War on Poverty. It is a **Cabinet** department. There are 15 Cabinet positions in the executive branch of the US government. Cabinet heads report directly to the president, create policy, and make decisions on national issues. HUD helps create affordable housing by guaranteeing mortgages for low- and moderate-income families and by subsidizing public housing for the poor, people with disabilities, minorities, Native Americans, the elderly, the homeless, and those with acquired immune deficiency syndrome (AIDS). The agency also awards grants to communities to help clear blighted areas and spur investment and development, turning declining neighborhoods into safer places that are more livable and attractive

45

to new people and businesses. Through the Federal Housing Administration (FHA), HUD has provided government-backed mortgages for almost 50 million single-family homes.

PROGRAMS OFFERED BY HUD

Housing and Urban Development's (HUD's) biggest program is **Federal Housing Administration (FHA) mortgages**. FHA mortgages are backed and insured by the US government. This program allows borrowers with lower credit scores and lower down payments to be approved for mortgages. Loans can be made with credit scores as low as 500 and down payments as low as 3.5 percent of the purchase price. Borrowers must pay mortgage insurance on these loans to protect lenders in the event of default. Another major program through HUD is community development block grants. These grants help communities improve housing and economic opportunity. Funds are awarded to communities for a variety of projects, but their use must meet one of three broad categories. The funds must be used to help those with low and moderate incomes with housing, prevent or eliminate blight, or correct urgent safety needs. Some of HUD's other programs include providing subsidized rentals (Section 8), educating consumers, enforcing housing laws, and providing homelessness assistance.

TYPES OF LOANS THAT TRIGGER THE REQUIREMENT FOR A COUNSELING AGENCY TO CONSULT WITH A BORROWER

There are two types of loans that require lenders to refer borrowers to loan counselors before the loan can be consummated:

- High-cost mortgages (first-lien mortgages with rates more than 6.5 percentage points above the prime rate, fees that exceed five percent of the total loan amount, or through which the lender can charge a prepayment penalty more than two percent of the amount prepaid or more than 36 months after consummation)
- Mortgages that involve **negative amortization** (a loan whose balance increases even after borrowers make their regular monthly payment because the payments are not enough to keep up with the interest—eventually, the payment increases enough to begin lowering the amount owed)

Lenders cannot choose counselors for borrowers. They are allowed only to provide a list of 10 Consumer Financial Protection Bureau (CFPB)-approved counselors (within three days of taking an application). Borrowers must show confirmation that they attended the counseling.

In addition, lenders must provide a list of counselors to all borrowers taking out a federally related mortgage, including home equity loans (within three days of taking an application). A federally related mortgage is any loan secured by a dwelling. Timeshare loans and reverse mortgages are exempt from the counseling requirements.

ENTITIES THAT HUD OVERSEES

In its mission to promote fair and affordable housing, Housing and Urban Development (HUD) oversees 16 departments that carry out HUD programming. There are also three agencies that fall under HUD: the Government National Mortgage Association (Ginnie Mae), the Federal Housing Administration (FHA), and the Federal Housing Finance Agency (FHFA). Ginnie Mae is a government corporation that strives to make homeownership easier and more affordable. Ginnie Mae guarantees mortgages that are packaged and sold in the global market, giving lenders more money to originate home loans and borrowers more access to mortgages. Ginnie Mae guarantees only government-issued mortgages. FHA insures mortgages. If a borrower defaults, FHA pays claims to the lender. FHFA was another entity born out of the subprime mortgage crisis. It was established in 2008 to oversee the mortgage markets, primarily by regulating Fannie Mae, Freddie Mac, and the Federal Home Loan Bank System. Fannie Mae and Freddie Mac are similar to Ginnie Mae. They repackage mortgages into securities and sell them. These two organizations nearly failed during the subprime mortgage crisis and now are in a **conservatorship** overseen by the FHFA. A conservatorship is when an entity is appointed as "guardian" over another entity to help manage the subordinate's financial affairs.

FAIR HOUSING LAW PROTECTIONS

The Fair Housing Act was enacted as part of the 1968 Civil Rights Act. Its aim is to protect prospective home buyers or renters by prohibiting discrimination based on race, disability, sex, religion, family status, or national origin. When it comes to mortgage lending, it is illegal for a lender to discriminate against a borrower based on any of these characteristics when providing mortgage information or originating a mortgage. Lenders cannot impose different terms, such as interest rates and fees; discriminate on appraisals; nor refuse to buy a mortgage based on any of these characteristics. When it comes to purchasing or selling a home, it is illegal to refuse to sell or deny that housing is available, set different terms for sale, impose different sales prices or charges, or **block bust** (encourage a homeowner to sell because people with protected characteristics are moving into the neighborhood) based on race, disability, sex, religion, family status, or national origin.

Uniform State Content

SAFE Act and CSBS/AARMR Model State Law

STATE MORTGAGE REGULATORY AGENCIES
REGULATORY AUTHORITY
REGULATORY POWER

State mortgage regulatory authority varies from state to state, but most—at a minimum—have the power to supervise the mortgage loan originators (MLOs) and lenders in the state and can suspend, terminate, or refuse to renew licenses for MLOs who violate state and federal mortgage laws. Most agencies have the power to ensure all MLOs are registered with the Nationwide Multistate Licensing System (NMLS). State agencies typically maintain processes for enforcing and ensuring the accuracy of information contained in the NMLS registry for the MLOs in the state. Agencies have the power to assess fines and penalties for violations of state and federal mortgage laws.

State agencies can establish rules that ensure all MLOs are bonded or maintain a pool of funds that MLOs pay into and that is set aside to help those wronged recover losses. Overall, state agencies must have the power to monitor MLOs in their state and have ways to ensure that all lenders act in the best interests of consumers.

NATIONWIDE MULTISTATE LICENSING SYSTEM (NMLS) REGISTRY

The registry was created to comply with new consumer protection laws enacted as a result of the creation of the Consumer Financial Protection Bureau (CFPB) and the passage of the Secure and Fair Enforcement for Mortgage Licensing (SAFE) Act. The registry was created as a way to monitor and track the activities of lenders and mortgage loan originators (MLOs). To be registered, all MLOs must meet certain minimum standards of training and education, character, and integrity; submit to fingerprinting and a criminal background check performed by the Federal Bureau of Investigation (FBI); furnish their names, contact information, and employment history; and disclose any civil or criminal actions taken against them. The MLO is tracked to support federal regulatory oversight and to provide the public with information on the MLOs' backgrounds and histories. The system also helps local, state, and federal agencies coordinate information sharing, increase system efficiencies, and improve enforcement.

CFPB AUTHORITY TO CONDUCT EXAMS

Lawmakers created the Consumer Financial Protection Bureau (CFPB) to improve consumer protection. The bureau examines financial institutions with an emphasis on determining whether they adhere to consumer protection laws. The exams are focused on consumer experience, whereas a traditional bank exam focuses on the bank's soundness. The bureau conducts exams on banks, savings associations, and credit unions with assets greater than $10 billion, consumer mortgage companies, payday lenders, private education lenders, and "any large participant in a market for financial products or services and anyone who engages in conduct that poses risks to consumers with regard to the offering or provision of consumer financial products and services." Who gets examined under these last two areas depends on the bureau's discretion. The consumer-centered approach means examiners are primarily looking for business practices that violate consumer protection laws, harm consumers, or put them at risk.

UNIQUE IDENTIFIERS FOR MLOS

The Secure and Fair Enforcement for Mortgage Licensing Act (SAFE) Act mandated that all mortgage loan originators (MLOs) have a **unique identifier** that would follow them throughout their careers. The unique identifier is a number that MLOs must display on their business cards. The number is meant to facilitate tracking and identification of MLOs, their records of employment, and any disciplinary action. MLOs must provide their identifier to consumers upon request and before acting as an MLO to help consumers apply for a loan, as well as on any written communication with a consumer. The Federal Housing Finance Agency requires Freddie Mac and Fannie Mae to include Nationwide Multistate Licensing System (NMLS) numbers, also known as unique identifiers, on all mortgage applications. The applications must also include the NMLS number for the MLO's company, or the company an MLO is representing or subcontracting for. If a loan is originated by a mortgage broker, the broker's NMLS number must be on the application.

CFPB PENALTY LIMITS

Since its inception in 2011, the Consumer Financial Protection Bureau (CFPB) has issued billions of dollars in penalties against mortgage companies and mortgage loan originators (MLOs). The fines have ranged from $1 billion to $2 billion against a mortgage company for servicing issues that put thousands of people across the country at risk of losing their homes. In general, any person who violates consumer financial laws, deliberately or by omission, can be fined an amount that falls into three tiers. Tier 1 violators can be fined up to $7,034 per day that the violation continues; Tier 2, up to $35,169 per day; and Tier 3, up to $1,406,728 per day (as of 2024). The maximum fines can change annually based on inflation. Tier 1 violations are more innocuous, Tier 2 violations are seen as reckless, and Tier 3 violations are reserved for those who knowingly violate consumer financial laws. Determining the size of the fine also depends on the size of the financial resources and the good faith of the person charged, the gravity of the violation, the severity of risks or loss to the consumer, history of previous violations, and any other pertinent factors.

CFPB LOAN ORIGINATOR RULE

After the subprime mortgage meltdown, legislators became concerned with the influence of mortgage loan originators (MLOs) and loan officers, especially when it came to steering borrowers toward more expensive loans to increase their compensation. To tamp down on this malfeasance, lawmakers began to look at ways to regulate MLO pay, resulting in the **Loan Originator Rule**. This rule regulates how MLOs and loan officers get paid on closed-end mortgages secured by a dwelling. The rule prohibits paying an MLO based on the terms of the loan or based on how profitable the loan is to the financial institution selling the loan. The rule also prohibits a loan officer from simultaneously receiving compensation from both the consumer and another person in connection with the same transaction. The rule prescribes allowable compensation, such as salaries, commissions, bonuses, and retirement plan contributions, as long as none of the compensation is tied to the terms of a loan. The Consumer Financial Protection Bureau (CFPB) Loan Originator Rule also establishes minimum criteria for MLOs, such as good character, criminal background checks that meet certain standards, and a requirement for MLOs to obtain training and education before originating loans.

DEFINITIONS
NMLS

NMLS stands for **Nationwide Multistate Licensing System**. This watchdog group was created in 2008 in response to the subprime mortgage crisis and the predatory lenders who helped fuel the crisis. The Secure and Fair Enforcement for Mortgage Licensing (SAFE) Act of 2008 requires all residential mortgage loan originators (MLOs) to register with the NMLS, which is a database created by the Conference of State Bank Supervisors and the American Association of Residential

Mortgage Regulators. MLOs must meet minimum requirements to be licensed and registered. The agency maintains licensing and information on MLOs across the country. Each originator or mortgage officer is assigned a unique identifier, also known as an NMLS number, that is used by the originator throughout the officer's career. NMLS maintains records on individuals seeking to apply for, amend, renew, and surrender the mortgage licenses. Regulators created the SAFE Act and the NMLS registry to help consumers feel confident that they are dealing with registered, reputable mortgage lenders.

SAFE ACT

The **Secure and Fair Enforcement for Mortgage Licensing (SAFE) Act** of 2008 was the federal government's response to the subprime mortgage meltdown of 2007. The goal of the act was to create minimum standards for licensing and regulation of mortgage loan originators (MLOs), reduce fraud, and bolster consumer confidence in the mortgage industry. The SAFE Act mandated that all residential MLOs register with the Nationwide Multistate Licensing System (NMLS). Each originator is given an NMLS number that he or she keeps throughout his or her career. The goal was to track mortgage professionals, share information with state agencies and consumers, and enhance consumer protections. To obtain an NMLS number, MLOs must submit to a background check by the Federal Bureau of Investigation (FBI); be fingerprinted; provide 10 years of employment history; register personal identifying information such as height, weight, Social Security number, and date of birth; and disclose all state or federal criminal history as well as any regulatory action that has been taken against them. Every year, MLOs must renew and attest to their registration information, report any changes to their address or employers, and attest to any criminal activity for which they have been charged or convicted.

MLO AND THE REQUIREMENT TO BE LICENSED WITH A STATE

The Secure and Fair Enforcement for Mortgage Licensing (SAFE) Act defines a mortgage loan originator (MLO, sometimes referred to as a mortgage loan officer) as an individual who, for compensation or gain, takes a residential mortgage loan application or offers or negotiates terms of a residential mortgage loan application. Anyone in such a role must be licensed or registered as an MLO. Individuals performing real estate brokerage services, underwriting, or loan processing do not have to be licensed in most instances. An MLO who works for a federal depository institution covered by federal laws, such as a bank, must be registered. An individual who works for a mortgage company or broker must be licensed by the state. Licensing requires passing a Federal Bureau of Investigation (FBI) background test, providing a credit report, studying for and passing a state license exam, receiving ongoing education, and maintaining registration with the Nationwide Multistate Licensing System.

LICENSE LAWS AND REGULATIONS
PERSONS REQUIRED TO BE LICENSED

Essentially, anyone who acts as an originator needs to be licensed. An originator is anyone who takes mortgage applications, discusses or negotiates mortgage terms and conditions for compensation or financial gain, or anyone who presents himself or herself as someone who takes mortgage applications or negotiates with borrowers the terms and conditions of a mortgage. Negotiating the terms of a loan can include showing borrowers loan terms, communicating terms with the goal of obtaining business, or guiding borrowers to specific terms. In most instances, an independent contractor who acts as a loan processor will also have to be licensed. There are many job roles in the mortgage industry that do not require a license—for example, processors, underwriters, and assistants—because these individuals are not negotiating loans. Because many states have unique licensing requirements, it is also important to check the licensing rules in the state where one is working in the mortgage industry.

MORTGAGE LICENSING EXEMPTIONS FOR CLERICAL AND SUPPORT ROLES

A mortgage loan originator (MLO) is defined as someone who takes mortgage applications, collects information on borrowers, negotiates mortgage terms, and prepares mortgage packages. MLOs must be licensed, but individuals in roles that fall outside of this definition do not. For example, individuals who perform administrative or clerical duties for an MLO do not need to be licensed. Real estate agents and those who sell timeshares do not need to have a mortgage license. Loan processors and underwriters do not need to be licensed either. Individuals in these roles typically are not representing themselves to the public as MLOs nor are they soliciting mortgage loans or negotiating the terms of a mortgage. As long as underwriters and loan processors are not presenting themselves as individuals who can solicit or negotiate mortgages and mortgage terms, they do not need to be licensed.

LICENSEE QUALIFICATIONS AND APPLICATION PROCESS
BACKGROUND CHECKS

Prior to registering with the Nationwide Multistate Licensing System (NMLS), a candidate must submit to fingerprinting and a criminal background check performed by the Federal Bureau of Investigation (FBI). The criminal background check must be requested through the NMLS website by either the candidate or the candidate's employer. Once this request has been made, the prospective mortgage loan originator (MLO) must schedule a fingerprinting session through Fieldprint. Fingerprinting can also be done at local police departments. It must be completed within 180 days of initiating the background check; failing to submit prints within 180 days will require a new background investigation request. The FBI checks a candidate's prints against its fingerprint databases to see if an applicant has a criminal history. Anyone convicted of a felony within seven years of the background check is ineligible to be licensed. Anyone with a felony related to financial services, such as fraud, bribery, or check forgery, is also ineligible to obtain a mortgage license.

REQUIREMENTS FOR BECOMING AN MLO

Licensing varies by state, but according to the Secure and Fair Enforcement for Mortgage Licensing (SAFE) Act, at a minimum, an individual must meet the following criteria:

- Has never previously had a mortgage loan originator (MLO) license revoked.
- Has had no felony convictions in the prior seven years.
- Demonstrates good character.
- Completes 20 hours of pre-licensing education that has been approved by the Nationwide Multistate Licensing System (NMLS) Registry. The education must include at least:
  - Three hours about federal laws and regulations
  - Three hours of ethics instruction on fraud, consumer protection, and fair lending
  - Two hours about lending standards for the nontraditional mortgage marketplace
- Achieves a test score of at least 75 percent on a written test developed by the NMLS.
- Is covered by either a net worth or a surety bond or pays into a state fund as required by state law.
- Submits fingerprints to the NMLS for a Federal Bureau of Investigation (FBI) criminal background check.
- Submits personal employment experience that includes authorization for the NMLS to obtain histories of any administrative, civil, or criminal findings, and also to obtain a credit report.

WAITING PERIOD FOR RETAKES

If an applicant fails to gain a score of 75 percent on an exam developed by the Nationwide Multistate Licensing System (NMLS), there are further opportunities to retake the exam. An individual may take the exam three consecutive times. With each retest, the NMLS requires an individual to wait 30 days from the date of the previous test before taking the test again. If an individual fails three times, there is further recourse. After failing three times, the budding mortgage loan originator (MLO) can wait six months, at which time the individual can take the test again. If a formerly state-licensed originator fails to maintain a license for five years or longer, not taking into account any time during which the individual is a registered MLO, the individual must retake the test and achieve a score of at least 75 percent. It is recommended that an aspiring MLO take a minimum of 20 hours of pre-licensing education before attempting the exam.

SPONSORSHIP REQUIREMENT

In most states, an individual needs to be sponsored by a company before working as a mortgage loan originator (MLO). Legitimate sponsorships require establishing a relationship between an employer and an MLO candidate. A sponsorship means that an employer will supervise the activities of the licensed MLO. If a candidate has already completed all the Nationwide Multistate Licensing System (NMLS) requirements to be licensed, including passing the mortgage license test, the individual will be granted status as "Approved-Inactive" until they are hired and sponsored by a financial institution. At any time, if an MLO becomes unsponsored, his or her license goes back into "Approved-Inactive" status until the MLO acquires new sponsorship. While inactive, MLOs cannot take mortgage applications or perform any duties related to originating mortgages. Sponsorships can only be initiated in the NMLS Registry by companies, but they can be removed by companies or MLOs.

GROUNDS FOR DENYING A LICENSE

REASONS FOR DENYING AN APPLICANT

An applicant who has committed a felony or a financial crime can be denied a mortgage license. The minimum licensing standards expressed by the Nationwide Multistate Licensing System (NMLS) Registry are that applicants shall not have been convicted of a felony within the last seven years prior to applying for a mortgage license. Also, an applicant cannot have a conviction at any time for a financial-related crime—for example, bribery, embezzlement, fraud, or check forgery. If an applicant does not meet the pre-licensure education requirement, the applicant can be denied a license. A person who does not demonstrate good character and financial responsibility can be denied a license. Someone who has tax liens or judgements filed against him or her, has had a foreclosure in the last three years, or exhibits a pattern of delinquency in paying bills might be demonstrating a lack of financial responsibility.

LICENSE MAINTENANCE

CONTINUING EDUCATION REQUIREMENTS

To renew a state mortgage loan originator (MLO) license, the MLO must continue to meet the minimum standards established by the Nationwide Multistate Licensing System (NMLS) Registry (no felony convictions, be bonded, etc.). Also, an MLO must take a minimum of eight hours of education approved by the NMLS. The eight hours of continuing education must include:

- Three hours of training on federal laws and regulations
- Two hours of ethics training, including instruction on fraud, consumer protection, and fair lending
- Two hours of training related to lending standards for the nontraditional mortgage product marketplace

An MLO must receive credit for a continuing education course in the year the course was taken, and he or she cannot apply for education credits for courses taken in one year to meet the continuing education requirements for subsequent years. MLOs cannot receive credit for approved courses more than once in the same year nor in successive years. An individual who is an instructor of approved continuing education courses may receive credit for his or her own individual continuing education requirements at the rate of two hours for every one hour taught.

RENEWAL PERIOD

The Nationwide Multistate Licensing System (NMLS) renewal period takes place annually from November 1 to December 31. During this time, anyone registered with the NMLS—including financial institutions—must renew registration. Anyone who does not renew is placed in an "Inactive" status and cannot originate loans or undertake any activities involving loan origination. To renew, mortgage loan originators (MLOs) simply access their files on the NMLS Registry website and review the contents for accuracy. At this time, MLOs are also required to update their files where needed. If an MLO is under investigation or has been charged with wrongdoing, these events need to be disclosed on the registry. After MLOs review their personal, employment, and background information, they then must attest that the information listed on the site is complete, true, and accurate. MLOs must also pay an annual fee to renew their NMLS registration.

CONTINUING EDUCATION COURSE APPROVALS

Continuing education courses and providers of education courses must be reviewed and approved by the Nationwide Multistate Licensing System (NMLS). The employer of the mortgage loan originator (MLO) can provide or contract with a third party for the provision of continuing education courses as long as the courses and the providers are approved by the NMLS. Continuing education can be offered in a classroom, online, or by any other means allowed by the NMLS. Credit for coursework can be given only in the year the work was completed. An MLO who completes continuing education in one state and subsequently moves to another state shall have his or her credits accepted by the new state as long as the coursework was approved by the NMLS. Each state shall allow provisions for making up continuing education work for any licensed MLO as established by the regulations of each state.

REQUIREMENTS TO RETAKE EXAM IF AN INDIVIDUAL HAS BEEN ABSENT FROM THE INDUSTRY

Credentials expire for a mortgage loan originator (MLO) who leaves the industry for five consecutive years, and retesting is required to obtain a new license. The Secure and Fair Enforcement for Mortgage Licensing (SAFE) Act says that "a state licensed loan originator who fails to maintain a valid license for a period of five years or longer shall retake the test." The creation of the Nationwide Multistate Licensing System (NMLS) Registry and the SAFE Act were done in the spirit of placing highly qualified and reputable individuals in the role of MLOs. In such a fast-moving, complex, and ever-changing industry, an MLO who has been out of the industry for five years or more will not be sufficiently familiar with the latest trends, rule changes, new regulations, and products to perform as a competent mortgage professional. The same retake rule pertains to individuals who do not obtain a valid license or active federal registration within five years of passing the MLO exam.

NMLS REQUIREMENTS
CHANGE OF EMPLOYMENT AND UPDATING NMLS

Originators who are already registered with Nationwide Multistate Licensing System (NMLS) must update their NMLS profiles reflecting any change of employers. All relevant information, such as the name of the employer, address, phone number, and any other employer information, must be updated in the NMLS Registry. In most cases, the mortgage loan originator (MLO) must also submit to fingerprinting and a background review before being hired by the new employer. The MLO's NMLS profile must be updated before the MLO may act as a loan officer for the new employer. An MLO who changes employers due to reorganization, mergers, or acquisitions has 60 days from the date of the change to register the change with the NMLS. If an MLO leaves a company, the company has 30 days to notify the NMLS. Also, if an MLO changes location while remaining with the same employer, the officer must register the new address and contact information with the NMLS within 30 days of the move.

REQUIREMENT TO PUBLICLY DISPLAY AN NMLS IDENTIFIER

To make sure consumers know who they are dealing with—or at least have the opportunity to easily research a mortgage loan originator's (MLO's) background—the Secure and Fair Enforcement for Mortgage Licensing (SAFE) Act requires loan officers to provide their Nationwide Multistate Licensing System (NMLS) identifiers upon request and upon representing themselves as licensed professionals. The identifier must be included in any written communication (e.g., commitment letter, Loan Estimate, and disclosures) and should also be included on general communication tools, such as stationery, business cards, note pads, and advertisements. The act also encourages MLOs to display their identifiers in other ways: on websites and in prominent locales in an MLO's workplace. It also requires employers to implement a process to accommodate public requests for MLOs to provide their unique identifiers. The SAFE Act was implemented in the spirit of transparency and fairness regarding the relationship between MLOs and consumers. Living up to good-faith ideals means being open and honest with consumers about an MLO's background.

LICENSES FOR NON-DEPOSITORY VS. REGISTERED DEPOSITORY EMPLOYEES IN NMLS

Mortgage loan originators (MLOs) or loan officers who work for a depository institution (banks, most credit unions, or mortgage companies owned by a bank) need to be registered on Nationwide Multistate Licensing System (NMLS), whereas MLOs who work for non-depository institutions need to be listed on the NMLS Registry as possessing a state license. Licensing requirements vary by state. Both non-depository and depository loan officers must be fingerprinted, undergo a criminal background check performed by the Federal Bureau of Investigation (FBI), and submit an individual credit report. Depository institutions are required to train their loan officers and most go through rigorous training before they begin originating loans. No matter whether someone works at a depository or non-depository institution, the Secure and Fair Enforcement for Mortgage Licensing (SAFE) Act defines an MLO or a loan officer as an individual who, for compensation or gain, takes loan applications or communicates, negotiates, or offers the terms on a residential mortgage or loan.

COMPLIANCE

PROHIBITED CONDUCT AND PRACTICES

The spirit of the Secure and Fair Enforcement for Mortgage Licensing (SAFE) Act calls for mortgage loan originators (MLOs) to act in good faith and in the best interests of consumers. Individuals shall not misrepresent, mislead, or defraud, either intentionally or by omission, or engage in any unfair or deceptive practices. MLOs shall not advertise, solicit, or negotiate the terms of a mortgage unless the terms are actually available to the borrower. MLOs must not conduct any business covered by the SAFE Act without being licensed. MLOs must make all state and federal disclosures covered by the SAFE Act and comply with all of the regulations set forth by the act. MLOs are prohibited from negotiating any terms of a loan and later changing those terms in a bait-and-switch scheme. MLOs are required to be truthful and to not mislead any regulatory agency, state or federal, regarding information included on the Nationwide Multistate Licensing System (NMLS) Registry. MLOs are also prohibited from threatening, bribing, or influencing third-party service providers with the intent of altering the results or influencing the decisions of third-party service providers such as appraisers or other officials.

REQUIRED CONDUCT

There are certain duties undertaken by mortgage loan originators (MLOs) that require them to be licensed under the Secure and Fair Enforcement for Mortgage Licensing (SAFE) Act—for example, taking a loan application. No matter how an individual receives a loan application, whether directly or indirectly, the individual must be licensed. Simply having someone else physically receive an application does not exempt the need for a mortgage license by the individual who ultimately acts on and negotiates the mortgage. Another example might be a mortgage broker who ultimately passes on an application to a lender who makes the final lending decision. The mortgage broker who receives the application must be licensed, even if this individual is not required to verify the information in the application. Finally, an individual who inputs information on a loan application using an online system must be licensed. This may seem more like a clerical duty, but this type of action is technically considered taking a mortgage application, and an individual must be licensed to do it.

ADVERTISING
REQUIREMENT TO INCLUDE NMLS UNIQUE ID IN ADVERTISEMENTS

Whenever mortgage originators advertise their services or a mortgage product, they are required to include a Nationwide Multistate Licensing System (NMLS) number in the promotional materials. This applies to both electronic and print advertising. If an originator is examined by the Consumer Financial Protection Bureau (CFPB), this is one of the first things they will look for. Including the NMLS unique identifier also helps consumers identify and learn more about an originator if the consumer wishes to investigate the originator's background. After the subprime mortgage meltdown, the CFPB implemented strict rules for advertising mortgage products. The primary aim was to ensure that ads are clear, straightforward, and not misleading in any way. The CFPB's rules regarding advertising are broad, and virtually any communication could be considered an advertisement, including social media posts, emails, and text messages. Mortgage loan originators should take this under consideration and include their NMLS numbers in communications.

General Mortgage Knowledge

Qualified and Nonqualified Mortgage Programs

FEATURES OF A QUALIFIED MORTGAGE

A qualified mortgage is a mortgage that protects lenders and borrowers by ensuring that lenders properly document borrowers' ability to repay their debt. The Dodd-Frank Wall Street Reform and Consumer Protection Act, passed in 2010, requires lenders to analyze a borrower's ability to repay based on income, assets, and debts. Dodd-Frank stipulates that a borrower's monthly debt obligations not exceed 43 percent of pretax income; that the lender charges no more than three percent in points and origination fees; and that the loan contains no risky terms like balloon payments or negative amortization, is not interest-only, and is not longer than 30 years. The new provisions shield borrowers from risky lending practices and protect lenders when borrowers sue, claiming they were given loans that they could not afford. The act also protects those wishing to buy mortgages in the secondary market. Only certain qualified mortgages are eligible for sale in the secondary market.

ALLOWABLE POINTS AND FEES FOR QUALIFIED MORTGAGES

As part of the ability-to-repay rules passed after the subprime mortgage crisis, lenders are capped on the amount of fees and points they can charge for a qualified mortgage. Again, the rules are intended to protect borrowers from predatory lending practices and to ensure that mortgages are fair and affordable. The limits change every year based on inflation. As of 2024, the limits include the following:

- 3 percent of the total loan amount for loans greater than $130,461
- $3,914 for loans between $78,277 and $130,461
- 5 percent of the total loan amount for loans between $26,092 and $63,095
- $1,305 for loans between $16,308 and $26,092
- 8 percent of the total loan amount for loans of less than $16,308

According to Consumer Financial Protection Bureau (CFPB) regulations, only qualified mortgages have limits on points and fees. Lenders can make nonqualified mortgages to borrowers and charge as much as the market will bear for points and fees.

INFORMATION USED TO DETERMINE WHETHER A LOAN IS QUALIFIED

For a mortgage to be qualified, it must be closed-end and secured by a one- to four-family home; contain no risky features like interest-only payments, balloon payments, or negative amortization; be no longer than 30 years; and have limited points and fees. In addition, the lender must ensure the borrower has the ability to repay. There are seven considerations that go into the ability-to-repay assessment:

- Current or reasonably expected income and assets
- Employment status
- Mortgage payment for the loan applied for
- Other loan payments on the residence used to secure the loan
- Monthly property taxes and insurance
- Debts, alimony, and child support
- Credit history

All of these payments and obligations are measured against the borrower's gross annual income to arrive at a debt-to-income ratio. For example, if a borrower makes $60,000 annually, that is $5,000 per month. The borrower's monthly obligations cannot exceed 43 percent of $5,000, or $2,150.

ANNUAL PERCENTAGE RATES THAT MAKE A MORTGAGE QUALIFIED

A qualified mortgage is higher-priced if it's a first-lien mortgage and its annual percentage rate (APR) is more than 1.5 percentage points higher than the average prime offer rate (APOR). For subordinate-lien mortgages, the APR cannot be more than 3.5 percentage points higher than the APOR. For example, if the APOR is five percent at the time a first-lien mortgage's rate is set, the loan is higher-priced if the rate is more than 6.5 percent. For a qualified mortgage issued by small or rural lenders, it is considered higher-priced if the rate is more than 3.5 percentage points higher than the APOR at the time the rate is set for both first-lien and subordinate-lien mortgages. Higher-priced qualified mortgages must meet all the same requirements as a qualified mortgage and meet the ability-to-repay requirements.

CATEGORIES OF QUALIFIED MORTGAGES

There are basically two types of qualified mortgages: those that must meet the 43 percent debt-to-income ratio and mortgages that only small lenders are allowed to make. The new rules became effective in January 2016 and were intended to help banks and credit unions lend in rural and underserved areas. The first type is the qualified mortgage we have already discussed, where borrowers must have a debt-to-income ratio of 43 percent or less. After Dodd-Frank was passed in 2010, lawmakers changed the definition for qualified mortgages for small and rural lenders. These changes allow qualified lenders to exceed the 43 percent debt-to-income ratio and also allow for balloon payments. A small lender is defined under the new rules as a lender originating fewer than 2,000 mortgages annually and retaining a portfolio of $2 billion or less in assets.

CONVENTIONAL/CONFORMING
RESPONSIBILITIES OF FANNIE MAE

Fannie Mae is the nickname for the quasi-governmental organization called the Federal National Mortgage Association. Congress created the agency in 1938, and by the 1970s, it had evolved into a private corporation. Fannie Mae's main responsibility is to buy mortgages from lenders, bundle the loans into securities, and sell the securities in the global market. Congress envisioned Fannie Mae as a way to create more mortgages and thus make the dream of homeownership more attainable. When Fannie Mae buys a mortgage from a lender, it gives the lender more funds to originate mortgages. It creates liquidity and access in the mortgage marketplace. The securities issued by Fannie Mae are often referred to as mortgage-backed securities (MBSs). They are similar to bonds. They have maturities and pay interest and principal monthly until the buyer recoups the investment. Fannie Mae guarantees the payments; if there is a default, Fannie Mae will continue to pay back investors. The federal government does not guarantee Fannie Mae debts. Fannie Mae shares are traded on the over the counter (OTC) market under the ticker symbol FNMA.

LIMITS ON CLOSING COST CONCESSIONS

Conventional loans are also known as conforming loans because they conform to Fannie Mae and Freddie Mac requirements for loans the agencies will buy. There are many closing costs in originating a mortgage. A good rule of thumb is that closing costs range from two to five percent of a home's purchase price. To make a purchase more affordable for home buyers, sometimes a seller will pay some of the closing costs. However, there are limits on how much a seller can contribute. For a conventional loan on primary and secondary home purchases where the borrower pays less than 10 percent down, the most a seller can contribute is three percent of the sale price. If the borrower pays 11 to 25 percent down, the seller can contribute up to six percent. If the borrower pays down more than 25 percent, the seller can contribute up to nine percent. For example, if the purchase price of a home is $250,000 and the borrower pays down three percent, the seller can contribute $7,500 toward closing costs. Setting limits on concessions helps keep real estate market prices and home values fair.

FANNIE MAE/FREDDIE MAC'S AUTOMATED UNDERWRITING SYSTEMS

Automated underwriting systems are desktop programs that mortgage originators use to screen and assess a borrower's risk. The systems determine whether a mortgage deal meets Fannie Mae and Freddie Mac requirements. Lenders insert data provided by borrowers and pull credit scores to get a snapshot of a potential borrower's financial health. Some of the data input by the lender is provided by the borrower, so the output is only as good as the information supplied by the borrower. The system also reports the credit scores from all three reporting agencies. Most lenders will throw out the highest and lowest score and go with the middle score. One of the requirements of the desktop underwriter is that none of the borrower's debts can include money that was borrowed to buy the home. The automated underwriter also takes into account the amount of the loan sought and calculates a monthly payment. This payment is compared to the income data reported to arrive at a debt-to-income ratio. Borrowers typically need an approval by the automated underwriter to move forward in the mortgage process.

REQUIREMENTS WHEN PURCHASING A NONOWNER-OCCUPIED RENTAL PROPERTY

Unlike with other government-backed mortgages, investors can use conventional mortgages to buy rental properties. Basically, all of the requirements are the same as buying a primary residence, except the investor will have to pay more down (20 to 30 percent) and the interest rates will be higher. For investment properties, higher cash reserves are also required. Cash reserves are the money the investor has on hand *after* the mortgage closes. The Federal Housing Administration (FHA) wants to see that an investor has enough cash on hand to handle unexpected expenditures like maintenance without jeopardizing the investors' liquidity and, ultimately, solvency. In many cases, investors must also meet higher credit score expectations to be approved for a conventional loan as well. There are also limits on how many investment properties one investor can mortgage conventionally, anywhere from six to 10, depending on certain scenarios.

ACCEPTABLE DOWN PAYMENT AMOUNTS

Another way to think of a conventional mortgage is as a loan that is backed by Fannie Mae or Freddie Mac. Freddie Mac is the nickname for the Federal Home Loan Mortgage Corporation. It has the same mission as Fannie Mae, which is to create liquidity and access in the mortgage marketplace by buying mortgages from lenders and bundling those mortgages into securities that are sold globally. The main difference between Freddie Mac and Fannie Mae is who they buy mortgages from. Fannie Mae buys mortgages from commercial banks, whereas Freddie Mac buys mortgages from small lenders. A conventional mortgage can be made with a minimum down payment of three percent. The down payment amount affects the cost of a loan. For example, for home purchase mortgages in which the borrower pays less than 20 percent down, private mortgage insurance (PMI) is required. Also, larger down payments allow lenders to offer lower annual percentage rates. Down payments may be made through gifts. Also, a mortgage can be structured into two separate loans when a borrower pays 10 percent down, borrows 10 percent for a second mortgage, and 80 percent for a conventional mortgage. This eliminates the PMI requirement.

HAZARD INSURANCE REQUIREMENTS

There are a host of stipulations around homeowner's insurance required for conventional mortgages. All homes purchased with a conventional mortgage must be insured for the life of the loan. The minimum insurance amount is 100 percent of a single-family home's value and 90 percent of a multifamily home's value. Policies must have provisions that preclude cancellation without a 30-day notice. Policies must be issued by carriers with the highest ratings and be issued in 12-month terms. In most instances, it is impermissible to finance insurance premium payments. Payments must be made through escrow or paid in full annually or monthly. If payments are not escrowed, the lender may require proof of payment. There must be proof of insurance before a mortgage closes. Insurance coverage must detail the name of the insurer, name of the insured or borrower, coverage amount, deductible, policy expiration date and term, description of the property, and coinsurer and percent if applicable.

GOVERNMENT

FHA MORTGAGE

An FHA mortgage is a government-backed mortgage insured by the Federal Housing Administration. They are popular among first-time homebuyers because they require smaller down payments and lower credit scores. The FHA was one of the first government agencies created to help more Americans become homeowners. It was established during the Great Depression when less than 40 percent of American households owned their homes. During the Great Depression, unemployment and foreclosure rates skyrocketed. Banks were reluctant to make mortgage loans. The FHA stepped in to reduce banks' risk by insuring mortgages. The FHA also made it easier for borrowers to qualify for loans. With lenders confident they would be protected in the event of default, rates of homeownership steadily increased to about 70 percent in the 2000s. The FHA does not actually lend the money for a mortgage. The loans are originated by FHA-approved lenders, and the FHA insures the mortgages.

FACTS ABOUT FHA LOANS

The most well-known facts about a Federal Housing Administration (FHA) mortgage are the low down payment feature (minimum 3.5 percent) and the low credit scores (a borrower can be approved with a FICO score as low as 500) that make a borrower eligible. FHA loans are available only for primary residences, and the borrower must be a lawful US resident with a Social Security number. The borrower's front-end debt-to-income ratio (mortgage payment, property taxes, homeowner's insurance, homeowners association fees if applicable, and mortgage insurance) must be under 31 percent, and the back-end (the mortgage and related payments plus all other debts, i.e., student loans, credit cards, and car loans) ratio must be under 43 percent. Borrowers need a credit score of at least 580 to get the maximum loan with a down payment of 3.5 percent. The property must be appraised by an FHA-approved vendor and meet minimum FHA appraisal standards. If the seller won't pay to fix a problem, the buyer must pay for the repairs or the loan will be declined.

FHA

FHA stands for the Federal Housing Administration. FHA mortgages are issued by FHA-approved lenders and are backed and insured by the US government. This program allows borrowers with lower credit scores and lower down payments to be approved for mortgages. Loans can be made with credit scores as low as 500 and down payments as low as 3.5 percent of the purchase price. Borrowers must pay mortgage insurance (often for the life of the loan, depending on the down payment) on these loans to protect lenders in the event of default. The difference between an FHA loan and a conventional loan is simple: both FHA and conventional loans are originated in the private sector; however, conventional loans are insured privately (hence the term private mortgage insurance, or PMI), and FHA loans are insured by the government. Because the government is insuring the mortgage, lenders are willing to take on more risk and loan to less-qualified borrowers because, in the event of default, they know they will recoup their losses. This makes the mortgage market fairer for people with dinged-up credit histories, and it makes homeownership more likely for more people.

VA LOANS

Department of Veterans Affairs (VA) loans are government-backed loans for military veterans, service members, and their spouses. The loans are made by commercial banks and lending institutions. Borrowers must meet both military service requirements and credit and income requirements to be eligible. VA loans came about as part of the 1944 GI Bill. The loans are generally easier to get and come with advantages like no down payments and no mortgage insurance. Today, there are more than 25 million veterans and service personnel eligible for this mortgage, making it popular and attractive. Generally, military personnel have to serve a minimum of 90 consecutive days during wartime or 181 days during peacetime to be eligible. Active members of the National Guard or Reserves need six years of service. A spouse is eligible if his or her military spouse died or was disabled during service. VA mortgages come with what is known as a funding fee to help offset taxpayers because these mortgages do not require mortgage insurance. The fees can range from around one percent to more than three percent, depending on the mortgage scenario. VA loans must be made for owner-occupied residences. Neither investment properties nor second homes are eligible for VA funding.

PROHIBITION ON MORTGAGE INSURANCE

Unlike Federal Housing Administration (FHA) loans, which require mortgage insurance (often for the life of the loan), and conventional loans, which require mortgage insurance with down payments of less than 20 percent, Department of Veterans Affairs (VA) loans do not require mortgage insurance. Although mortgage insurance ends when a homeowner obtains 20 percent equity, not paying mortgage insurance at all can be a huge savings and a big selling point for VA mortgages. A mortgage insurance payment of $100 per month comes out to $6,000 for five years of mortgage payments. On a 30-year loan, that equals $36,000. Also, FHA mortgage insurance has to be prepaid the first year, which can add to closing costs. For VA loans, the money saved on mortgage insurance can go toward other things, like paying off other debts, paying down mortgage principal, or paying for homeowner costs and maintenance.

TYPES OF GOVERNMENT GUARANTORS

There are several government agencies that guarantee mortgages for the purchase of a primary residence. Federal Housing Administration (FHA) and Department of Veterans Affair (VA) loans are two of the largest providers of government-backed mortgages. Other agencies are Ginnie Mae, a government agency that backs mortgage securities, and Fannie Mae and Freddie Mac, two quasi-governmental entities that also back mortgage securities. The US Department of Agriculture (USDA) runs another popular government-backed loan program. It is similar to the FHA and VA programs, helping low- to moderate-income families and individuals buy homes. The difference with the USDA program, run by the agency's Rural Housing Service, is that it focuses on rural development. It lends to people in rural areas, offering low down payment options and low interest rates. Sources of funds for USDA loans come mostly from banks, but the USDA will also lend directly to borrowers who qualify, usually for very low-income borrowers. Another program is the Office of Public and Indian Housing, which guarantees loans for Native Americans.

ENTITLEMENT

The entitlement is the amount of a loan that the Department of Veterans Affairs (VA) guarantees it will repay to a lender should a borrower default on a VA mortgage. The basic entitlement on a VA loan is $36,000. Eligible service personnel are allowed to borrow up to four times the basic entitlement, for a loan amount of $144,000 ($36,000 × 4 = $144,000). Entitlement is a confusing topic for some borrowers, who mistakenly believe it is their maximum loan amount or a lump-sum payment the VA provides to buy a home. It is neither of these things. Some eligible service members can qualify for a bonus entitlement of up to $70,025 for loans over $144,000. This makes for a maximum loan size of $424,100 ($144,000 + $70,025 × 4 = $424,100). In some high-cost counties in states like California, New York, and New Jersey, loan amounts can go even higher, giving veterans a chance to purchase homes in line with higher-priced markets.

COE REQUIREMENT

Borrowers applying for a Department of Veterans Affairs (VA) mortgage must prove they are eligible for the loan. The proof required is called a certificate of eligibility (COE). Generally, military personnel must have 181 days of peacetime service, 90 consecutive days of wartime service, six years in the National Guard or Reserves, or be a surviving spouse. Proof can be obtained in minutes from lenders who have access to a service database. Borrowers can also apply for a COE online or through the mail. Documentation of service is required and depends on a borrower's type of service. For veterans, a DD214 form will suffice, as long as it shows the type of service and reason for leaving. An up-to-date statement of service will also suffice if it is signed by the borrower's commanding officer, adjutant, or other qualified leader and includes the borrower's name, Social Security number, date of birth, details concerning dates of service, and the name of the command in which the borrower served.

ACCEPTABLE FUNDS FOR DOWN PAYMENT AND CLOSING COSTS

All Federal Housing Administration (FHA) loans require a minimum down payment of at least 3.5 percent. Down payments are subject to scrutiny and often must be documented to prove their source and legitimacy. Remember, down payments cannot come from borrowed funds. Acceptable down payment sources can be checking and savings balances, cash saved at home, savings bonds, IRA and 401(k) accounts, investments, gifts, and the sale of personal property. Gifts are limited to those that come from family, the borrower's employer or union, a close friend, and charitable or government organizations. It is prohibited to receive a gift from the seller, a real estate agent, or the home builder. This list of acceptable sources gives the most common sources, but there are more that are considered acceptable. Down payment money is considered separately from and in addition to closing cost funds but can come from the same list of acceptable sources.

PROPERTIES ELIGIBLE FOR FHA PURCHASE TRANSACTIONS

Most borrowers assume that Federal Housing Administration (FHA) loans can be used to buy a single-family home. Although it is true that FHA loans require the borrower to live in the home that is being mortgaged, there are still other options. An FHA mortgage can be used to buy a multifamily home as long as the borrower plans to live in one of the units. This requirement is true for homes with a maximum of four units. For example, if a borrower is using an FHA loan to buy a duplex or a four-family building, the borrower must live in one of the units to qualify for the mortgage. This type of purchase might be attractive for homeowners who want to pay off their mortgage faster. Generally, the borrower can use the rent drawn from the other units to pay extra principal against the mortgage. To buy a multifamily home, the borrower must show that the other units are either already rented or show prepared rent agreements and deposits for the additional units prior to closing. The rent from the additional unit(s) cannot be counted as income for the mortgage application.

FHA LOAN LIMITS

FHA loan limits vary from county to county across the country. Limits depend on home prices in a specific area. For example, the median home price in San Francisco, California, is about $1.3 million, whereas the median home price in Cincinnati, Ohio, is about $265,000. For 2024, the maximum loan in an expensive market like San Francisco is $1,149,825. In Cincinnati, the maximum is $766,550. Every year the limits can change based on inflation. Most years the limits go up, but sometimes they go down or stay the same. For 2024, the upper limit for the least expensive real estate markets is

$498,257. The US Department of Housing and Urban Development provides a searchable database where users can look up FHA loan limits in their specific counties. The limits are stated for single-family homes. Limits are also set for two-, three- and four-family homes.

VA Funding Fees

Nearly all Department of Veterans Affairs (VA) loans require the borrower to pay a funding fee. The thinking behind the fee is that because these loans require no down payment or mortgage insurance, the fee must be collected to reduce the cost to taxpayers, who ultimately pay for VA mortgages. The fee is a percentage of the loan amount and varies based on military personnel's service, whether the borrower is a first-time home buyer, and the down payment. The fee can be rolled into the loan amount and financed or paid at closing. Veterans disabled during their service and surviving spouses of military killed in action or who died from a service-related disability do not have to pay the fee. For example, a first-time homeowner who pays no money down would pay a fee of 2.15 percent of the loan amount. On a $100,000 mortgage, the fee comes to $2,150. If the same borrower pays down 10 percent, the fee drops to 1.25 percent.

Up-Front Mortgage Insurance Premiums

Federal Housing Administration (FHA) mortgages require borrowers to pay mortgage insurance as an up-front cost at closing and monthly during the term of the mortgage. Currently, borrowers pay 1.75 percent of the loan amount for the up-front costs of mortgage insurance. Often, the lender will send the fee to the government and roll the amount of the up-front cost into the loan. Therefore, the loan amount would be equal to the funds needed to purchase the home plus the amount of the up-front mortgage insurance. Typically, the ongoing cost of mortgage insurance falls between 0.5 and one percent of the loan amount. On a $100,000 mortgage at one percent, the annual insurance premium would total $1,000, or about $83 per month. The monthly mortgage insurance premium is not always for the life of the FHA loan. It does last the life of the loan for 30-year and 15-year mortgages where the down payment was less than 10 percent; however, on a 30-year mortgage with a down payment of greater than 10 percent, the mortgage insurance premium would last the first 11 years of the loan.

Residual Income Qualification Test

Department of Veterans Affairs (VA) loans have a low default rate. That might be due to income requirements that are unique to VA loans (and some Federal Housing Administration [FHA] loans). To qualify for a VA loan, borrowers must meet debt-to-income ratios of about 41 percent. In addition, the VA wants to make sure that borrowers, after paying the mortgage and all debts, have money left over for things like day-to-day expenses, entertainment, food, and housing maintenance. The money left over after all debts—including the mortgage—have been paid is **residual income**. Lenders use sufficient residual income and debt-to-income ratios to determine how much to loan to an eligible borrower. The VA sets expectations for residual income based on where a borrower lives and the size of the borrower's family. For example, a family of five living in the Northeast would need to show a residual income of at least $921 to qualify for a loan of $79,999 or less and $1,062 for a loan of $80,000 or more.

Required Documentation

All institutions have basic documentation requirements, but for Federal Housing Administration (FHA) mortgages, certain documents need to be collected regardless of the lender's internal policies. All borrowers must complete the Form 1003 Universal Residential Loan Application and then sign an addendum to this application known as the HUD-92900-A. The addendum certifies that all of the information the borrower has provided in the application is true. The lender also signs this addendum, certifying that the loan is eligible for federal backing. Proof of Social Security is required. Usually, a photocopy of the borrower's Social Security card suffices. A credit report is also required, as is proof of employment, which can be as simple as showing a pay stub with the employer's name, address, and phone number. Two years' tax returns are required. A sales or purchase agreement is mandatory, signed by both the buyer and the seller. The FHA Amendatory Clause form must be included, which gives the buyer the right to cancel the purchase without losing the deposit if the house appraises for less than the sale price. The Real Estate Certification form is required, whereby all parties attest to the terms and conditions of the sales contract. Finally, an appraisal is mandatory as well.

MONTHLY MORTGAGE INSURANCE PAYMENT SCENARIOS

Federal Housing Administration (FHA) mortgage insurance premiums are calculated based on the borrower's down payment, the loan amount, and the term of the loan. Remember, all FHA loans require an up-front mortgage insurance payment equal to 1.75 percent of the loan amount. On a $100,000 mortgage, the up-front mortgage payment would be $1,750. The FHA uses a different multiple to determine the monthly mortgage premium, which ranges from 0.45 to 1.05. For example, for a $100,000, 15-year loan with a down payment of five percent, the monthly mortgage payment would be calculated like this: $100,000 \times 0.7\% = \$700$. The monthly premium is $\frac{\$700}{12} = \$58.33$. Another example is a $250,000, 30-year mortgage with a 10 percent down payment: $\$250,000 \times 0.85\% = \$2,125$. The monthly premium comes to $\frac{\$2,125}{12} = \$177.08$. Most FHA borrowers pay down the minimum of 3.5 percent on a 30-year mortgage, which means their monthly mortgage insurance premium would be 0.85 percent of the loan amount divided by 12.

MINIMUM DOWN PAYMENT FOR FHA LOAN

The possibility of a low down payment is one of the most popular features of a Federal Housing Administration (FHA) loan. As of 2024, a borrower can pay down as little as 3.5 percent of a home's purchase price and still qualify for an FHA mortgage. A borrower needs a credit score of at least 580 to be eligible to make the minimum down payment. Borrowers with credit scores between 500 and 579 can still qualify for an FHA mortgage but will have to pay down a minimum of 10 percent. Compared to a conventional mortgage, where borrowers need a credit score of at least 620 and down payments of three to 20 percent, the FHA mortgage is much easier for many potential homeowners to obtain. Borrowers who cannot pay down 20 percent, cannot qualify for PMI, or who have lower credit scores should be encouraged to consider an FHA loan.

CONVENTIONAL/NONCONFORMING
FACTS ON JUMBO LOANS

Beginning in 2024, a jumbo loan is a mortgage higher than $766,550 for a single-family home in most US counties—an increase of six percent over 2023. The upper limit for high-cost counties in 2024 is $1,149,825. Jumbo loans exceed Fannie Mae and Freddie Mac limits; therefore, they are not government backed and are ineligible for purchase and resale on the secondary market. For banks, more money means more risk, so qualifying for a jumbo loan is harder. Credit scores often need to be in the 700s. Some lenders require debt-to-income levels around 36 percent instead of the 43 percent needed for a conforming loan. Often, required down payments are at least 20 percent, although some lenders might go as low as 10 percent. Cash reserve requirements are often higher than for conforming loans as well. Because these loans are riskier, lenders want to fully justify them and may require two appraisals instead of one. Luxury home prices can be more volatile than lower-priced homes, so lenders want to be sure.

NONCONFORMING LOAN

Basically, a **nonconforming** loan is one that fails Fannie Mae and Freddie Mac guidelines, that is, a loan they won't buy. Conforming loans are mortgages that do meet Fannie Mae and Freddie Mac criteria and are purchased for resale on the secondary market, giving lenders more money to lend to more borrowers. Most nonconforming loans are jumbo loans. The maximum loan Fannie Mae and Freddie Mac will buy in 2024 is $766,550 (or as high as $1,149,825 in some high-cost markets like California and New York). Anything higher is a jumbo loan. There are other reasons a loan might not conform—for example, when credit scores are too low; when there is too much debt in relation to income (high debt-to-income ratio); too small of a down payment, affecting debt-to-value ratios; or property issues. As one might discern, lenders view nonconforming loans as less desirable and charge higher interest rates and fees.

NONTRADITIONAL LOANS

Nontraditional loans are mortgages that do not follow standard amortization schedules or do not follow standard payment schedules. Examples are loans with balloon payments, interest-only loans, and adjustable-rate mortgages (ARMs). Because these loans are out of the norm, they carry heavier risks and are associated with higher interest rates and fees. Balloon-payment loans require a large principal and interest payment at the end to pay off the loan. It gives borrowers low payments in the beginning in exchange for the risk of having to make a large, one-time payment at the end. Interest-only loans require the lender to collect payments only for interest initially, then a large principal payment at maturity. These two types of loans are often used for short time periods by developers. An ARM is a loan that has a fixed rate and payment initially, typically for three, five, or seven years. After this initial period, the rate becomes variable, and payments will adjust accordingly. ARMs can be good for a borrower who intends to stay in his or her home for a short time.

REQUIREMENTS FOR AN ESCROW ACCOUNT ASSOCIATED WITH A HIGH-PRICED LOAN

A qualified mortgage is high-priced if it's a first-lien mortgage and its annual percentage rate is more than 1.5 percentage points higher than the average prime offer rate (APOR). Federal Truth in Lending Act (TILA) regulations require certain escrow account terms. First, an escrow account is mandatory for at least the first five years of the loan (first lien, secured by a principal dwelling). The escrow account can be canceled after five years if the loan is paid off or the borrower requests the escrow account to be canceled. However, the borrower must be current on the mortgage and have at least 20 percent equity in the home to cancel. Lenders do not have to escrow for condominiums or other common-interest facilities where homeowners participate in governance and master insurance policies are required. Some predominantly rural areas are exempt from the TILA escrow rules.

ESCROW REQUIREMENTS FOR A HIGH-COST LOAN

In general, a high-cost loan occurs when the loan's annual percentage rate (APR) exceeds the Average Prime Offer Rate (APOR) by more than 6.5 percent for first-lien transactions or when fees and costs exceed five percent of the loan amount. High-cost mortgages have all of the same regulations as regular mortgages plus some additional, such as mandatory homeownership counseling. As far as escrow requirements, the Truth in Lending Act (TILA) escrow regulations apply. Escrow accounts must be established for the collection of property taxes, homeowner's insurance, and mortgage insurance for the first five years of the loan. After five years, escrow can be canceled if the loan is canceled or paid off or if the borrower requests that the escrow be canceled. The borrower must be in good standing on the mortgage and have at least 20 percent equity in the home to be eligible to cancel the escrow. Some predominantly rural areas are exempt from the TILA escrow rules.

STATEMENT ON SUBPRIME LENDING
PAYMENT SHOCK

Payment shock occurs with nontraditional loans when the borrower initially enjoys a low monthly payment and then struggles with the loan after the payments increase dramatically. Payments increase when interest-only features expire and principal payments are added, adjustable-rate mortgage (ARM) interest rates skyrocket, or payment option features like negative amortization gradually include more and more principal in the payment. Consumers want these loans because they like the low initial payments, but they sometimes don't realize what can happen if interest rates spike or their income does not keep pace with mortgage payments. Many lenders try to prevent payment shock by calculating the risk that a borrower might default. One way to do this is to measure debt to income and set limits on what is acceptable—for example, not lending to someone whose mortgage and debt obligations exceed a certain threshold, like 36 percent, or the commonly used 43 percent for some government-backed loans.

SUBPRIME

Subprime loans are loans made to borrowers with poor credit histories. The rates are higher because the risk of default is greater when credit scores are lower. Around 2007, many subprime borrowers began to default on their loans, a precursor to the recession. Scores of these borrowers did not understand their mortgages and did not have sufficient income to afford them. Many homeowners had taken on outsized mortgages with some of the nontraditional features—interest-only payments and negative amortization—discussed in this section. When loan payments increased, borrowers were swamped. After the bottom fell out of the economy, home values tumbled, leaving homeowners owing more on their homes than the homes were worth. Many homeowners capitulated and walked away. Some of this lending activity turned out to be predatory, whereby lenders made loans they knew would default. There is a market for subprime loans for people with dinged-up credit histories, but these loans require due diligence.

ARM LOANS

An **adjustable-rate mortgage (ARM)** is a mortgage in which the rate periodically adjusts. The vast majority of mortgages today are fixed-rate mortgages; the rate stays the same for the life of the loan. For lenders and borrowers, there are many more considerations to understand when contemplating an ARM: indexes, caps on rates, payment options, recalculating the loan, and more. Many ARMs start with rates that are lower than fixed rates initially but rise higher than fixed rates over time. This is the adjustment period. Typically, for the first months up to five years or more, the rate is lower and will remain lower during this time. After this period, rates will begin to increase. Lenders must evaluate whether a borrower's income is likely to increase enough to support the higher payments. Borrowers must make the same analysis. If the borrower does not plan to stay in the home for long, can make extra payments, and does not have any other lending needs in the near future—that is, for cars or school—ARMs can make sense.

DTI RATIO ASSESSMENT

Besides credit history, **debt to income (DTI)** is probably the most important factor to consider when assessing a borrower's ability to repay a loan. DTI measures the percentage of a borrower's income that will be used to repay the mortgage he or she is applying for and any existing debts. Most lenders like to see DTI around 36 percent but will sometimes go as high as 50 percent in special circumstances. DTI is debt divided by income. For example, if a borrower's monthly gross income is $3,000, the new mortgage payment is $800 (including taxes and insurances), and other debts (credit card, student loan, and car payment) total $200 per month, DTI would be 33 percent: $\frac{\$1,000}{\$3,000} = 0.33$. DTI does not take into account everyday expenses (food, entertainment, travel, gym memberships, utilities, etc.). A high DTI is an indication that the borrower may have more debt than his or her income can support.

CREDIT RISK CHARACTERISTICS

An easy way to think of credit risk characteristics is to consider **the five Cs**: character, capacity, capital, collateral, and conditions. A lender can discern a lot about a borrower by looking at his or her credit report.

- One indication of good character would be a person honoring his or her obligations. A good payment history and history of paying off debts with no liens, bankruptcies, or judgements all indicate good character.
- Capacity is the debt-to-income ratio we have discussed. Does the borrower have the cash flow to maintain all of his or her debts?
- Capital is the down payment. Borrowers who are willing to put their own money down up front are better risks. It is a sign of commitment to the loan. Large down payments also lessen the chance of default.
- Collateral is the home being purchased. Whether the home is a primary home, a vacation home, or an investment is a factor that affects risk. Other factors concerning the collateral affect risk as well, such as the condition of the home and its location.
- Conditions are the terms of the loan: the number of years to repay, the type of mortgage, and the size of the loan.

STATED INCOME LOANS

Stated income loans, also known as non-income verification or alternative document loans, are loans provided to borrowers with little or no proof of income. These loans are rare and usually approved for borrowers who have trouble documenting their income, for example, people who work on commission, business owners who keep all their assets in the business, seasonal workers, and freelancers. Instead of using traditional methods to verify income, like W-2s and income tax returns, lenders use bank statements, both personal and business, to verify income. Stated income loans are often considered subprime because they are riskier and therefore have higher interest rates and fees. These types of loans were popular before the subprime mortgage crisis and contributed to the 2008 recession. Their popularity was fueled by a lethal combination of skyrocketing home prices and relaxed lending practices. Many stated income loans failed during the mortgage crisis.

SCENARIOS IN WHICH A BALLOON LOAN MIGHT BE APPROPRIATE

A balloon loan is one that has a normal monthly payment initially (usually based on a 30-year amortization schedule), then the entire loan becomes due in one final payment. An example is a $200,000 loan with an interest rate of three percent and a monthly payment of $843 for the first seven years. After seven years, a final payment of $168,000 is due. Balloon loans are attractive because the rates are typically lower than for most other types of traditional mortgages. The dilemma is how to handle this last payment. Some loans have reset options, but most require this final lump-sum payment. This type of loan could work for someone who knows he or she will soon be selling a house or someone who is expecting his or her income to increase significantly over time. It could also work for someone with low credit scores now who wants to refinance again when his or her credit scores improve.

SUBPRIME BORROWERS

A subprime borrower is someone whose credit history is dinged up. Lenders will loan to subprime borrowers but at higher rates than those with good credit histories. FICO refers to dings on a credit history as derogatory information—anything from missed payments to bankruptcy. A subprime borrower typically has a low credit score, in the 600 range or lower. Banks give their best rates to borrowers with credit scores in the 700 range or higher. A subprime borrower usually has a history of delinquencies, two or more 30-day delinquencies in the last 12 months, or one 60-day delinquency in the last 24 months. Subprime borrowers will often have loans that have been charged off; this is, a lender has stopped trying to collect on the debt and assigned it to a collection agency for repayment. A borrower would fall into the subprime category with a foreclosure in the past 24 months or a bankruptcy in the last 60 months. Subprime borrowers usually have debt-to-income ratios in the 50s and show a history of troubles with budgeting for everyday expenses.

NONTRADITIONAL MORTGAGE LOAN

A **nontraditional mortgage loan** is any mortgage that is not a fixed-rate, fully amortizing mortgage. Examples are balloon mortgages, adjustable-rate mortgages (ARMs), and interest-only mortgages. Subprime borrowers willing to pay higher interest rates are good candidates for nontraditional mortgages, as are borrowers who want a mortgage with more flexibility. A payment-option ARM is a good example of a nontraditional mortgage. This type of mortgage follows the ARM framework but allows the borrower to choose each month what type of payment he or she wants to make. Payment options can be interest only, 15-year or 30-year amortization payments, or negative amortization payments. These types of loans can be complicated, and it is important that the borrower fully understands all of the payment options. For example, with negative amortization, because the unpaid interest and/or principal is added onto the outstanding balance, the borrower will pay more interest over time.

NONQUALIFIED MORTGAGE

A **nonqualified mortgage** is a loan that does not comply with the guidelines of the Consumer Financial Protection Bureau (CFPB) for qualified mortgages. A qualified mortgage is simply a loan that the borrower can repay and that is easy to understand, safe, and not overly expensive. Therefore, a nonqualified loan might have risky features—for example, having balloon payments or negative amortization, or being interest only. These types of features are not allowed with a qualified mortgage. The borrower's debt-to-income ratio would be higher than 43 percent (the ceiling set by CFPB guidelines for a qualified mortgage). With nonqualified mortgages, the points and fees would exceed three percent of the loan amount, the limit for a loan to be considered qualified. For a qualified mortgage, lenders use tax returns, pay stubs, and W-2s to assess the borrower's income. For a nonqualified mortgage, a lender might rely on bank statements or other alternative documents. Because nonqualified loans tend to be riskier, they are not sold on the secondary market. In most cases, the lender remains the servicer for the life of the loan.

Mortgage Loan Products

PURCHASE-MONEY SECOND MORTGAGES

A **purchase-money mortgage** is a mortgage offered by the seller of a home. As part of the deal, the seller takes the place of the bank, setting the terms of the mortgage. This type of loan is often referred to as seller financing.

A **purchase-money second mortgage** is often used in conjunction with traditional mortgages to help buyers avoid paying mortgage insurance. The loan basically takes the place of a down payment when the borrower chooses to pay less down or cannot afford a larger down payment. Sometimes referred to as a piggyback loan, the financing in this scenario looks something like this: a primary mortgage covering 80 percent of the purchase price, a second mortgage covering 10 percent of the purchase price, and a 10 percent down payment. Technically, having the first mortgage at 80 percent allows the homeowner to get to the 20 percent equity threshold needed to avoid paying mortgage insurance.

FIXED

FIXED-RATE MORTGAGE

The **fixed-rate mortgage** is the most popular mortgage offered. These mortgages have rates and payments that are fixed for the life of the loan. The most common fixed-rate loans are for terms of 15, 20, and 30 years. The loans are amortized over the life of the loan, which means the payment is calculated so that each month, the payment is the same and includes principal and interest. With each payment, the portion that goes toward paying down the principal gradually increases. If the borrower does not make any additional payments during the life of the loan, the mortgage is completely paid off with the last monthly payment in the last year of the loan. All lenders must provide an amortization schedule when originating a loan. Because extra payments go toward principal, a fixed-rate mortgage can be paid off sooner by making extra payments or by paying more than the minimum each month. Paying extra will not lower a borrower's monthly payment, but it will pay down the loan sooner. For example, making one extra payment each year on a 30-year mortgage would satisfy the loan in about 25 years.

TYPES OF LOANS

Most lenders predominantly issue fixed-rate mortgages with terms of varying lengths, that is, 30, 20, or 15 years. During the life of the loan, the rate remains fixed, and the payments are amortized into equal monthly installments so that the loan is paid off with the final payment. Another way to think of a fixed-rate loan is as one that is not amortized; that is, it does not have equal monthly payments for the life of the loan. For example, a balloon loan can have a fixed rate with equal monthly payments for some set time initially—say, three, five, or seven years—then the remainder of the loan is due in one large final payment. An interest-only loan might be based on a fixed rate, but at least initially the monthly payment due is interest only. Borrowers do not begin to pay down loan principal until some later specified time from months to years.

PERCENTAGE OF DOWN PAYMENT REQUIRED TO LESSEN MONTHLY PAYMENTS

The more a borrower pays down, the less he or she will have to borrow and the more it will reduce the potential monthly payment. In an ideal world, the borrower would pay down at least 20 percent. A 20 percent down payment reduces the need to pay monthly expenses for mortgage insurance (mortgage insurance protects the lender from borrower default and is required on purchases in which the borrower pays down less than 20 percent). Mortgage insurance can cost anywhere from 0.05 percent to one percent of the loan amount. On a $150,000 mortgage, mortgage insurance would potentially cost anywhere from $63 to $125 per month. Not having to pay mortgage insurance would be a significant savings. In another example, if a home costs $200,000, and a borrower pays down 10 percent, he or she would have to borrow $180,000. The principal and interest payment alone would run about $966 on a 30-year loan at a fixed rate of five percent. Paying down $40,000 would reduce the monthly payment to $859 per month, a significant savings, and there would be no mortgage insurance.

ADJUSTABLE

MARGIN AND INDEX

Once an adjustable-rate mortgage (ARM) enters the adjustable rate period of the loan, there are two rates that make up the mortgage's interest rate. One is the **margin**, which is fixed, and the other is the **index**, which floats. The two rates added together make up the **fully indexed** rate for the mortgage. All ARMs have an introductory rate period during which the rate is fixed. After this stage, the rate begins to adjust, and the payment will change as well. The index portion of the adjustable rate is usually a popular measure; for example, it could be the rate on a 10-year Treasury note or the prime rate. The index reflects economic conditions. The margin is a set rate chosen by the lender. Therefore: $index + margin = interest\ rate$. The current 10-year Treasury is about 2.86 percent; a margin of two percent would make the rate for this ARM example 4.86. If the Treasury yield changes to 3.5, the mortgage rate would be 5.5 percent.

FULLY INDEXED RATE

A **fully indexed rate** is a variable interest rate on a mortgage. The rate is derived by adding a fixed margin to an index rate. The combination equals the full rate for the mortgage. Fully indexed rates are used on mortgages with variable rates, mostly commonly with adjustable-rate mortgages (ARMs). ARMs typically start with a period of time during which the rate is fixed. When this stage ends, the formula for devising the rate during the adjustable period is found by adding an index to a set margin. For example, the index could be the rate for the 10-year Treasury note, four percent, and the margin, two percent. The margin is set by the lender and does not change during the life of the mortgage. These two numbers added together give the fully indexed rate of $4 + 2 = 6$. ARMs change rates according to the mortgage terms. Typically, the rate adjusts annually. If in the following year, the 10-year Treasury rate rises to five, the fully indexed rate will be $5 + 2 = 7$.

ARMS

There are many types of adjustable-rate mortgages (ARMs). The most common are 3/1, 5/1, and 7/1 ARMs. The first number refers to the number of years the rate initially remains locked. The second number refers to how often the rate can reset after the initial locked period. For a 3/1 ARM, the rate remains locked for the first three years and then resets every year thereafter. There are many variations, for example, a 5/5 ARM (fixed for five years, resets every five years). At the end of the fixed-rate period, the rate increases based on an index plus a set margin. An example of an index might be the prime rate or US Treasury note rates. The margin is a fixed amount that remains the same for the life of the loan. For example, you arrive at the adjustable rate by adding the 10-year Treasury to a margin of two, as follows: $2.86 + 2 = 4.86$. In the following year, if the 10-year Treasury rate changes to three percent, the rate for the mortgage loan goes up to five percent.

TIMELINE FOR NOTIFYING A CUSTOMER OF A RATE CHANGE

Adjustable-rate mortgages typically have a period of time in the beginning when the rate and payment are fixed, usually for the first three, five, or seven years. After this initial period, the rate will normally adjust annually. The first time the rate changes, the lender must notify the borrower seven to eight months before the first payment at the new rate is due. All subsequent rate change notices must be provided to the borrower two to four months before the payment at the new rate is due. The advance notice is designed to give borrowers a chance to adjust to the new payment or refinance their mortgages. The first notice must include options to explore if the borrower cannot afford the new payment and information on how to contact a Housing and Urban Development (HUD)-approved mortgage counselor. The subsequent notices must show the current rate and the new rate, the current payment and the new payment, and the date the new payment is due.

BALLOON MORTGAGES

A **balloon mortgage** is a mortgage in which a large portion of the loan is due in one large payment at the end of the loan. A balloon mortgage does not have a fixed payment for the life of the loan like a fixed-rate mortgage. It is also similar to an adjustable-rate mortgage (ARM) in that there is an initial period during which the rate and payment are predictable. For example, with a balloon mortgage, for the first three, five, or seven years, the payment can be fixed, typically calculated on a 30-year amortization schedule with a fixed rate. During this initial period, however, some lenders might also allow interest-only payments or some other arrangement that keeps the payment low. When this initial period ends, the remaining balance of the loan is due in one final payment. Obviously, this final payment will be large compared to the monthly payments preceding it. Balloon mortgages are much less popular today than they were before the subprime mortgage crisis, but they are still appropriate in limited circumstances.

REVERSE MORTGAGE

Think of a **reverse mortgage** as making a loan to an elderly homeowner, but instead of collecting payments, the bank pays the homeowner. Reverse mortgages require the borrower to be 62 or older. Payments can be made in a lump sum or monthly. The entire balance on the mortgage is due when the homeowner sells the home or dies. Reverse mortgages are structured so that the balance on the loan is not larger than the value of the home. This is done so that the homeowner's estate or heirs will owe nothing additional after the home is sold and the loan paid. However, the loan amount could exceed the home value if the housing market suffers a decline, causing home prices to drop. If there are proceeds left over after the house is sold and the loan is satisfied, those funds go to the homeowner or his or her heirs. With a reverse mortgage, the homeowner retains the title on the house until he or she sells or dies. Reverse mortgages can be good for elderly people who have a lot of equity in their homes but little cash or other marketable securities to pay for everyday expenses.

REQUIRED AMOUNT OF TITLE INSURANCE

Title insurance protects lenders and homeowners in the event there is ever a dispute over ownership of a property. In general, most policies are issued in an amount that equals the value of the property. Some policies state this as the maximum amount that a homeowner might be able to claim in the event of a dispute. The maximum claim amount is the value of the property. Title insurance policies can be purchased separately to protect the lender and to protect the borrower. Unlike homeowner's insurance, which protects borrowers against future events, title insurance protects homeowners from past events. Some past occurrences that could come back to haunt a homeowner are forged title documents, liens, unknown easements, outstanding lawsuits, and more. The dangers of forgoing title insurance are dire. For example, if the previous owner of a home defaulted on property taxes, a lien would be placed against the home. If this lien goes undetected when the home changes hands, the current homeowner becomes responsible for the tax debt.

SCENARIOS THAT CAUSE THE FULL BALANCE TO BECOME DUE

The most common scenarios requiring the full balance to be paid on a reverse mortgage are when the homeowner dies, no longer resides in the home, or sells the property. Reverse mortgages require homeowners to annually certify that the residence borrowed against is still their primary home. The home is not considered primary if the homeowner is absent for the majority of a year for nonmedical reasons or absent for more than 12 consecutive months for medical reasons. Co-borrowers can continue living in the home after the co-borrower passes or moves out. A reverse mortgage can also become due if the borrower fails to pay taxes or homeowner's insurance or does not keep the home in good repair. Otherwise, the reverse mortgage must be paid when the last surviving homeowner moves out, dies, or sells the house.

REQUIREMENTS OF REVERSE MORTGAGE ADVERTISEMENTS

Advertisements for reverse mortgages must meet certain federal regulations. The use of Housing and Urban Development (HUD) or Federal Housing Administration (FHA) names, seals, or logos is prohibited. Ads cannot mislead or deceive. The regulations require specific disclaimers and record retention, and they also impose sanctions. Using HUD or FHA names, seals, or logos could indicate to borrowers that the reverse mortgage program is a federal program or endorsed by the federal government, which would be misleading or false. Lenders must fully explain reverse mortgages in plain language. Lenders must issue a disclaimer saying that neither the HUD nor the FHA distributes or approves the advertising materials. Advertisers are prohibited from saying that any federal organizations endorse or are affiliated with their products. All advertising materials must be retained for two years. Advertisers who violate federal regulations can be sanctioned, fined, or subject to administrative actions.

HELOC

A **home equity line of credit (HELOC)** is a revolving loan using a borrower's residence as collateral. This type of loan is sometimes referred to as open-ended because the credit can be used over and over again. HELOCs have draw periods. This is the time period that the borrower can access the line. For example, a lender might issue a line of credit for $50,000 with a ten-year draw period. This means the homeowner can borrow as much as he or she wants for the next ten years until he or she reaches the $50,000 limit. There is no monthly payment if there is no balance on the line. Once the borrower uses the line, a minimum monthly payment becomes due, much like a credit card. The lender charges interest based on some index, often the prime rate plus some set margin, making these loan rates variable with a set maximum. Payments can be interest only or principal and interest. At the end of the draw period, the borrower can no longer access the line of credit and must pay off the remaining balance. Depending on the loan terms, lenders might allow borrowers up to 20 years after the draw period to pay off the remaining balance.

CONSTRUCTION MORTGAGES

A **construction loan** provides temporary funding to build a home. A builder or a homebuyer obtains this type of loan through the build and then seeks permanent financing once the home is completed. Because construction loans are seen as riskier, the rates are higher, and some banks do not offer them. After the construction is complete, the borrower refinances the temporary loan, typically into a more traditional loan with a competitive interest rate. Often the builder requires the temporary loan to be paid off by the time the home is completed. Construction loans can be obtained to build new homes from the ground up and also to rehabilitate existing homes. Large down payment requirements and the lack of collateral can be problematic for both lenders and borrowers when assessing whether to originate a construction loan, which results in higher rates when a lender is willing to provide such a loan. Smaller credit unions and regional banks tend to be primary sources for construction loans because these institutions are more familiar with the local real estate market.

INTEREST-ONLY MORTGAGES

An **interest-only mortgage** requires the borrower to pay only the interest due monthly and to defer paying principal to a later date. At some point, the borrower must pay the principal. After the initial period of interest-only payments, the borrower has a few options. Usually, the interest-only period lasts a short time, for example, five years. At that point, mortgage converts to a more traditional loan in which monthly payments include interest and principal until the loan is satisfied. Some borrowers might opt for a balloon payment through which the entire principal is paid in one lump sum. The loan could also be refinanced completely into a traditional, fixed-rate mortgage. Finally, the homeowners might opt to sell the home. The risk with interest-only mortgages is correctly calculating how to manage the increased monthly payments or the balloon payment. These types of loans are risky but might be good for someone who expects their income to increase dramatically in the near future.

Interest-only mortgage payments pay only the interest that accumulates on the mortgage, not the principal. A fixed-rate mortgage, the most common mortgage type, includes interest and principal with each monthly payment. With every payment, the borrower is slowly paying off the loan, usually over a 15-, 20-, or 30-year term. Interest-only mortgages are usually made for short terms, perhaps three to five years. At the end of the term, the borrower usually makes a large payment to satisfy the debt, refinances, or sells the home. The upside of interest-only payments is that they provide a smaller monthly payment. The downside is that the borrower is not creating equity in the home. To calculate the payment, take the mortgage balance, multiply it by the interest rate, and divide by 12, the number of monthly payments in a year: $\frac{\$100,000 \times 0.05}{12} = \$416$ per month. The same mortgage with a principal and interest payment for 30 years would be \$516.

TERMS USED IN THE MORTGAGE INDUSTRY

LOAN TERMS

SUBORDINATE LIENS

Subordinate liens can be second mortgages or judgements filed against a homeowner. Both can cause problems when it comes to closing a new mortgage. A **subordinate lien** can also be a home equity loan or line of credit, loans that are often taken out in addition to a first mortgage to do repairs or upgrades on a home. These loans are called subordinate because they are paid off second when a homeowner defaults and the home has to be sold to pay off debts. When the holder of the first mortgage forecloses on a homeowner, the lender in first position gets to collect its debt first, then if there are any remaining funds, subordinate liens are paid. Sometimes subordinate liens are placed when a judgment is filed against a homeowner. For example, a subordinate lien can be placed for unpaid real estate taxes or other unpaid bills. Sellers must pay off these subordinate liens before the title can be cleared and the home can be transferred to a new owner.

ESCROW ACCOUNTS

Escrow accounts are established by lenders to collect payments for real estate taxes, homeowner's insurance, and mortgage insurance. Lenders collect funds for these items monthly and pay them on behalf of the homeowner when they are due. Lenders are also required to issue **annual escrow account statements**. The annual statement must detail the account history for the computation year and the next year. The following items must be clearly itemized:

- The borrower's current monthly mortgage payment and the portion placed in escrow
- The amount of the past year's monthly mortgage payment and the portion placed in escrow
- The total amount paid into escrow in the past computation year
- The total amount paid out of escrow for the same year for taxes, insurance, and other charges
- The balance of the escrow account at the end of the period
- An explanation of how any surplus will be handled
- An explanation of how any shortage will be paid by the borrower
- If applicable, an explanation of why the low monthly balance was not reached as a comparison of the most recent account year and last year's projection

TABLE FUNDING

Table funding is when the originator of a loan, often a mortgage broker, does not have sufficient funds to make loans and hold the loans until they can be sold on the secondary market. The originator teams up with a larger lender who provides the funds at closing and immediately takes assignment of the mortgage. Under Department of Housing and Urban Development (HUD) regulations, the business relationship between originator and lender must be disclosed to the borrower. All premiums paid to the originator (the originator's profit) for this type of funding must also be disclosed in the closing documents. The funding of the loan and the transfer to the lender occur on the same day as closing. Loans sold on the secondary market do not have to make this disclosure. Table funding is illegal in some states.

RATE LOCK AGREEMENT

The mortgage process can be lengthy, with some deals taking up to 90 days to close, and most deals closing in about 45 days. Interest rates can change daily, even hourly. To avoid the risk of rates increasing while the borrower is waiting to close, lenders offer a **rate lock**, fixing the rate so it does not fluctuate during the remainder of the underwriting process. The rate lock agreement binds both the lender and the borrower and fixes the rate until the loan closing. The rate remains the same unless there are some extenuating circumstances; for example, the loan amount changes, there is new information introduced about the borrower's income or credit score, or the borrower chooses a different type of loan. The borrower also risks locking into a rate only to find that, at closing time, rates have dropped. Because the agreement is binding, the borrower must accept the higher rate or pay a fee to lock again at the lower rate. Rate locks usually last anywhere from 10 to 60 days. If the agreement expires before the loan closes, it may be possible to request an extension.

TOLERANCES

According to TILA-RESPA Integrated Disclosure (TRID) rules, lenders are supposed to quote fees and costs for a mortgage in good faith. This good-faith standard is measured by comparing the fees disclosed in the Loan Estimate to what the borrower actually pays. There will be times when the actual costs exceed what was detailed in the Loan Estimate. As long as what the borrower actually pays does not exceed certain **tolerances**, the fees quoted were disclosed in good faith. There are three tolerance thresholds specified by TRID: zero tolerance, 10 percent cumulative tolerance, and no or unlimited tolerance. These tolerances apply to fees quoted on page two of the Loan Estimate: origination fees, fees for services that cannot be shopped for, and fees for services that can be shopped for.

Zero-tolerance fees are paid directly from the borrower to the lender or mortgage broker, that is, an origination fee. Other zero-tolerance fees are transfer taxes and fees for services that the borrower cannot shop for. All of these zero-tolerance fees are known ahead of time and therefore should never fluctuate.

Ten percent cumulative tolerance fees are recording fees and third-party service fees. As long as the cumulative total of these fees does not increase by more than 10 percent, they are quoted in good faith.

The last category is for fees the lender has no control over and that may increase by any amount: fees for services the borrower shopped for, prepaid interest, homeowner's insurance premiums and the amount placed in escrow, title insurance fees, and fees for services the lender does not require.

LIENS

A lien is the right to make a claim against a property until the owner of the property repays a debt to the lienholder. Liens are either granted by property owners or placed against property owners for statutory reasons. When a mortgage is granted, the lender's main recourse in the case of default is to retake the home. If the homeowner does not make payments, the lender evicts the owner and takes possession of the home. At the time of closing and recording, the lender places a lien on the house. This is the legal notice that the lender has the right to foreclose on a homeowner in the event of default. A lien can also be placed by authorities other than lenders. For example, if a property owner fails to pay real estate taxes, the local government can place a lien on the property to force collection of the back taxes. When a homeowner pays off the mortgage, the lien filed against the home with local authorities is released, and the homeowner then owns the home free and clear assuming there are no other liens against the property.

DELINQUENT LOAN

A **delinquent loan** is one in which the borrower has failed to make a payment by the due date. Failing to make payments for a mortgage on time can result in foreclosure, where the lender evicts the owner, takes possession of the property, and sells it to recoup losses. Lenders typically lose money in a foreclosure and will work with borrowers who find themselves in financial straits to try and resolve payment issues before initiating foreclosure procedures. If the borrower's payment struggles are more of a temporary situation, some lenders might offer forbearance, whereby borrowers are allowed to suspend monthly payments for a short period of time. Lenders might also arrange for lower payments for a brief period as well. These alternatives give homeowners a chance to recover financially and stay in their homes. In situations that are more dire and of a long-term nature, lenders might agree to modify a mortgage so that it is more affordable for the borrower.

HIGH-COST LOANS

Typically, **high-cost mortgages** are first-lien loans with rates more than 6.5 percentage points higher than the prime rate or with fees that exceed five percent of the total loan amount, or a mortgage in which the lender can charge a prepayment penalty of more than two percent of the amount prepaid for more than 36 months after consummation. A mortgage of less than $50,000 with a rate greater than 8.5 percentage points above prime is also considered high cost. A subordinate or junior mortgage with a rate more than 8.5 percentage points higher than prime is considered high cost as well. Federal regulations prohibit balloon payments with high-cost mortgages as well as many fees. Lenders cannot charge early payment fees or fees greater than four percent for late payments. Lenders are also prohibited from charging fees for modifications to a high-cost mortgage. Borrowers are also required to meet with a HUD-certified mortgage counselor before taking out this type of mortgage.

DISCLOSURE TERMS

YIELD SPREAD PREMIUMS

Mortgage brokers are paid by either origination fees or yield spread premiums, or some combination of both. The origination fee is a flat fee assessed against the loan amount. For a $100,000 loan, an origination fee might be one percent, or $1,000. The **yield spread premium** is a fee paid directly to the broker by the lender for selling a mortgage with a rate that is higher than market rates or higher than what the borrower is qualified to receive. Borrowers can use it to offset loan costs. Yield spread premiums must be disclosed to borrowers. If a borrower does not pay a broker an origination fee, then mostly likely the broker's fee is made by using a yield spread premium. In this scenario, the borrower is trading lower up-front costs for a higher rate. Borrowers whose cash reserves are limited might view this as a good trade-off. Also, for borrowers who will not stay in the house long, lowering up-front fees with a slightly higher interest rate might still end up costing less overall.

SERVICING TRANSFERS

A **servicing transfer** happens when a lender sells a mortgage to another institution that then assumes all of the administrative aspects of the loan—for example, collecting the payments, calculating escrows, and printing and mailing monthly statements. Most borrowers barely realize that their loans have been transferred. All of the original terms of the loan remain unchanged, and the original loan contract is recognized by the new servicer in its entirety. Federal regulations require lenders to notify borrowers of any potential transfer and of the transfer itself. A Mortgage Servicing Disclosure Statement must be given to a borrower during the loan process, explaining that the lender may at some point transfer the borrower's loan to another institution for servicing. When a loan is transferred, the lender is also required to alert the borrower. The borrower will also receive a notice from the new servicer.

LENDER CREDITS

Lender credits are funds that the lender provides to offset closing costs on a mortgage. Closing costs, for things like title insurance, inspections, legal fees, filing fees, and so on, run anywhere from two to five percent of a home's purchase price. This can be a hefty sum, especially considering that the borrower also needs to bring a down payment to closing and most likely fund the escrow account. A **lender credit** of several thousand dollars to offset mortgage closing costs can make a big difference for a borrower. Most lenders will charge a higher interest rate in exchange for a lender credit. Paying a higher interest rate in exchange for a lender credit means the buyer will pay more in the long run. Many buyers would rather take the credit, especially if it can potentially save the mortgage deal or if the buyer would rather have the extra cash to cover other incidental costs that come with buying a home, like furniture or new appliances.

FINANCIAL TERMS
DISCOUNT POINTS

Discount points, sometimes referred to as mortgage points or "buying down the rate," are fees that borrowers pay to the lender for a reduction in the interest rate. Typically, a one percent reduction in rate would cost one percent of the mortgage amount. On a $100,000 mortgage, the borrower would have to pay $1,000 to lower the interest rate by one percent. Lowering the interest rate can be attractive for borrowers because this will also lower their monthly payment and total interest expense over the life of the loan. On a $200,000, 30-year mortgage, one discount point would save more than $10,000 in interest, and two points would save the borrower over $20,000 in interest— not a bad return on the initial $2,000 and $4,000, respectively, it would cost to buy down the rate. A borrower should consider how much cash he or she has up front and how long he or she plans to stay in the home to evaluate whether buying points is worth the costs. If cash up front is no problem, and the borrower will remain in the house long enough to recoup the cost of buying the points, then buying down the rate makes sense.

2-1 BUYDOWN

A 2-1 buydown helps homebuyers lower their monthly mortgage payments in the first two years of the mortgage. The terms for 2-1 buydowns vary among lenders. Some lenders collect the cost of the buydown and put the funds into a separate account. Each month the lender draws out an amount equal to the difference between the lower monthly payment and what the payment will be beginning in the third year. Other lenders treat the buydown the same as buying a mortgage point. A buydown helps a borrower afford a larger loan than he or she might otherwise qualify for without the buydown. It also gives homebuyers a chance to build up their finances during the first two years of the loan. With Federal Housing Administration (FHA) loans, the buydown reduces the monthly mortgage payment for the first two years by two percent the first year and by one percent in the second year. On a 30-year mortgage, the payments for the remaining 28 years are fixed at the full monthly amount.

ACCRUED INTEREST

Accrued interest is interest that has accumulated on a mortgage but has not yet been paid to the lender. Mortgage interest accrues daily or weekly depending on the loan. Mortgages are paid in arrears because the interest accrues before the payment is made. If a borrower pays on the due date, all of the interest due has accrued. Any extra payment will all go to principal. On a $200,000 mortgage at five percent, the interest accrues at a rate of $27.77 per day $\left(\frac{\$200,000 \times 0.05}{360} = \$27.77 \right)$.

When a borrower requests a payoff quote for a mortgage, the lender will provide a quote that is good up to a certain date; it includes the accrued interest. After that date, the payoff will increase each day by the amount of interest that accrues daily. This daily accumulation of interest outside of the standard repayment period is sometimes referred to as the **per diem**.

LOAN-TO-VALUE RATIO

Loan-to-value ratio is the measure of the mortgage amount versus the value of the home. If a home is worth $300,000, and the loan amount is $250,000, the loan-to-value ratio is 83 percent. Lenders use loan-to-value to assess the risk of making a mortgage, refinancing, or providing home equity loans. The higher the loan-to-value ratio, the higher the risk. Lenders prefer that the borrower have some equity in the home before making the loan. In the event of default, if the loan-to-value ratio is high, the lender may not be able to sell the home for enough money to recover the mortgage balance and the loan costs. This is where mortgage insurance comes in. With loan-to-value ratios greater than 80 percent, lenders make the borrower buy insurance. The insurance helps lenders recoup costs in the event of foreclosure.

SETTLEMENT

Settlement, also known as closing, is the final stage of the mortgage process. This is when the borrower, seller, and lender meet to legally transfer the home into the borrower's name, pay the seller, and establish the new mortgage. The settlement includes a flurry of documents that must be signed to make the transaction binding: settlement sheets, the mortgage note, truth-in-lending documents, and any others that might be required by state or federal laws. Settlement is when the borrower brings the down payment, as well as funds that will be used to pay the closing costs and fund an escrow account. All of these funds are normally aggregated into one cashier's check that the borrower brings to the closing. Once all of the documents are signed, then the seller is paid, the mortgage is in place, and the buyer receives the keys and is a proud new homeowner.

DAILY SIMPLE INTEREST

The main difference between most mortgages, which calculate interest monthly, and a **daily simple interest** mortgage is that the latter calculates interest on a daily basis, leading to higher payments and higher interest charges. On a simple-interest mortgage, the interest is calculated by dividing the interest rate by 365 days and then multiplying that number by the outstanding loan balance. A traditional mortgage that is calculated monthly has five fewer days ($30 \times 12 = 360$), resulting in lower interest charges overall. It is a small difference but can add up over time, especially for larger loans. In a traditional mortgage, it doesn't matter when the borrower makes a payment; no additional interest accrues. With simple interest, interest is always accruing, so paying later than the due date will result in paying more interest. Paying during the grace period for a traditional loan does not result in more interest. Borrowers who want a little more payment flexibility are better off with a traditional mortgage.

GENERAL TERMS
SUBORDINATION

Subordination happens when there is more than one mortgage against a home. The first mortgage takes precedence over the second mortgage in the event of foreclosure; the lender of the first mortgage gets paid first. Often when a lender originates a mortgage to a borrower who already has a mortgage on the home, the lender will ask the other mortgage company to sign a subordination agreement. For example, a borrower has two loans against the home and refinances the first one. The second loan would move into first position, and the new loan would move into second position. However, the lender who is refinancing can ask the holder of the second loan to sign a subordination agreement, allowing the refinanced loan to take first position. In the event of a default, the lender in first position is guaranteed to get paid before the lender in second position.

CONVEYANCE

Conveyance in real estate refers to the act of transferring ownership rights from one party to another. Conveyance most often occurs with a written sales deed that transfers title from the seller to the buyer. Conveyance is a contract that legally binds both parties to the terms and conditions in the contract. The process of conveying a property from the seller to the buyer is thorough; financing is verified and searches are undertaken for any loans, liens, or encumbrances that must first be settled, as well as title searches to ensure there are no other owners on the current deed besides the sellers. It is typically the buyer's responsibility to ensure he or she has obtained free and clear rights to the property. This is why title insurance is purchased by buyers in most real estate deals. Title insurance protects the home buyer if someone should try to claim ownership on the property after the deal has closed.

CASH-OUT REFINANCE

Cash-out refinance occurs when a homeowner refinances an existing mortgage for more than he or she owes and retains the additional funds after closing. This type of refinancing is often used by homeowners to lower their interest rates and to use the additional funds to make improvements to their homes. A homeowner must have enough equity built up to qualify for this type of loan. For example, if a homeowner's current loan is $100,000, and the home is worth $200,000, he or she would be eligible for a new loan of up to $200,000, depending on the lender. After the first loan is paid off, the homeowner retains the additional $100,000 to use how he or she pleases. Many lenders place limits on how much they are willing to lend in a cash-out refinance. Some are willing to lend only 80 percent of the home's value. In this example, the maximum loan the homeowner could take would be $160,000, which would leave $60,000 in cash after the mortgage is refinanced.

PREPAIDS

Prepaids are items that the borrower is required to pay in advance of closing for items like homeowner's insurance, taxes, and mortgage insurance (if mortgage insurance is required). These funds are placed into an escrow account, and the lender pays them on behalf of the homeowner when the items are due. They are called **prepaids** because the funds are collected before the funds are actually needed to pay future bills. Prepaids typically require the borrower to escrow two to three months of expenses for taxes and insurance. Prepaids differ from closing costs because they are ongoing expenses that come with homeownership. Closing costs are one-time expenses paid at closing. Collecting these funds in advance protects the lender in the event of an immediate disaster like a flood or storm damage. During the life of the loan, the homeowner pays into the escrow account every month. Funds accumulate until the annual bills for property taxes and homeowner's insurance are due.

UNDERWRITING

Underwriting in the mortgage world is the process of analyzing a borrower's creditworthiness and deciding whether to lend to the applicant and at what terms. The word "underwriter" originates from the early days of lending when people would write their names under the amount of debt they were willing to accept at a specific premium. Mortgage underwriters are the people who take all of the documents that a mortgage loan officer collects—credit reports, tax returns, W-2s, pay stubs, appraisals, bank statements, and so on—and analyze them to determine if an applicant has the ability to repay the mortgage he or she has applied for. Underwriters have the final say on whether a loan is approved or denied. They also determine how risky a deal is, which affects the rate a borrower is offered. Most financial institutions have appeals processes for cases in which a loan is denied, but some good reasoning and evidence must be used to overturn an underwriter's denial.

SECONDARY MARKET

The **secondary mortgage market** is where mortgages and servicing rights are traded by investors and lenders. Lenders have only a finite amount of money to lend. To obtain more funds to extend to borrowers, lenders sell their mortgages to institutions like Fannie Mae and Freddie Mac. Lenders get cash in exchange for the mortgage. Fannie Mae and Freddie Mac then package the mortgages they have purchased into securities that they then sell to investors in the secondary market. The instrument that Fannie and Freddie create is called a mortgage-backed security. The value of these securities is "guaranteed," or backed by the mortgages. Homeowners make their payments, and the payments are portioned back out to the holders of the mortgage-backed securities. Mortgage-backed securities were largely implicated in the 2008 subprime debt crisis. As homeowners began to default, so did the mortgage-backed securities, creating a ripple effect through the economy. Fannie Mae and Freddie Mac nearly failed, and some large institutions that had bet heavily on mortgage-backed securities lost everything when it turned out these investments were worthless.

THIRD-PARTY PROVIDERS

The mortgage process is complicated and has many moving parts. Lenders rely upon many separate companies and services to originate loans. **Third-party providers** perform services like inspections, appraisals, title searches, and more. "Third party" means these service providers are wholly separate from the lender. Real Estate Settlement Procedures Act (RESPA) laws require lenders to be transparent about these business relationships. RESPA states that if a lender refers business to a settlement service provider or maintains more than a one percent ownership stake in the service provider, this is called an **Affiliated Business Arrangement,** and the lender is required to disclose the relationship to the borrower. The lender must also disclose an estimate of the charges or range of charges the provider demands. Further, the lender may not require the borrower to use these settlement service providers. However, the lender can require the borrower to pay for the services of an alternate provider.

PRIMARY MORTGAGE MARKET

The **primary mortgage market** is made up of borrowers, banks, mortgage brokers, credit unions, savings and loans, and other institutions who meet to negotiate and originate mortgages. Primary lenders originate loans and sometimes service the mortgages for the life of the loans. Borrowers meet with lending officers in a financial institution and negotiate mortgage terms, and the lenders originate or issue the funds used by borrowers to buy homes. This is all part of the primary market.

The secondary market is where third parties buy mortgages and servicing rights from the primary lender. Fannie Mae and Freddie Mac are examples of entities working in the secondary market. The primary mortgage market is a good gauge for the health of the economy. When the primary mortgage market is strong, it indicates consumers are comfortable with their jobs and wages and confident that they can commit to a mortgage and the purchase of a home. A strong demand for mortgages indicates that prices and rates are in line with consumers' expectations as well. Conversely, a weak economy can make it harder to attract borrowers who are not feeling as confident.

CONSUMER CREDIT

The most common form of consumer credit is a credit card. Sometimes referred to as consumer debt, this type of credit involves purchasing goods or services with some type of loan—either revolving, installment, or a line of credit. Consumer credit involves purchasing non-investment type items, things that depreciate quickly, like cars, appliances, and everyday items. Consumer credit does not include debt used to purchase real estate or debt used to buy investments on margin. Someone who buys a 60-inch plasma television with a credit card is using consumer credit. Retailers, banks, department stores, and other financial institutions all offer consumer credit, which allows consumers to obtain expensive items and push the payments off into the future. Consumer credit usually comes with higher interest rates because, unlike a home loan, these types of debts are unsecured. There is no collateral that a lender can seize in the event of default, so there is more risk, hence the higher interest rates.

ASSUMABLE LOAN

An **assumable loan** is an existing mortgage that a home buyer takes over from the seller after purchasing the home. Even though the lender must approve the assumption, often the mortgage is assumed with little or no change to the original terms, including the rate. By transferring the original mortgage, the buyer avoids having to obtain a new mortgage. Depending on the interest rate (assumable mortgages work best in high or rising rate environments when the existing rate is lower than market rates), taking over an existing mortgage can save time and money, especially considering the rigorous process of getting approved and obtaining a mortgage on one's own. In this type of scenario, buyers will often need to take out an additional mortgage. For example, if a home sells for $250,000 and has a remaining mortgage balance of $100,000, the borrower will either have to pay down $150,000 or borrow at least some portion of the additional funds needed to purchase the home.

ASSIGNED LOAN

Financial institutions often buy and sell mortgages to and from each other. When a bank sells a mortgage to another institution, it assigns the loan or transfers it. An assignment transfers all of the interests, rights, and responsibilities for the loan to the new institution. The borrower must be notified of the transfer, and the transfer must also be recorded in public records. An assignment can be nullified if it is not recorded correctly. All future payments will be made to the new owner of the loan. It is not uncommon for a mortgage to be sold many times during its life. The institution assigning a loan to a new lender often does so to improve its own liquidity and to improve its debt portfolio. Borrowers will not recognize any disruption with regard to a mortgage assignment, other than having to change who their mortgage check is paid to and where it is mailed.

APOR

Average prime offer rate (APOR) is a benchmark used to measure interest rates. APOR is based on the average prime interest rate, fees and terms offered to highly qualified borrowers across the United States. APOR is determined by surveying annual percentage rates (APRs) currently being offered to applicants. The primary sources of data used to calculate APOR are the rates obtained by Freddie Mac data as well as other sources. The rates are published for fixed-rate and adjustable-rate mortgages. The Federal Financial Institutions Examination Council calculates and publishes APOR weekly. APOR is also used under Regulation Z to determine if a loan is higher priced. A mortgage used to buy a residence is considered higher priced if the rate offered is a certain percentage amount higher than the APOR at the time of origination. For first-lien mortgages, if the APR is 1.5 points higher than the APOR, it is a higher-priced mortgage.

Mortgage Loan Origination Activities

Loan Inquiry and Application Process Requirements

FORM 1003

The Uniform Residential Loan Application (Form 1003) is the standard mortgage application used by lenders. The application asks for basic information about the borrower and the loan: name, Social Security number, monthly income, loan amount, the address of the home being purchased, and its estimated value. It also asks for the borrower's date of birth, marital status, previous employers, borrower's current address, whether the home being purchased is a primary or secondary residence or investment property, phone numbers, years of education, and the borrower's other assets and liabilities. A mortgage is likely a borrower's largest purchase and a big commitment on behalf of a lender. Understandably, the 1003 is quite thorough, but it is just the beginning of the information-gathering process. The mortgage application provides a sketch that the borrower must fill in with supporting documentation, like tax returns, income, assets, bank statements, credit checks, and more. Only after all stones are turned can a lender assess a borrower's ability to repay and render a decision.

HANDLING CREDIT

Lenders want to work with borrowers who have a history of obtaining credit and handling the repayment of all debts responsibly. The credit report is the primary teller of tales for borrowers. The overall score is usually one of the best indicators of whether a borrower will be a good risk. Scores of 740 or higher indicate that a borrower has consistently taken on debt and repaid it in a timely and reasonable fashion. Lenders would be comfortable extending their most favorable terms and conditions to a borrower of this caliber. A credit report with lower scores, say in the 600 range, indicates that a borrower has had problems handling credit responsibilities in the past. In these instances, mortgage loan originators (MLOs) may need to delve deeper into why problems have arisen and learn more about the circumstances around the borrower's credit history. Medical problems are often the source of dings to a borrower's credit report; these often involve mitigating circumstances that underwriters should know about and that will improve an application despite low credit scores.

REPORT DISCREPANCIES

Credit scores make or break a mortgage application. But even good credit reports can be derailed by inaccurate information. Unfortunately, inaccuracies are fairly common. Under the Fair Credit Reporting Act, consumers have the right to dispute inaccurate information. And by law, credit reporting agencies must respond to a dispute within 30 days. Unfortunately, correcting a discrepancy might take much longer, and disputes may linger for months or years, sometimes without the borrower even realizing it. Disputes on a credit report raise red flags for lenders, and many will insist that a borrower resolve disputes before moving forward with a mortgage application. Fannie Mae and Freddie Mac often will not approve a mortgage with credit reports that contain unresolved disputes. Federal Housing Administration (FHA) mortgages can be obtained with flawed credit reports, but the approval process can be lengthy. Because credit reports and FICO scores are crucial, lenders should counsel customers to be proactive with their reports and monitor them regularly. Other common discrepancies involve name misspellings, address errors, or Social Security number mistakes. Lenders like accurate information. Mistakes create inaccurate or incomplete credit histories, leading to lower credit scores for borrowers.

Copyright © Mometrix Media. You have been licensed one copy of this document for personal use only. Any other reproduction or redistribution is strictly prohibited. All rights reserved. This content is provided for test preparation purposes only and does not imply an endorsement by Mometrix of any particular political, scientific, or religious point of view.

ACCEPTABLE GIFT DONORS

Rules regarding gifts used to purchase a primary residence vary depending on the mortgage and the lender. According to Federal Housing Administration (FHA) guidelines, acceptable gifts are limited to those that come from family, the borrower's employer or union, a close friend, and charitable or government organizations. It is acceptable for the borrower to obtain 100 percent of the down payment from gifts. However, if the borrower has a credit score under 620, he or she must provide at least 3.5 percent of the down payment. For a conventional mortgage, gift sources primarily need to be from relatives. A relative can be a spouse, child, dependent, an individual related to the borrower by blood, marriage, or adoption, or a legal guardian. Gifts from a fiancé, fiancée, or domestic partner are also acceptable. For conventional mortgages, five percent of the down payment has to come from the borrower's personal funds unless the gift funds are for 20 percent or more of the sales price. It is prohibited to receive a gift from the seller, a real estate agent, or the home builder. These types of gifts can unduly influence a potential homebuyer and are unacceptable.

LOAN INQUIRY PROCESS

APPLICATION ACCURACY AND REQUIRED INFORMATION ON AN APPLICATION

The lender needs to know, at a minimum, six basic pieces of information about the borrower and the home when taking a mortgage application:

- The borrower's name
- The borrower's Social Security number
- The borrower's monthly income
- The loan amount
- The address of the home being purchased
- The home's estimated value

Once the lender receives this basic information, the lender will provide a Loan Estimate. It is up to the borrower to then notify the lender that he or she is ready to proceed with the application. At this point, the lender will ask for additional information and documents (e.g., tax returns, pay stubs, and W-2s) to support information provided on the application. Generally, the more information provided to a lender, the better. The lender will then notify the borrower of any clarifications that might be needed. If no clarification is required, the lender will render a decision, approving or denying the application.

PERMISSIBLE QUESTIONS ON AN APPLICATION

Lenders primarily want to know about borrowers' income and employment, credit history, assets, and other liabilities that might be pertinent to an application. In addition to asking borrowers questions in these areas, lenders will also ask for supporting documentation, that is, tax returns, bank statements, a credit report, and more. Lenders will also ask applicants about their sex, race, and ethnicity. Lenders record this information to show that they are following federal laws and guidelines that prohibit discrimination. Lenders also want to know if borrowers are subject to lawsuits or bankruptcies or if they are borrowers or co-borrowers on any notes or liabilities like business or personal loans that could affect their ability to repay a potential mortgage. Lenders might also ask about foreclosures or whether a borrower is in the midst of divorce proceedings. A divorce settlement could affect a borrower's ability to repay.

APPLICATION PROCESS

QUESTIONS ON A BORROWER APPLICATION

HOW MLOS ACCEPT LOAN APPLICATIONS

The most common ways that mortgage loan originators (MLOs) accept loan applications are in person, via the internet, and by phone. With the rise of programs such as Rocket Mortgage, offered by Quicken Loans, more and more mortgage applications are going digital. Use of online applications—in which borrowers do almost everything from home—continues to grow, especially among men and borrowers under 45 years old. Taking applications electronically puts pressure on companies to ensure their networks are secure. Consumer expectations of privacy remain the same whether they apply online or in person. More and more consumers like the convenience of providing loan documents, such as tax returns and insurance information, through secure portals offered by lenders. In addition, more and more closings are happening electronically. With consumers embracing technology in their everyday lives, more and more are applying for mortgages online, and most originations use some combination of in-person and digital processes.

HOW MLOS MANAGE INFORMATION ON AN APPLICATION

Mortgage professionals are privy to their customers' most personal financial information. MLOs must use customer information strictly for business purposes and safeguard customer files at all times. Confidentiality is key to the success of any MLO or lender. MLOs must use client information only for its intended purposes and never share this information with family, friends, or coworkers who do not need the information to assist with the mortgage transaction. Ethically, lenders should never use customer information for their own personal gain either. Confidentiality goes beyond not using or sharing a customer's personal financial information; lenders should have a plan established for securely storing and protecting customer information from prying eyes. It's important to have strong information storage systems and strong systems for destroying customer information. Customer information must remain confidential even after the transaction is completed.

SERVICE CHARGES SUBJECT TO 10 PERCENT TOLERANCE

According to TILA-RESPA Integrated Disclosure (TRID) rules, there are three classes of closing costs: some that cannot increase at all, some that can increase by up to 10 percent, and some that can increase by any amount. Fees that cannot increase by more than 10 percent are recording fees and fees for required services provided by third parties that the borrower chooses from the lender's list of approved providers (if the provider is an affiliate of the lender, the fee cannot change at all). One caveat is that if there is a change in circumstances, these fees can increase by any amount. However, if there is no change in circumstances, the fees can increase by no more than 10 percent. A change in circumstances happens due to forces beyond anyone's control, like war or natural disaster. Also, a change in circumstances happens due to the introduction of new information concerning the borrower or the property that was not known at the time of application.

VERIFICATION AND DOCUMENTATION

FORMS USED TO AUTHORIZE THE RELEASE OF INFORMATION

The Certification and Authorization form is a document that lenders require borrowers to sign, certifying that all the information borrowers have provided in the application is true and complete. This form pertains to a borrower's statement of assets and liabilities, employment and income, the purpose of the loan, and the source of the down payment. It also authorizes the lender to verify a borrower's credit history and to verify the borrower's employment information. When signing the form, the borrower is also stating that he or she made no misrepresentations and did not omit any pertinent information that the lender might need to make a decision on the application. It is a federal crime to falsify a mortgage application. Often this form also gives the lender the right to sell a borrower's mortgage and to share the borrower's information with companies that might buy the mortgage.

METHODS OF VERIFYING EMPLOYMENT

Employment income is the primary means borrowers use to repay mortgages, so verifying employment is essential to the lending process. Lenders verify employment early in the application process, usually by calling a borrower's workplace. Some lenders also verify by fax or email as well. Lenders also request documentation such as pay stubs and W-2s. Some lenders also use verification of employment (VOE) software. These programs can automatically send a verification request to a borrower's employer based on the information the lender gathers from the borrower's application. Borrowers must sign a form authorizing the lender to contact employers. The process involves verifying dates of employment, income, and job title. The lender may also inquire about a borrower's prospects for continued employment. Lenders use these verifications to calculate debt-to-income ratios to see if a borrower can afford the mortgage. The front-end ratio looks at the borrower's monthly mortgage payment versus income, and the back-end ratio looks at a borrower's total debt-to-income ratio. The front-end ratio needs to be around 30, and the back end around 45, to satisfy most lenders.

SUITABILITY OF PRODUCTS AND PROGRAMS
REFLECTING THE TYPE OF LOAN ON A MORTGAGE APPLICATION

The first section of the 1003 mortgage application details the type of loan and the terms. The application asks if the loan is Federal Housing Administration (FHA), Department of Veterans Affairs (VA), US Department of Agriculture (USDA)/rural, conventional, or other. This section of the application also details the loan amount, interest rate, number of months, and type of amortization: fixed, adjustable-rate mortgage (ARM), graduated payment mortgage (GPM), or other. It is important for mortgage officers to have a thorough conversation with borrowers before recommending a mortgage. Every borrower's situation is unique, and every borrower's level of understanding and financial acumen is different. Before making a recommendation, a lender must fully understand the borrower and his or her needs. Is the borrower:

- A first-time home buyer?
- Self-employed, or a wage earner?
- A younger buyer just starting a career or someone established in a career?
- Someone with great financial acumen or poor money and budgeting skills?
- Someone with poor credit scores or outstanding scores?

These are some of the things a mortgage officer should be considering.

DISCLOSURES
INFORMATION INCLUDED IN THE TRUTH-IN-LENDING DISCLOSURE

The truth-in-lending disclosure details important information about a borrower's loan. The borrower must receive this disclosure before being legally bound to repay the loan. The disclosure includes:

- The annual percentage rate (APR) for the loan and total finance charges (finance charges are the cost of securing and paying off the loan)
- The total amount of fees and the total interest that would be paid if the borrower made every payment on time for the full term of the loan
- The amount of the loan

- The total payments required to pay off the loan, including paying all of the interest
- The amount of the monthly loan payment, the number of payments, and late fees
- Whether there are prepayment penalties
- Other important information about the terms of the loan

DISCLOSURES ON LOAN ESTIMATES

Borrowers receive the Loan Estimate document after applying for a mortgage. The Loan Estimate details the estimated interest rate, monthly payment, closing costs, and taxes and insurance. It also describes features of a loan—for example, whether the interest rate is fixed or variable; the term; whether there will be a balloon payment; and whether there are penalties for paying off the loan early.

The Closing Disclosure lists all the costs and fees associated with closing a mortgage, as well as the terms and the monthly payment. Lenders are required to provide this document to borrowers three days prior to closing. Because it is a lengthy document, the three-day window gives borrowers a chance to review it or retain an attorney. Having the Loan Estimate and the Closing Disclosure together allows the borrower to confirm that the loan he or she had requested is what he or she is getting.

CHARM BOOKLET

The Consumer Handbook on Adjustable-Rate Mortgages (CHARM) is an informational booklet that seeks to educate borrowers on ARMs. Lenders provide the booklet to borrowers who apply for an ARM. The booklet is published by the Consumer Financial Protection Bureau. As prescribed by Regulation Z and the Truth In Lending Act, lenders are required to give the booklet to borrowers interested in ARMs. It contains general information about ARMS, how they work, the types of ARMs, cautions about undertaking this type of mortgage, a glossary of definitions, and a list of sources that provide more information on ARMs. The booklet is designed to educate borrowers considering an ARM, especially those who are unfamiliar with this product; however, it is not specific to the loan a borrower is applying for. For in-person applications, the booklet must be provided at the time of application. For all other applications, it must be mailed or delivered within three business days.

REQUIRED DISCLOSURES

For most mortgages, there are two main disclosures that lenders are required to deliver to borrowers: the Loan Estimate and the Closing Disclosure. The Know Before You Owe rule, mandated by Dodd-Frank, simplified the mortgage process by making it easier to understand and easier for borrowers to compare offers from multiple lenders. After a borrower applies for a mortgage, he or she should receive the Loan Estimate from the lender within three business days. At least three days prior to closing on the mortgage, the lender is required to deliver the Closing Disclosure. These forms are meant to give the borrower all the information he or she needs to make a decision and to be fully informed of the costs and terms of a mortgage before committing. The timing of the delivery of the forms is also meant to give borrowers sufficient time to review the terms, ask questions, and accept a deal offered by a lender.

REVERSE MORTGAGES

Truth in Lending (Regulation Z) details the mortgage disclosure requirements that are specific to reverse mortgages. Basically, lenders must be clear and transparent about the costs of obtaining a reverse mortgage. First, lenders must disclose to borrowers that borrowers are not required to complete the reverse mortgage transaction merely because they have submitted an application or obtain the disclosures from a lender. Next, the lender must provide an itemized summary of the loan terms and charges, the youngest borrower's age, and the property's appraised value. The lender must provide a good faith projection of the total annual cost of the loan as well as an explanation of the total annual costs. A reverse mortgage can be a good tool for some retirees, but it is important that lenders explain the true costs as well as the benefits before initiating this type of transaction. After applying, borrowers must also receive a Good Faith Estimate and a truth-in-lending disclosure. At closing, borrowers receive the Housing and Urban Development (HUD)-1 Settlement Statement and the truth-in-lending disclosure.

TIMING

TIMING OF NOTIFICATION OF ACTION TAKEN

A lender must notify an applicant of action taken within 30 days of application. This applies to decisions to grant or deny credit. The denial of credit is an **adverse action**, which can negatively impact someone's credit report. An adverse action could also refer to denying an application to increase credit or terminating a credit account. Lenders must also notify borrowers within 30 days of an adverse action taken on incomplete applications. The adverse action notice must be in writing and must include the specific reason for the denial, name and address of the creditor, description of the type of loan being applied for, credit agency information, and how to obtain a credit report. For joint applicants, it is acceptable to provide notification to the primary applicant when it is clear who the primary applicant is.

DISCLOSURE TIMELINES FOR THE LOAN ESTIMATE

The lender must give the Loan Estimate to the borrower no later than three business days after a borrower applies for a mortgage. The TILA-RESPA Integrated Disclosure (TRID) defines a completed application as one that includes the borrower's name, income, and Social Security number (SSN is required to obtain a credit report), the property address, an estimate of the value of the desired property, and the desired loan amount. Lenders generally cannot charge borrowers any fees until they provide borrowers with the Loan Estimate and the borrowers have expressed their desire to move forward. The only exception is charging a fee to obtain a borrower's credit report. The Loan Estimate provides important information about rates, fees, charges, monthly payment, and estimates of taxes and insurance for which a borrower has applied. If the loan has special features like prepayment penalties or negative amortization, these must be mentioned in the Loan Estimate.

EXPIRATION OF CHARGES AND TERMS IN A LOAN ESTIMATE

Many consumers will obtain more than one Loan Estimate to compare lenders. Under this assumption, a Loan Estimate provided to a potential borrower is good for 10 business days. A lender is required to honor a Loan Estimate submitted to a borrower for 10 business days. To proceed, it is up to the borrower to notify the lender that he or she wants to move forward with the application. After 10 business days, the lender has the right to revise the Loan Estimate. For example, if a borrower waits 15 days to tell a lender he or she wants to proceed, the lender has the right to revise the initial Loan Estimate provided to the borrower. A lender can never assume that silence means the borrower wants to move forward with the application. It is incumbent on the lender to explain this 10-day rule and make sure the borrower knows what is required to proceed.

REISSUING A LOAN ESTIMATE

Loan Estimates are supposed to be issued in good faith. According to TILA-RESPA Integrated Disclosure (TRID) rules, the Loan Estimate generally cannot be changed after the fact. However, sometimes circumstances arrive that necessitate revisions. TRID states that there are six situations that can trigger a new Loan Estimate:

- Changes in circumstances that increase settlement charges
- Changes in circumstances that affect the borrower's eligibility for the loan
- Consumer-requested changes
- Expired interest rate locks
- The Loan Estimate expiring
- Construction delays

Changes in circumstances include events beyond control, like war or natural disasters. Changes in circumstances can also occur when new information arises concerning the borrower or the property that was not known at the time of application. If the Loan Estimate does have to be reissued, it must be delivered or placed in the mail to the borrower no later than three business days after the triggering event that prompted the Loan Estimate revision.

TIME PERIOD FOR THE DELIVERY OF THE AFFILIATED BUSINESS DISCLOSURE

In general, the Affiliated Business Disclosure needs to be provided to a borrower at the time that a lender provides a referral to the borrower; or, if the lender requires use of a specific service provider, the disclosure must be made at the time of application. The disclosure must be in writing; it must explain the nature of the business relationship, including ownership and financial interests, between the maker of the referral and the provider of the settlement service; and it must detail the estimated charge or range of charges that might be incurred by the borrower. "Affiliated relationship" means a relationship between business entities where one entity has control over the other through a partnership or other agreement. "Control" means that a person is a partner, director, or employer acting in concert with others or influencing others and retains more than 20 percent ownership.

TIME PERIOD FOR THE DELIVERY OF THE SPECIAL INFORMATION BOOKLET (KNOW BEFORE YOU OWE)

As prescribed by the Real Estate Settlement Procedures Act (RESPA), all lenders, at the time of taking an application from a borrower, are required to give borrowers a Special Information Booklet. Originally, the booklet was called the "Shopping for Your Home Loan: Settlement Cost Booklet." Today it is called "Your Home Loan Toolkit: A Step-By-Step Guide." The booklet is designed to familiarize borrowers with mortgage buying and homeownership and guide them through the tricky, complex journey toward owning a home. The booklet walks borrowers through the home-buying process from start to finish and explains topics such as annual percentage rates (APRs), disclosures, fees, the different kinds of mortgages, down payment options, points, and the ongoing costs of maintaining a home. Lenders are required to deliver or mail the booklet no later than three days after obtaining a mortgage application from a borrower. However, regulators encourage real estate professionals to provide this booklet even sooner in the home-buying process. The booklet is also designed to be emailed.

TIMING OF THE REISSUING OF LOAN ESTIMATES

A revised Loan Estimate must be produced within three business days of the event that triggered the need for a revision. Revision of a Loan Estimate should be rare, but the need for revisions will arise. The most common triggering events are changes in circumstances involving closing costs, changes in circumstances involving the borrower's eligibility or new information being provided about the property, the borrower requesting changes, construction delays, interest rate lock issues, and expiration of Loan Estimates. The three-business-day rule for producing new Loan Estimates is a tight window but must be followed or the lender will be violating federal TILA-RESPA Integrated Disclosure (TRID) rules. A Loan Estimate cannot be revised on or after the day the Closing Disclosure is delivered. To avoid having to revise the Loan Estimate, it is crucial that the lender is thorough and collects all relevant information before the Loan Estimate is delivered.

CHANGE IN CIRCUMSTANCE

A **change in circumstance** is an unexpected event beyond anyone's control that changes the loan process. A change in circumstance also happens when new information specific to the borrower or the transaction comes to light that is significant enough to impact loan variables. Furthermore, a change in circumstance involves information given to a lender that is found to be inaccurate or is changed after the Loan Estimate has been provided. Some examples of changed circumstances would be natural disasters, service providers going out of business, challenges made to a survey by a third party (for example, the neighbor of the seller), or the lender determining the borrower's income is only $75,000 when the borrower reported income of $100,000 on an application. TILA-RESPA Integrated Disclosure (TRID) rules say that a new Loan Estimate must be provided within three business days of discovering the change in circumstance that requires revising the Loan Estimate. A revised Loan Estimate does not have to be provided seven business days prior to closing. The seven-day rule applies only to the original Loan Estimate.

DELIVERY METHODS ALLOWED FOR THE LOAN ESTIMATE

Electronic, face-to-face, standard mail, and overnight delivery are all acceptable ways to deliver the Loan Estimate. The timing of the delivery of the Loan Estimate is the most important consideration. The lender must deliver the Loan Estimate no later than three business days after receiving a mortgage application. To comply with federal guidelines for electronic delivery of the Loan Estimate, the lender must first obtain permission from the borrower to receive disclosures by email. The disclosure is deemed received three business days after sending when using email. The borrower's consent to receive emailed disclosures and a read receipt are acceptable proof of delivery within three business days. Snail mail is deemed received three days after placing the disclosure in the mail or by proof-of-delivery receipt signed by the borrower when using overnight services. For in-person delivery, the disclosure is deemed received the day it is signed.

TIMING OF THE CLOSING DISCLOSURE

The Closing Disclosure must be provided to borrowers at least three business days before the mortgage closing. This three-day window gives the borrower time to compare the Closing Disclosure to the final terms and costs detailed in the Loan Estimate. If the lender gives the Closing Disclosure to the borrower, then makes significant changes before the closing, in many instances the lender will have to submit a new Closing Disclosure, and a new three-day waiting period will ensue. The three changes that require an additional three-day waiting period are changes to the rate, changes to the type of loan, or addition of a prepayment penalty. Any other changes would not necessarily require another three-day waiting period. The Closing Disclosure is a five-page form that provides final details about a borrower's mortgage. It includes the loan's terms, projected monthly payment, and all fees and closing costs.

DEFINITION OF A BUSINESS DAY FOR DELIVERY PURPOSES

For the purposes of the Loan Estimate or delivering a revised Loan Estimate, the definition of a business day is any day that the lender's office is open to the public for carrying out substantially all of its business functions. For all other purposes, the definition of a business day is every day except Sundays and federal holidays. The federal holidays are: New Year's Day, Martin Luther King Jr.'s birthday, George Washington's birthday (Presidents' Day), Memorial Day, Juneteenth, Independence Day, Labor Day, Columbus Day, Veterans Day, Thanksgiving Day, and Christmas Day. If a closing is scheduled for Thursday, then a borrower must receive the Closing Disclosure by Monday. If the following Monday happens to be a federal holiday, the Closing Disclosure must be delivered by Saturday. Loan Estimates must be provided no less than three business days after an application is received.

HOMEOWNERSHIP COUNSELING DISCLOSURE

As part of Housing and Urban Development's (HUD's) desire to educate borrowers on home buying and owning, the agency requires lenders to help borrowers identify and locate counselors who can provide assistance. The counselors educate borrowers on a range of topics, from how to buy a home to preventing foreclosure. HUD sponsors and trains these counselors, and they are available across the country. They are well equipped to help in all aspects of the homeownership process. Lenders are required to provide a list of 10 names to prospective homebuyers. HUD maintains a database of approved counselors. Access is free and open to the public as well as to lenders. Lenders can compile and maintain their own lists of approved and certified counselors from the bureau's database and give these names to borrowers as well. The list must be written and provide the names and contact information for counselors in the borrower's geographic location.

Qualification: Processing and Underwriting

BORROWER ANALYSIS
VERIFICATION OF DEPOSIT SCENARIOS
ACCEPTABLE ASSETS THAT MAY BE USED FOR A DOWN PAYMENT

Acceptable assets for down payments will vary according to the type of mortgage and the lender. The most common source of down payment funds is checking and savings accounts. However, some of these funds may require verification, for example, newly deposited funds or deposits great than 50 percent of the borrower's gross monthly income. This 50 percent rule is typical but can vary by lender. Funds coming from investment and retirement accounts are acceptable. Gift funds and proceeds from the sale of personal property are also acceptable. Some lenders may require borrowers to provide proof of the sale of personal property, especially for personal items like coin collections or other valuables. In some mortgage situations, a second mortgage can be the down payment. Federal Housing Administration (FHA) rules allow "mattress money" or cash saved at home, whereas other lenders may not. Any asset or deposit that cannot be sourced cannot be used for down payment.

ASSETS PERMISSIBLE TO BE USED TOWARD RESERVE FUNDS

Reserve funds are liquid assets a borrower has on hand *after* closing on a mortgage. Lenders like to reduce risk. Borrowers that have emergency funds after purchasing a home are less risky. Some federal loans require reserves, whereas other lenders prefer that borrowers have reserves or may require them in some situations. Most lenders measure reserves in months. For example, if a borrower's monthly mortgage payment is $1,500, and the lender requires three months of reserves, the borrower would need to have $4,500 on hand after closing. Acceptable sources are funds from checking and savings accounts, certificates of deposit (CDs), money markets, investments, vested retirement account funds, and cash value life insurance. Unacceptable funds are borrowed funds, cash-out real estate funds on the subject property, funds inaccessible until a borrower retires or dies, unlisted stock, interested-party contributions (e.g., from the borrower's realtor), and funds that have not vested.

LIABILITIES LISTED ON A LOAN APPLICATION

Liabilities listed on a Form 1003 mortgage application include monthly loan payments, such as car loans, credit cards, revolving credit lines, lines of credit, real estate loans, present mortgages, alimony and child support, and maintenance payments. Additional debts might be student loans, payday loans, or secured or unsecured personal loans. Job-related expenses like child care or union dues must also be listed on the application. On the application, liabilities are subtracted from assets to compute a borrower's net worth. Liabilities reveal a lot about a potential borrower. Liabilities that significantly exceed assets on a mortgage application can be problematic. The type of debt is also revealing. A young applicant with lots of student loan debt is understandable, and this might lead to higher-paying jobs, but an applicant with high levels of credit card debt might indicate a borrower who is not good at saving or managing debt.

INCOME DOCUMENTATION REQUIRED FOR A SELF-EMPLOYED APPLICANT

Today's gig economy requires lending to more and more applicants whose income is sometimes irregular. Self-employed workers, as well as some small business owners, sometimes have difficulty proving their income, making it harder for them to get a mortgage. Lenders like to originate mortgages for borrowers who have regular, steady income. At the same time, they do not want to eliminate a growing segment of workers who also make a good living. Some of the documents lenders will ask self-employed workers to provide—in lieu of W-2s and pay stubs—are two years of business and personal tax returns, IRS Form 4506-T (giving permission for the lender to request tax return transcripts), profit and loss statements, business bank statements, a business license, canceled checks for a borrower's current rent or mortgage, accountant statements, or proof of Social Security or disability payments. Many lenders want to see at least two years of steady self-employment. Two to three consecutive years of strong earnings makes lenders less concerned about income instability.

SOCIAL SECURITY AND DISABILITY INCOME ON A MORTGAGE APPLICATION

According to Federal Housing Administration (FHA) guidelines, all income from the Social Security Administration (SSA), including Supplemental Security Income, Social Security Disability Insurance, and Social Security income, can be used to qualify a borrower for a mortgage if the income has been verified and the payments are likely to continue for at least three years from the date of the mortgage application. Borrowers can use income tax returns, bank statements, benefits letters and statements, and award letters from the SSA to verify the income. The Equal Credit Opportunity Act makes it illegal for lenders to discriminate against borrowers based on age. Lenders are obligated to take mortgage applications from seniors, and Social Security income can be used to analyze senior borrowers' ability to repay the loan. Qualifying for a mortgage based solely on Social Security income might be challenging, so many seniors will likely need other sources of income or assets to qualify for a mortgage.

CALCULATING MONTHLY INCOME

For salaried and hourly workers, calculating income is fairly straightforward. Lenders look at borrowers' W-2s, tax returns, and pay stubs and use those numbers to determine income. If a borrower earns commissions, lenders may first want some kind of proof that the commissions will continue. They may also want to see a history of bonuses for the two years prior to the borrower's application. Lenders will add up the two-year bonus or commission total, divide it by 24, and include this as part of the borrower's monthly income. For part-time and seasonal work, lenders will use the figures found on W-2s and pay stubs. For self-employed workers and business owners, lenders will go by what is reported on tax returns. If it is not on the tax return, it cannot be calculated as monthly income. For teachers, seasonal employees, and construction workers, lenders will generally take the total from their last two years of W-2s and divide that by 24 to arrive at monthly income.

INFORMATION INCLUDED ON A CREDIT REPORT

A credit report contains information on an individual's credit history. The information is gathered by three credit bureaus and used by lenders to access a borrower's creditworthiness. The reports contain a credit score, which is a snapshot of a borrower's risk, followed by detailed information on the borrower's present and past credit accounts. A strong credit score is crucial for a mortgage and for getting the best rates. In addition to the FICO score (an analysis of someone's credit reported as a number between 300 and 850, produced by the Fair Isaac Corporation), the reports contain these types of information:

- Personal information like name, address, Social Security number, and birthdate.
- Credit accounts, which include the type of credit (credit card, student loan, etc.), when the account was opened, credit limit, balance (if any), and payment history.
- Inquiry information, which reports when a company pulls a copy of a consumer's credit report. "Hard" inquiries happen when someone applies for credit, and "soft" inquiries can simply be offers or a borrower's request for his or her own report. Soft queries show only for the borrower. Lenders do not see soft queries.

The reports also detail bankruptcies and collections.

CAPACITY

Capacity is the ability of a borrower to repay a mortgage. Lenders prefer borrowers who have a stable work history, predictable and sufficient pay, and low debt levels. Most lenders calculate a borrower's capacity by evaluating current income against the borrower's new mortgage payment and existing debt payments. This is called the debt-to-income ratio. According to the Consumer Financial Protection Bureau, borrowers need a debt-to-income ratio of 43 percent or lower to ensure that they can comfortably repay a mortgage. Lenders evaluate W-2s, income tax returns, and pay stubs to access a borrower's income. A borrower's income is then compared to debt payments as reflected on the borrower's credit report plus the payments that will be required to repay the new mortgage. If a lender confirms a borrower's gross income is $4,000 per month, total debt and mortgage payments should not exceed $1,720.

LOAN-TO-VALUE RATIOS

The loan-to-value ratio is determined by taking the loan amount and dividing it by the assessed or market value of a home. For example, if a borrower needs $150,000 to purchase a $200,000 home, the loan-to-value ratio is 75 percent $\left(\frac{\$150,000}{\$200,000} = 0.75\right)$. Another way to calculate the loan-to-value is to take the market value of a home and subtract the down payment. This produces the required loan amount, which—divided by the home value—equals the loan-to-value. For example, if a home sells for $200,000, and the borrower pays down $50,000, he or she will need to borrow $150,000. This produces a loan-to-value of 75 percent $\left(\frac{200 - 50}{200} = 0.75\right)$. It is important to understand the loan-to-value because in some situations, such as refinances or home equity loans, lenders set limits on how much they will lend based on loan-to-value. For example, many banks will not lend more than 80 percent of a home's value when refinancing a loan or originating a home equity line of credit.

CALCULATION OF DEBT-TO-INCOME RATIO

The debt-to-income ratio is an important measure of a borrower's ability to repay a mortgage. If a borrower's debt-to-income ratio is too high, he or she may be declined by lenders or may not qualify for certain kinds of mortgages, like qualified mortgages. Calculating the housing-to-income ratio, sometimes known as the front-end ratio, means measuring a borrower's housing payment versus income. For example, if the housing payment (mortgage principal and interest, taxes, and insurance) is $1,000, and the borrower's gross pay is $3,000 per month, the ratio is 33 percent. Most lenders prefer to see this ratio under 28 percent. Calculating the total debt ratio, or back-end ratio, means measuring the housing payment and all other debt payments (e.g., student loans, car payment, and credit cards) against income. If a borrower's housing payment is $800, all other debt payments are $500, and his or her gross monthly income is $4,000, then the total ratio would be 33 percent. Lenders like to see total ratios under 40. The total debt-to-income ratio to qualify for a qualified mortgage is 43 percent.

REVIEWING AN APPLICANT'S ABILITY TO REPAY A LOAN

Several factors must be considered when reviewing an applicant's ability to repay a loan. One of the first things to look at is the applicant's employment history. Has the borrower been working consistently for at least the last two years? Is his or her current employment status likely to continue or perhaps improve, or do prospects look dim—for example, are layoffs pending? Does the borrower earn enough income from his or her job to pay for all of his or her debts, including the new mortgage, property taxes, and insurance? Has the borrower done a good job of managing debt in the past? This is where the credit report is vital. Does the credit report indicate any missed payments, judgements, or unpaid debts, or does it show consistent payments and proper utilization of debt (i.e., the borrower shows no signs of overextending himself or herself)? Is the borrower buying a home that he or she can afford, and is the home in good condition?

DETERMINING A BORROWER'S ABILITY TO REPAY

A borrower's ability to repay is an assessment of the borrower's financial health and whether he or she can make good on all debts. The Dodd-Frank Act specifically calls for lenders to prove that borrowers have the "ability to repay" a mortgage before lending. The primary standard for determining ability to repay is quantifying whether a borrower has enough income to comfortably cover all debts. This determination is called the debt-to-income ratio. For most situations, if a borrower's debt payments—including the new mortgage—are less than 43 percent of gross income, then the borrower meets the ability-to-repay standards. For example, if a borrower grosses $5,000 per month, the total monthly debt burden (all outstanding debt plus the new mortgage payment, taxes, and insurance) should not exceed $2,150 ($5,000 × 0.43 = $2,150). Before the Dodd-Frank Act, lenders routinely made loans to borrowers without having to prove the borrowers could repay the mortgage, which led to the housing bubble in the 2000s and the subsequent mortgage crisis of 2007.

ALLOWABLE DEBT-TO-INCOME RATIO AT LOAN CONSUMMATION

According to Federal Housing Administration (FHA) guidelines, a borrower's debt-to-income ratio should be no higher than 31 percent on the front end and 43 percent on the back end. The front-end ratio looks at monthly housing payments, that is, mortgage payment, taxes, and insurance; the back end looks at all debts, housing payments, credit card debts, student loans, car payments, and so on. These numbers are compared to the borrower's monthly income. A housing payment total of $1,000 and monthly income of $5,000 results in a 20 percent front-end ratio. If total debts equal $2,000, the back-end ratio would be 40 percent. The ratios can be as high as 40/50 for borrowers with credit scores over 580 and who have greater cash reserves. For nongovernment-backed loans, most lenders will hew close to these parameters, but all lenders have their own internal guidelines and standards.

SAFE HARBOR PROVISIONS

Safe harbor provisions protect lenders against distressed borrowers who claim they were put in a loan that the lender knew they were unable to repay. After the subprime mortgage meltdown in 2007, Congress enacted the Dodd-Frank Act to protect borrowers from predatory lenders and to improve the quality of the mortgages sold into the secondary market. The act defined an ideal mortgage, one that was good for borrowers and good for mortgage investors, otherwise known as a qualified mortgage. To meet the qualified mortgage standard, a lender had to certify the following: that a borrower could repay the loan, the borrower's debt-to-income ratio was under 43 percent, fees for the loan did not exceed three percent, and the loan contained no risky features like balloon payments. As long as lenders made this type of mortgage, they were safe from lawsuits brought by distressed homeowners. Investors buying qualified mortgages were also reassured that the debt was a good investment.

TANGIBLE NET BENEFIT

When borrowers refinance their mortgages, they need to be better off financially with the new mortgage than they were with the old mortgage. That is **tangible net benefit**, improving the terms of a mortgage through refinance. A tangible net benefit could be a lower monthly payment or a lower interest rate, as long as the costs to refinance are not greater than the savings to the borrower. Many borrowers have Federal Housing Administration (FHA) loans. The FHA has specific guidelines concerning refinancing FHA mortgages, which state that the tangible net benefit must reduce the borrower's monthly mortgage payment, including private mortgage interest (PMI), by five percent. For FHA refinancing, going from an adjustable-rate mortgage (ARM) to a fixed rate also satisfies its tangible net benefit criteria. Borrowers refinance mortgages primarily for four reasons: to lower rates, to get cash, to lower their payments, or to reduce risk by going from an ARM to a fixed rate. There are always costs involved in refinancing. As long as the cost to refinance does not outweigh the benefit to the consumer, then there is tangible net benefit.

OCCUPANCY TYPES

There are three types of occupancy to consider in a mortgage application: principal, secondary, and investment. The most common form of occupancy is when a borrower seeks a mortgage to buy a home where he or she will live the majority of the year, which is often close to the borrower's workplace and where he or she votes. This is the least risky type of occupancy. Secondary occupancy is for a mortgage to purchase a home where borrowers live for portions of the year, typically summer or vacation homes. Secondary homes can be rented out subject to certain occupancy and income tax constraints. The last type of occupancy is an investment property. These are typically owned by the borrower and leased to other occupants. Lenders view investment as the most risky type of occupancy. Interest rates will be lowest for principal residences and highest for investment properties.

APPRAISALS

PURPOSE OF APPRAISALS

Lenders need an immense amount of information before deciding whether and how much to lend to a home buyer. A complete analysis is required on the borrower and on the property. A lender will not provide funds without first knowing the true value of a property, and the best way to find the property's value is to appraise it. Appraisals provide an estimated market value of a home. The real estate is the lender's collateral, its recourse should the borrower default, so it is essential that the lender fully understand the property's value. Appraisals also protect buyers. Purchasing a home can be an emotional and exciting experience. Buyers might be so giddy about a home upon viewing it that they are willing to pay whatever the seller is asking. Appraisals take the emotion out of the process and provide a clear picture of the property's exact value, which protects buyers from overpaying potentially thousands of dollars.

MARKET APPROACH

There are basically three ways to value a property: the market, income, and cost approaches. The market approach is the most common and looks at recent sales of similar properties in the vicinity to estimate a home's value. The other properties are often referred to as comparables. The cost approach considers the replacement value of a property, in other words, how much it would cost to rebuild a similar home in a similar location. The income approach is primarily used with investment properties or properties a buyer intends to rent. For these types of investments, owners want to know how much income they generate. The income generated is the prime determiner of the property's value. Evaluations of apartment buildings and duplexes are examples of where an appraiser might use an income approach. Some of the basic things appraisers look at are the home's appearance, size, and condition; whether improvements have been made; or if there are extras, such as pools, fireplaces, garages, or insulated windows.

USING COMPARABLE INFORMATION TO ESTABLISH VALUES

Comparing properties is one of the most common ways appraisers valuate a home. With this method, appraisers look at sales of nearby homes that are similar to the home being appraised to assign a value. This method is considered one of the most reliable in determining a home's market value. If the appraiser is looking at a three-bedroom home with 2,000 square feet, and a three-bedroom 2,000-square-foot home half a mile away just sold for $200,000, it's a fairly safe bet that the home being appraised will be valued somewhere near $200,000. The appraiser must take into account other factors, such as the condition of the home, amenities, number of bathrooms, and so on, but the values will be close to each other. According to Fannie Mae, it is up to the appraiser to choose the best comps for the home he or she is appraising. Fannie Mae says comps should have similar physical and legal characteristics, such as the number of rooms, site sizes, gross square footage, style, and condition.

REQUIREMENT/TIMELINE TO INFORM APPLICANT OF THE RIGHT TO RECEIVE AN APPRAISAL

Lenders must provide written appraisals or any other form or written valuations to borrowers promptly upon completion or no later than three business days before closing the loan, whichever is earlier. For example, if a loan closes on Friday, April 4, the appraisal must be delivered no later than Tuesday, April 1. Borrowers can waive this three-day rule and elect to receive an appraisal at or before closing. The waiver must be submitted at least three business days prior to closing. Also, lenders must provide, within three business days of taking a loan application, disclosures detailing a borrower's right to obtain a copy of any appraisal performed in relation to the application for a loan secured by a dwelling. Creditors cannot charge borrowers for copies of their own appraisals but may charge borrowers for the appraisal itself. Borrowers have the right to a copy of the appraisal regardless of whether the loan is made or denied.

APPRAISALS

An **appraisal** is an unbiased assessment of a property's market value performed by a qualified and trained professional. Virtually any home purchase requires an appraisal. It's needed to assure all the parties involved—the lender, buyer, and seller—that the home's value is truly accurate. Neither lenders nor borrowers can choose the appraisal company or appraiser. This process must be completely unbiased. Allowing the borrower to choose an appraiser could be a conflict of interest, especially if the buyer knows the appraiser. Most lenders have a list of approved appraisers that they use, and the actual appraiser for a specific home is chosen randomly from the list. Some lenders also use appraisal management companies who select the appraiser. A lender's officers and staff are prohibited from having direct contact with appraisers. An appraisal is different from a home inspection, which is also a necessary part of the home-buying process. An appraisal seeks to determine the value of a home. The inspection seeks to uncover any needed repairs or defects with the home and the cost to fix them.

APPRAISAL REQUIREMENT WITH A HIGH-RISK MORTGAGE

This appraisal rule was put in place to prevent fraud when consumers are buying a property that has been flipped. For all home purchasers, borrowers have the right to request a copy of the home appraisal. Lenders cannot charge a fee to the consumer for appraisal copies, although they can charge the borrower a fee for the actual appraisal. High-risk mortgages require a second appraisal, at no cost to the borrower, if the home sold for less money in the prior six months. The second appraisal must include an analysis of the difference in home price, changes in market conditions, and any improvements made to the property between the two transaction dates. High-risk mortgages also involve homes where the annual percentage rate (APR) exceeds the average prime offer rate (APOR) by 1.5 for first-lien mortgages, 2.5 percent for first-lien jumbo mortgages, and 3.5 percent for second-lien loans. For all high-risk mortgages, the lender cannot originate a loan without first obtaining a written appraisal from a qualified appraiser.

APPRAISER

An appraiser is a qualified, licensed professional who inspects a home to determine its market value. Appraisers should be unbiased and independent in their assessment of a property's value. Their role is to assemble facts and statistics and render those facts into a market value that is fair based on sound judgement and analysis. All states require appraisers to be licensed before they can render judgement on homes purchased with federally regulated lenders. Licensing usually requires passing a state exam. Appraisers also need to have a firm understanding of the real estate market in which they are working. They need to be aware of trends and be familiar with neighborhoods, local politics, and anything that can affect home values. Appraisers need to understand comparable values of homes in a neighborhood and need to be able to understand future values as well. Appraisers also need to be good communicators, knowing how to listen and how to ask good questions to get people talking.

TITLE REPORTS

A preliminary title report allows buyers and sellers to determine if there may be any liens or judgements placed against a property that might hold up a deal. A preliminary title report shows who the rightful property owner is; if there is anyone, from banks to construction crews, who have placed liens against the home; or if any back taxes are owed on the home. Any liens or taxes have to be paid before the deal can be finalized. For sellers, providing a preliminary title report helps assure buyers that there will not be any problems conveying the title. The preliminary report is issued prior to issuing an actual title insurance policy. The preliminary report allows lenders and buyers to see problems earlier in the buying process and devise a plan to eliminate encumbrances. If problems with the title are not remedied before the deal is finalized, any potential title insurance policy will exclude coverage for the existing encumbrances; however, this is not the best alternative for a buyer or lender.

INSURANCE

FLOOD INSURANCE

FLOOD INSURANCE REQUIREMENTS

Most homeowner's insurance policies do not cover damage from floods. To protect against flooding, homeowners need to purchase a separate policy that specifically covers floods. The federal government maintains maps of flood zones. If a home is being purchased in a high-risk flood zone with a mortgage provided by a federally regulated or insured lender, the borrower must purchase flood insurance. Homes purchased in moderate- to low-risk zones do not require flood insurance, but many lenders may still insist on it. Federal regulations require flood insurance to help reduce the impact of flooding. The regulations also encourage communities to adopt floodplain management activities, which (among other things) restrict building in zones considered vulnerable to flooding. These activities help mitigate flood damage and minimize losses from flooding. Borrowers who have paid off their homes are not required to carry flood insurance.

DESIGNATED ZONES FOR FLOOD INSURANCE

Flood zones are everywhere, not just on coastlines and next to rivers and waterways. Nearly 41 million Americans live in a flood zone, according to some studies. A home located in a landlocked subdivision might not look flood prone, but it very well could be situated in a flood zone. Those who live in high-risk zones—designated with the letters A or V on a Flood Insurance Rate Map (FIRM), drawn by the Federal Emergency Management Agency—are usually required by mortgage lenders to purchase flood insurance. A regular homeowner's policy will cover water damage due to burst pipes but not flood damage from storms or natural disasters. Even if a homeowner is not in a flood zone, flood insurance could be a lifesaver, and the premiums will be much lower than for homeowners living in designated flood zones. One foot of water in a home can be disastrous, causing up to $72,000 in damage, according to some experts.

LIMITS OF FLOOD INSURANCE

Flood insurance limits are set by the National Flood Insurance Program and are not particularly generous. For residential structures, flood insurance is limited to $250,000 for rebuilding and repairs and $100,000 for contents and personal belongings. For commercial properties, the rebuilding and repairs limit is $500,000. Flood policies typically cover personal items (e.g., beds, clothes, shoes, electronics) for the amount of their value, not what it would cost to buy new items. Flood policies cover contents of basements differently. For basements, items such as foundation walls, drywall, walls and ceilings, furnaces, water heaters, central air conditioners, washers and dryers, and freezers (and the food in them) are covered. Nothing else in basements is covered (e.g., clothing, personal items, books, electronics). People who have finished basements and live in a flood zone should be aware of these policy limitations.

PMI

PURPOSE OF PMI

Private mortgage insurance (PMI) is insurance that protects lenders from borrower default and foreclosure. It is often required for buyers who pay down less than 20 percent on a home purchase. Today, with the increase in home prices and slow wage growth, many borrowers are unable to afford a 20 percent down payment. The insurance is arranged by the lender and provided by private insurance companies. Premiums for PMI are paid monthly by adding them to the monthly mortgage payment. Homeowners must pay for PMI until they have 20 percent equity in the home. At this point, the insurance can be canceled. It is uniformly agreed that once a homeowner obtains 20 percent equity, PMI is no longer needed. A 20 percent equity gives the homeowner enough incentive to continue payments and gives a lender enough equity to help it recover foreclosure costs.

BENEFITS OF PMI

Private mortgage insurance (PMI) protects lenders if a borrower should default on a loan. Even though borrowers pay for the insurance, it protects lenders. On the surface, it would seem lenders benefit more from PMI than borrowers. However, without PMI, many borrowers would fail to qualify for a mortgage. Lenders like to see a down payment of 20 percent. On a $250,000 home, that's $50,000. The average consumer under 35 years old has less than $1,000 in a savings account; 35- to 45-year-olds have about $5,000. PMI allows borrowers access to the home market more quickly and allows them to buy a home with less than 20 percent down. Also, borrowers can cancel PMI once they have 20 percent equity in their homes. PMI protects lenders and also gives them an expanded pool of buyers. By lowering down payment requirements, PMI is critical to expanding the opportunity of homeownership.

REQUIREMENT GUIDELINES TO ENDING PRIVATE MORTGAGE INSURANCE

Once a borrower has paid down a mortgage to the point where he or she has a minimum of 20 percent equity in the home, he or she can make a written request to the lender to cancel the private mortgage insurance (PMI). Lenders are also required to cancel PMI once a borrower reaches 20 percent equity. Some lenders will cancel PMI using the original appraised value of a residence, whereas others will ask the borrower to present them with a new appraisal showing that the borrower has reached the 20 percent equity threshold. With some Federal Housing Administration (FHA) loans, borrowers are not allowed to cancel mortgage insurance. Some ways borrowers can get rid of PMI sooner include prepaying on their mortgage (that is, paying a little extra each month), adding on to the home, finishing a basement to increase the home's value, or refinancing the loan.

HAZARD/HOMEOWNER INSURANCE
FORCED-PLACED INSURANCE

Lenders require properties to be insured and will force insurance on a property if the borrower's policy lapses. Forced-placed insurance is also known as lender-placed, creditor-placed, or collateral protection insurance. Force-placed policies are more expensive than policies purchased by the homeowner and often offer less coverage. The policies are in place strictly to cover the lender's potential losses in the event of damage, not to reimburse the homeowner for loss of contents or for the full amount of a homeowner's loss. There are many reasons for forced-placed insurance. Homeowner's policies must be renewed by the owner annually. If the homeowner forgets, the policy can lapse. Also, the insurance company may view the home as too risky to insure because the home's neighborhood is seen as having high crime or the home is flood-prone. If the homeowner makes excessive claims, the insurance company might refuse to renew a policy. If a home is too old or the insurer believes adequate upkeep has not been maintained, the insurance company might refuse to insure the home.

Closing

TITLE AND TITLE INSURANCE
TITLE INSURANCE COVERAGE

Title insurance protects the owner of the policy from financial loss due to defects in the title of a property. Title insurance can be purchased by the lender and by the borrower. Most lenders require borrowers to purchase title insurance that protects lenders' interests in the property. Before a title policy is written, an extensive search is performed. A "clean" title means there are no defects in the title. The borrower is assured that he or she is the rightful owner of the property and that he or she is protected against any future claims. In reality, few challenges to property titles occur. Perhaps four to five percent of all owners of title insurance policies file a claim. The most common instances triggering a title claim are errors in the public record, undiscovered liens, omitted heirs, and fraud. Title insurance is still prudent even though claims are rare. A title search is the only way to be certain there are no defects in a title that could be devastating to a home buyer.

EASEMENT

Easements are rights that allow people to use land that does not belong to them. Easements are most often granted to local governments to build roads or to utility companies to bury cables or access existing lines that run through private property. Practically every homeowner has easements on their property for utility lines. Easements are listed in title documents and public records and prohibit homeowners from building on these portions of the property. During the process of purchasing a home, easements will be shown in the title insurance preliminary report or in the title commitment. An example might say something along the lines of, "Building any structure is prohibited within five feet of the western property line." The prohibition would apply to any permanent structure or fence. Another common easement is a shared driveway or a road that runs through private property used by a neighbor to access a property. It is important to understand the locations of any easements before purchasing a home, especially if the homeowner is considering excavating the property.

ENCUMBRANCES

An **encumbrance** is a claim, limitation, or liability placed against real estate. Common encumbrances include liens, easements, judgements, and other restrictions. Liens and judgements must be satisfied before the real estate can be sold or transferred. Encumbrances can also lower the value of the real estate. Liens are probably the most common form of encumbrance. Liens can come from many sources: unpaid property taxes, unpaid income taxes, unpaid debts to contractors, or any other work or maintenance on a property that the owner has failed to pay for. Unpaid utility bills and homeowners association bills could also result in liens against a property. A restriction is also an encumbrance. For example, a restriction might limit a parcel of land to agricultural use. Easements are also encumbrances against a piece of real estate. An easement is a right to cross or otherwise use someone else's land.

RECONVEYANCE

A deed of **reconveyance** is an official document releasing a borrower from a mortgage debt. This document is proof that the mortgage has been paid in full. Some states also use a similar document called a satisfaction of mortgage. A deed of reconveyance is also recorded in the county where the property is located. The recording proves to anyone searching the records that the lien has been satisfied and removed from the property. The deed of reconveyance also proves that the lender no longer has a security interest in the property and can no longer foreclose on the homeowner. Without the deed of reconveyance, and absent recording it in county records, there is no way for a

97

homeowner to prove that he or she has paid the mortgage in full. It is possible for a homeowner to ask a lender for a new satisfaction letter, but the process can be cumbersome. These days it is uncommon for a homeowner to pay off the original mortgage. Most will refinance it at some point. Many deeds of reconveyance happen due to refinances rather than paying off mortgages.

SETTLEMENT/CLOSING AGENT

BORROWER/SELLER'S ABILITY TO REVIEW THE CLOSING DISCLOSURE

The Know Before You Owe rule (also known as the TILA-RESPA Integrated Disclosure rule), which went into effect in October 2015, requires lenders to make the Closing Disclosure available for review three days prior to closing. The three-day rule was implemented to give borrowers time to review the document and to get their attorneys or home buying counselors involved to clarify issues or answer questions borrowers might have. If the lender makes significant changes to the loan terms after submitting the Closing Disclosure for review, another three-day review period must commence with the issuance of a new Closing Disclosure. Things that might prompt a new Closing Disclosure would be increasing the annual percentage rate (APR) for the loan (by more than an eighth for fixed rates or by more than a quarter point for adjustable loans); adding a prepayment penalty; or switching the type of loan, that is, going from fixed to adjustable.

USE OF A POWER OF ATTORNEY

Power of attorney allows someone to act on another's behalf. When a real estate closing is scheduled, sometimes not all parties are able to attend. The individual who cannot attend can grant someone else the power to attend the closing on his or her behalf and sign all of the required documents. Power-of-attorney signatures are just as binding as signing in person. Commonly, a husband and wife cannot be at the closing at the same time. In this instance, one party will often give the other spouse power of attorney to sign on his or her behalf. Power of attorney can be all-encompassing, allowing someone to make all decisions on one's behalf, or limited to a single event or type of transaction. Usually, for real estate transactions, a limited power of attorney is used and is allowable and exercised solely for the real estate transaction.

EXPLANATION OF FEES

FEES/CHARGES LISTED ON HUD-1 SETTLEMENT STATEMENT

The Closing Disclosure is a five-page document that fully explains a borrower's loan in a way that is easy to read and understand. It includes the loan terms, the monthly payment, and fees and charges. Page 2 of the Closing Disclosure lays out the fees and charges. Section A, Loan Costs, lists the origination charges. Section B lists Services Borrower Did Not Shop For: fees for the appraisal, credit report, flood determination, and other fees. Section C lists fees for Services Borrower Did Shop For: pest inspection, survey, title, and so on. Finally, page 2 details Other Costs: Taxes and Other Government Fees, which includes recording fees, transfer tax, and so on. Next is Prepaids: homeowner's insurance premiums, private mortgage insurance (PMI) premiums, property taxes, and prepaid interest. There is also a section for Initial Escrow Payment at Closing for homeowner's insurance, mortgage insurance, and taxes. Finally, other fees are listed—for example, fees for homeowners associations, home inspection, and home warranty.

PREPAID FEES

Prepaid fees are fees the lender collects at closing on a mortgage. These fees are placed in escrow and cover the costs of things like real estate taxes, hazard insurance, mortgage insurance, and homeowners association fees. These fees are considered prepaid because the borrower pays for them ahead of when they are actually due. Prepaids typically cover the expense required to pay these premiums for about three months. Mortgage interest is also considered a prepaid item.

Interest accrues from the day of closing to the first of the month. Prepaids are necessary to decrease some of the risk for lenders. Lenders want to be protected from losses as early as possible in the origination process. Prepaids accumulate in the escrow account until they are needed. Going forward—and, normally, continuing for the life of the loan—the borrower will continue to pay some monthly expenses into the escrow account.

TYPES OF ESCROW EXPENSES

The most common escrow expenses are private mortgage insurance (PMI), real estate taxes, and homeowner's hazard insurance. Financial institutions establish escrow accounts for their mortgage borrowers to ensure that these homeowners' expenses get paid. Most borrowers who paid down less than 20 percent on their home purchase will be required to pay monthly into an escrow account. The escrow is calculated as part of a borrower's monthly mortgage payment. A portion of the monthly payment goes to actually pay down the mortgage, whereas the remainder of the monthly payment is collected for the previously mentioned escrow expenses. There are laws protecting consumers when it comes to escrow accounts. Financial institutions are prohibited from collecting excessive escrow amounts and must make a full accounting of the collected funds annually. However, it is common for financial institutions to collect a couple months' worth of escrow as a cushion in addition to the amount needed to satisfy PMI, real estate taxes, and homeowner's insurance for the year.

LOAN ORIGINATION FEES

An origination fee is how a lender gets paid for selling a mortgage. Lenders charge borrowers origination fees up front as the price of processing the mortgage application and putting a loan together for them. The fee can range anywhere from 0.5 to one percent of the loan amount. With a one percent fee, if the loan is $100,000, the lender makes $1,000 up front. Before the subprime mortgage crisis of 2008, some lenders charged origination fees as high as four to five percent. The borrowers who paid these fees often possessed marginal credit or had unverifiable income and, because they had few options, were targeted by predatory lenders. After the recession, new laws changed the way lenders could be compensated. Consumers today are also better educated and have more information about mortgages, which forced lenders to lower their fees.

EXPLANATION OF DOCUMENTS
REQUIRED DOCUMENTS AT A CLOSING

There are primarily two documents required to close a mortgage deal. The first is the **promissory note**, and the second is the mortgage or deed of trust. The promissory note is the agreement between the lender and the borrower. The borrower promises to repay the funds extended by the lender. The note includes important information such as the date of the loan, the names of the borrower and lender, the amount of the loan, the terms of the loan, and all the legalese that goes with a mortgage, that is, how defaults will be handled, prepayment penalties, and so on. The borrower must sign the promissory note. The second document is the mortgage or deed of trust. This document basically allows the borrower to live in the house while acknowledging that if he or she defaults on the loan, the lender can take back the residence. The mortgage is the agreement between the borrower and the lender that the house will be used as collateral for the loan.

ASSUMPTION CLAUSES

An assumption clause is a provision in a mortgage contract that allows a homeowner selling his or her home to transfer the existing mortgage to the new buyer. The new buyer would then be responsible for the loan and take over the monthly payments. In a rising-rate environment, when current rates are likely to be higher than rates on existing mortgages, an assumption clause could be a nice selling point. Most conventional loans do not contain assumption clauses. Banks want to be sure borrowers can afford to repay mortgages, and qualifying someone who is assuming a loan can be challenging. There are too many unknowns in a deal like this, so most banks are unwilling to offer assumptions due to the risks involved. However, assumption clauses are often included in government-backed mortgages from the Federal Housing Administration, Department of Veterans Affairs, and the US Department of Agriculture. The new homeowner must still meet eligibility criteria.

PROVIDING THE ESCROW ANALYSIS STATEMENT

Regulation X, also known as the Real Estate Settlement Procedures Act (RESPA), requires lenders to conduct an escrow analysis before establishing escrow accounts for borrowers. The analysis is used to determine borrowers' initial escrow payments. After conducting the analysis, the lender must deliver the statement at closing or no later than 45 days after closing for escrow accounts required as a condition of the loan. For escrow accounts not established at closing as a condition of the loan, the analysis must be provided to the borrower within 45 days of establishing the escrow account. In both instances, the analysis must itemize the payment, taxes, insurance, and any other charges to be paid from escrow. The disbursement dates of payments from escrow must also be included in the analysis as well as the amount of cushion required. A trial running balance must be included in the analysis as well. Annually, the servicer must provide the borrower an escrow account analysis no later than 30 days prior to the end of the year. The annual analysis must include a comparison of the previous year with the upcoming years, the ending year balance, any shortfalls, and an explanation of how the shortfalls will be paid.

FUNDING

END OF RESCISSION PERIOD

Rescission is a borrower's right to cancel a loan. The rescission period is a three-day window that begins on the day borrowers sign their loan closing documents. Mortgages cannot be canceled after signing the closing documents, but borrowers can cancel refinances and home equity loans. Borrowers have until midnight on the third business day after closing to cancel. The three-day clock starts after borrowers receive the credit contract or Promissory Note, the Closing Disclosure, and two copies of the rescission notice, which explains the borrower's rescission rights, the timing of the rescission, and how to exercise rescission rights. Saturdays count as business days for the purposes of rescission, but Sundays and legal public holidays do not. Borrowers must use the form provided by the lender to rescind or write a letter. The form or letter must be mailed or delivered before midnight on the third business day after the closing. If borrowers did not receive the rescission notice, or the Closing Disclosure or these documents were incorrect, the borrowers may have up to three years to rescind.

FUNDING REGARDING RESCISSION PERIODS

The three-day rescission period is a cooling-off time that allows borrowers to back out of a refinance or home equity loan. Some borrowers immediately experience remorse when they think about loans against their homes. It is a big financial decision. It is in the lender's and the borrower's best interest that the borrower is certain he or she wants to take out this kind of loan. That is why the rescission period was built in. This three-day period is basically a waiting period for the lender, in which nothing happens. All of the documents have been signed and collected, but the lender does not initiate funding. Funding happens only after midnight on the third business day after the loan closing. If no rescission notice has been filed, the lender proceeds to fund the loan on the fourth business day after the loan closing.

Financial Calculations Used in Mortgage Lending

PERIODIC INTEREST

Periodic interest is the rate lenders charge over a period of time. Most lenders charge interest on an annual basis, but interest compounds monthly. Therefore, the periodic interest rate is the annual interest rate divided by 12. A loan with an annual percentage rate (APR) of 12 percent would have a periodic rate of one percent. **Compounding** means interest on interest. It is calculated based on the initial principal and accumulated interest from prior months. Compounding comes into play with negative amortization loans, in which the principal increases because borrowers do not pay the full amount of interest owed each month. The periodic rate is a smaller number, but that does not mean it is less interest. The rates are equal. Periodic rate is merely the APR expressed over a shorter period of time. However, due to compounding, the actual rate a borrower pays can be higher.

INTEREST PER DIEM

Per diem is the amount of interest that accrues on a mortgage each day. "Per diem" is Latin for "by the day." Per diem usage in mortgage originations normally happens when calculating closing costs. Lenders are allowed to begin charging interest on a mortgage the day the funds are disbursed. Most mortgage payments are due on the first of the month. Interest is paid in arrears.

Say a mortgage is disbursed on August 29. The first payment is due on October 1. The October payment will include all the interest that has accrued since September 1. That leaves three days of unpaid interest for the days August 29–31. Most lenders will require borrowers to pay these three days of interest at closing. The amount of interest is the per diem for each day, or the interest that accrues daily for three days. If the mortgage interest rate is 4.75, to get the per diem, divide 4.75 by 365, which is 0.013. On a $100,000 mortgage that translates to a per diem of $13 ($100,000 × 0.013% = $13). The lender will require the borrower to pay an extra $39 at closing to cover the interest that accrued August 29–31.

PAYMENTS

CALCULATION SCENARIOS FOR MORTGAGE INSURANCE

Mortgage insurance is required when a borrower pays down less than 20 percent for a home purchase. The insurance protects the lender should the borrower default on the loan. Most lenders charge a percentage that ranges anywhere from 0.3 to 1.15 percent, depending on the size of the down payment and the loan amount. For example, on a $250,000 mortgage with a 10 percent down payment, that might equate to a mortgage insurance premium rate of 0.5. The cost of the mortgage insurance would be $93.75 per month $\left(\frac{\$225,000 \times 0.005}{12} = \$93.75\right)$. Every lender charges their own rates for private mortgage insurance (PMI). Some will post their rates on their websites. Also, mortgage insurance is calculated differently with Federal Housing Administration (FHA) loans. FHA loans require an up-front mortgage insurance payment of 1.75 percent of the loan amount. For the term of the loan, the monthly insurance premium is calculated the same way.

CALCULATION SCENARIOS FOR INTEREST RATES

A mortgage's interest rate is the single greatest contributor to the cost of a mortgage. Take a $200,000 mortgage financed over 30 years with a rate of 3.75; the borrower will end up paying $926 per month and pay back a total of $333,443. In addition to the $200,000 mortgage, that's an extra $133,443. Take the same mortgage at a rate of 4.75. The borrower will pay $1,043 per month and a total of $375,586 over the life of the loan. That's almost double what the homeowner borrowed. As one can see, small adjustments to the interest rate can increase the mortgage payments and costs dramatically. Consider a higher-priced mortgage, which would be 1.5 points higher than the average market interest rate. Using the initial figure of 3.75, the higher-priced mortgage would have a rate of 5.25. Using the same mortgage example here, the payment would be $1,104 per month, and the borrower would pay back a total of $397,587. The additional cost to the borrower with a higher-priced mortgage is greater than $64,000.

EFFECT OF ESCROW ON A MORTGAGE

Escrow payments are likely to change several times during the life of a loan, primarily due to insurance and tax payments. Escrow payments are made up of taxes and insurance. For most homeowners, property taxes will increase at some point during the time they own the home, perhaps several times. Communities raise property taxes to pay for schools, parks, utilities, roads, and more. When taxes increase, monthly mortgage payments increase to cover the corresponding increase in taxes. Even with a fixed-rate mortgage, the monthly payment can change due to changes in the amount of money needed to fully fund the escrow account. The principal and interest portion of the monthly payment will remain the same for the life of the loan, but changes in escrow requirements will cause the payment to change. The same is true for insurance. Homeowner's insurance increases with inflation and with the changing needs of homeowners. As a home increases in value—due to inflation, improvements, and adding additions—insurance needs will increase as well. Payments to escrow will have to increase to cover increases in homeowner's insurance. If a homeowner pays mortgage insurance, his or her monthly escrow and mortgage payments will drop when he or she has enough equity in the home to eliminate these insurance payments.

CLOSING DISCLOSURE INFORMATION

The Closing Disclosure details all the costs involved in closing a mortgage and must be delivered three business days before closing. An important section of this document details the mortgage monthly payment. The document details the principal and interest portion of the payment. This is the part that pays down the mortgage. The payment never changes with a fixed rate and may increase with an adjustable-rate mortgage. The next section details the portion of the monthly payment that covers mortgage insurance. Mortgage insurance protects the lender from borrower default and must be paid for borrowers who pay down less than 20 percent. Mortgage insurance can be canceled when the borrower obtains 20 percent equity in the residence. The last section details the escrow account. Escrow is where payments for property taxes, hazard insurance, and other bills are held until funds are disbursed to cover these annual premiums.

DOWN PAYMENT

A down payment is the cash a borrower pays up front before taking out a mortgage. If a home costs $200,000, and the borrower pays down $7,000 or 3.5 percent, the borrower would need a mortgage of $193,000. Some loans, like Federal Housing Administration (FHA) loans, require a minimum down payment of 3.5 percent. Down payment calculations are also determined by a borrower's credit scores and income. Some lenders will require borrowers with lower credit scores and income levels to pay more down to lessen the lender's risk. Today, some mortgages can be made with no down payment at all. However, borrowers who pay less than 20 percent down must purchase mortgage insurance, an added monthly expense. Does it always make sense to pay down 20 percent? Borrowers need sufficient funds on hand as a cushion to transition into homeownership. Also, deploying funds elsewhere in a low-rate environment might be more beneficial. If a mortgage is four percent, a borrower's return on funds used for a down payment is four percent. Those same funds invested in other assets, like stocks, might garner returns greater than four percent over the long run.

LOAN-TO-VALUE RATIOS

Loan-to-value is calculated by measuring the value of a home against the total loan used to refinance a mortgage or purchase a property. The loan-to-value ratio is important for many reasons. The lower the ratio, the lower a borrower's interest rate might be. Loan-to-value goes hand in hand with risk. Lenders like it when borrowers have some skin in the game; that is, when they use a good chunk of their own funds to purchase a home. Paying down more, thus reducing the loan-to-value, will often lower a borrower's interest rate. For refinances, many lenders will not allow borrowers to exceed 80 percent loan-to-value. The same holds true for home equity loans for some lenders. Also, if there is a first mortgage, the two loans combined should not exceed 80 percent loan-to-value. A high loan-to-value might also disqualify a borrower for a mortgage, unless the borrower is applying for a Department of Veterans Affairs (VA) loan or US Department of Agriculture (USDA) loan, which can be originated without a down payment. For lenders, 80 percent loan-to-value is the sweet spot. Anything less is seen as higher risk.

DEBT-TO-INCOME RATIOS

The debt ratio is one of the most common calculations in mortgage origination. With the advent of federal mortgage rules that require lenders to ensure that a borrower has the ability to repay the loan, debt ratios are crucial to the underwriting process. In calculating the debt ratio, the debts a lender looks for are basically debt payments that show up on a borrower's credit report: auto loans, student loans, credit card debt, line of credit, and other debts. A lender may also inquire about personal loans a borrower may owe to family, friends, or business colleagues. Other types of monthly obligations—for example, utility and insurance payments, groceries, and other cost-of-living items—are not included in the calculation of debt ratios. Once the lender has calculated a borrower's monthly debt payments, the number is compared against the borrower's income to determine whether he or she has the ability to repay a mortgage. As a rule of thumb, most lenders want to see debt-to-income ratios under about 45 percent. For example, if a borrower's total monthly debt payments are $1,200 and his or her gross monthly income is $5,000, the debt-to-income ratio would be 24 percent without the mortgage payment. If the mortgage payment (including escrow) is $1,000, the total debt-to-income ratio would be 44 percent.

DISCOUNT POINTS: FIXED INTEREST RATE BUYDOWNS

CALCULATION OF DISCOUNT POINTS

Discount points are a way to pay for a discounted interest rate on a mortgage. The borrower pays a fee directly to the lender. In exchange, the lender lowers the interest rate for the loan. Calculating the cost of one discount point is fairly simple. Take the amount of the loan and divide by 100. For example, on a $200,000 mortgage, the fee for the discount point would be $2,000 $\left(\frac{\$200,000}{100} = \$2,000\right)$. One point typically lowers the interest rate by 0.25. So if the lender was offering a rate of 3.75, after buying a discount point for $2,000, the rate would be lowered to 3.5. The fee for the discount point is included in the closing costs, thus increasing the cash a borrower will need up front. However, in exchange for higher closing costs, the borrower will have a lower monthly payment and will pay less interest over the life of the loan. On a 30-year mortgage using this example, the borrower would save approximately $10,000 over the life of the loan. Not a bad way to invest $2,000.

PURPOSE OF DISCOUNT POINTS

The purpose of discount points is to decrease the interest rate on a mortgage. Borrowers must pay a fee for discount points. Discount points increase a borrower's up-front mortgage costs, but the trade-off makes sense if the lowered rate saves the borrower more than he or she paid for the points. Points are usually priced as a percentage of the loan. For example, on a $100,000 mortgage, discounting the interest rate by one point would cost one percent of the loan value, or $1,000. Points aren't always round numbers. A point might also cost 1.25 percent, or $1,250 on a $100,000 mortgage. Points must be paid at closing. Lenders are required to list these costs on the Loan Estimate and Closing Disclosure. By law, points must be directly related to the discounted interest rate. It is important to realize that discount points will vary among lenders. Each lender has unique pricing structures, and some lenders may be more or less expensive than others.

CLOSING COSTS AND PREPAID ITEMS
CALCULATION OF CLOSING COSTS AND PREPAID ITEMS

Most closing costs are flat fees charged by banks, fees charged by third parties for services rendered, or payments made to government entities for taxes. Examples of closing costs are origination fees, appraisal fees, and property taxes. Prepaids are items that lenders collect at closing and set aside in an escrow account for the borrower. For most mortgages, the borrower is asked to pay a portion of the property taxes, homeowner's insurance, and mortgage insurance (if the borrower paid down less than 20 percent) in advance. Most lenders collect anywhere from one to a few months of these items in advance, depending on the loan. These funds are set aside in escrow. Going forward, all of these items are paid as part of the borrower's monthly mortgage payment. The lender may also collect any accrued interest at closing as well. How much depends on when the closing happens. Interest is paid in arrears. When a borrower makes June's payment, he or she is paying May's interest. For example, if you close on April 15 and the first payment is due June 1, the June 1 payment will cover all of May's interest. However, the interest that accrued from April 15 to May 1 still needs to be paid. These 15 days of interest are collected as a prepaid item at closing.

HAZARD INSURANCE COLLECTION

Most insurance companies require homeowners to pay their hazard insurance in a one-time payment that covers the entire year. Therefore, most lenders will collect the full cost of one year of hazard insurance from a borrower at closing. This pays for the borrower's first year of hazard insurance. Going forward, the lender will require the borrower to place $\frac{1}{12}$ of the annual hazard insurance premium into an escrow account each month. The hazard insurance is then paid annually out of the escrow account. If the homeowner lives in a flood zone, the same is true for this type of insurance as well. The homeowner will be required to pay the annual flood insurance premium up front. Going forward, $\frac{1}{12}$ of the annual flood insurance premium is placed into escrow until the next annual premium must be paid. Lenders want to protect their investment from calamity and likely will not close until the residence is fully insured.

ARMs
PAYMENT-ADJUSTMENT CALCULATIONS WITH ARMs

Most adjustable-rate mortgages (ARMs) have an initial period during which the rate remains fixed. Let's look at a 5/1 ARM. The interest rate is guaranteed for the five years. Let's say it is five percent. After five years the rate will adjust. For the first five years, the payment is calculated as if the rate will not change for the life of the loan—let's say 30 years, which is the most common term. On a $150,000 mortgage, the monthly payment for the first five years will be $805. In year six, the rate adjusts to 5.5, 25 years remain on the loan, and let's say the principal is $130,000. The monthly payment for each month of year six would be calculated as if the $130,000 mortgage was for 25 years at 5.5 percent. The payment would be $798.

Ethics

Ethical Issues

VIOLATIONS OF LAW

In the 1990s, when large financial institutions started offering more services and merging with other companies, the federal government became concerned about the privacy of consumer personal information. Lawmakers passed the Gramm-Leach-Bliley Act, mandating financial institutions to disclose their information-sharing practices and to provide safeguards for the protection of personal financial information. The rule requires companies to provide a written privacy notice at the time a relationship is established and periodically thereafter. The notice must give customers the right to opt out. Not providing a privacy notice is a violation of the act. The rules require companies to vigorously protect consumer private information. One example of a violation might be a company allowing employees to work remotely, accessing company mainframes from home, without encrypting customer files. The act also prohibits pretexting, which is collecting personal information under false pretenses. Scammers who call consumers, win their trust, and convince them to reveal personal financial information are pretexting. Usually, the stolen financial information is sold or used to open new accounts in the victim's name, a form of identity theft.

PROHIBITED ACTS

REDLINING

Redlining is the practice of denying a mortgage to an individual based on where the individual lives, not on the individual's creditworthiness. The practice refers to bankers literally drawing a red line on a map around an area or neighborhood where the bank refuses to invest. Lenders have refused to provide mortgages to borrowers from these areas. Most of the excluded neighborhoods were primarily black or inner-city. Examples of redlining can be found in not just mortgage lending but also student lending, credit cards, car loans, and insurance. The Community Reinvestment Act, passed in 1977, outlawed the practice of redlining, although it still occurs. 50 years after the passage of the Fair Housing Act, which also prohibited redlining, a 2018 study by the Center for Investigative Reporting found significant instances of redlining in 61 metro areas across the United States. The study found a pattern of troubling mortgage denials for people of color across the country.

PROHIBITED ACTS

The Real Estate Settlement Procedures Act (RESPA) prohibits anyone involved in a real estate deal from receiving kickbacks, fees, or anything of value for work they did not perform. RESPA also prohibits compensation for any referral of settlement services. The act prohibits giving, accepting, or splitting any charge or fees for the rendering of settlement services in connection with a transaction involving a federally related mortgage loan other than for services actually performed. The act prohibits sellers from forcing buyers to accept their settlement services. The act also limits how much money a lender can require a borrower to hold in an escrow account and prohibits lenders from charging excessive amounts for the escrow account. RESPA also provides borrowers with protections for the servicing of their mortgages and requires lenders and service providers to respond to borrower complaints and concerns in a timely fashion. When a borrower makes a written complaint or request, the loan servicer must acknowledge receipt within 20 days and make any appropriate corrections within 60 days.

KICKBACKS

An unearned fee is a **kickback**. Federal law and the Real Estate Settlement Procedures Act (RESPA) regulations prohibit kickbacks. If someone receives funds that are not part of his or her regular fees, salary, or commission in a real estate deal, then they have received an illegal kickback. If a title company pays a loan officer to get business from the loan officer, that is a kickback. If a loan officer pays a real estate agent a fee to receive referrals from the agent, that is a kickback. Often kickbacks result in inflated fees to the consumer to cover the cost of the kickback. In the previous example, the mortgage banker has likely bumped up the origination fee paid by the borrower to cover the cost of the kickback to the real estate agent. Kickbacks do not have to be in the form of cash. Offering anything of value to obtain business can also be seen as a kickback. For example, if a title company offered to provide free marketing services for a local lender in return for more business from the lender, that could be viewed as a kickback to the lender from the title company.

DUTIES A LOAN PROCESSOR MAY OR MAY NOT PERFORM

A loan processor is someone who works at the direction of a loan officer or mortgage loan originator, performing clerical and support duties. The duties typically involve collecting and analyzing documents from borrowers that are common in the underwriting process, such as tax returns, pay stubs, and insurance documents. The loan processor communicates with borrowers to obtain all the information needed to process a loan application; however, the processor does not offer or negotiate loan rates or terms and does not counsel applicants on mortgages or any rates or terms associated with mortgages. The loan processor keeps an eye open for red flags in the application and makes sure the application is in order before submitting it to underwriting. Loan processors do not typically need to be licensed. Some processors who work as independent contractors may need to be licensed.

FAIRNESS IN LENDING

REFERRAL

The Real Estate Settlement Procedures Act (RESPA) defines a referral as "any oral or written action directed to a person which has the effect of affirmatively influencing the selection of settlement service . . . when such person will pay for such settlement service. A referral also occurs whenever a person paying for a settlement service is required to use a particular provider of a settlement service." In these instances, if the referrer has a business arrangement with the settlement service, the arrangement must be disclosed to the borrower at the time of the referral or before the referral is made. The Affiliated Business Arrangement disclosure must describe the nature of the relationship and provide an estimate of possible fees. The lender cannot require the borrower to use the settlement services, except in cases where the lender refers a borrower to an attorney, appraiser, or credit reporting agency that the lender has chosen as its representative in the transaction.

COERCION SCENARIOS

An appraiser has a conflict of interest when there is an event that prevents the appraiser from acting independently and exercising professional judgement. An appraiser has a duty to act independently and objectively with the singular goal of arriving at a fair appraisal. A conflict of interest could arise if the appraiser is related to one of the parties involved in the real estate transaction: (e.g., the buyer, seller, real estate agent, or mortgage officer). A conflict could arise if the appraiser has a stake in the outcome of the real estate transaction; for example, if the appraiser owns the property. A conflict of interest can also occur if for any reason an appraiser will be paid based on the outcome of his or her appraisals, that is, the appraiser makes more for higher appraisals. A conflict can occur if, for example, an appraiser owns a restaurant and is appraising the building for a competing restaurant.

DISCRIMINATING AGAINST AN APPLICANT

Mortgage discrimination can occur in a plethora of ways. Federal lending laws prohibit discriminating against borrowers based on age, sex, religion, race, and ethnic origin. It is illegal to refuse to work with an applicant based on one of the prohibited categories, as well as to provide different levels of service based on an applicant's race, gender, ethnic origin, age, and so on. For example, lenders cannot offer better or worse rates to an applicant based on the applicant's race or gender. Discrimination occurs when lenders refuse to work with applicants from a particular neighborhood, a practice known as redlining. Despite these protections, recent studies have shown that black applicants as a whole tend to pay more for mortgages and are denied mortgages more often than white applicants. A 2016 study published by Zillow showed that white applicants were denied mortgages eight percent of the time, whereas black and Hispanic applicants were denied 21 and 15 percent of the time, respectively.

REQUIREMENT TO TREAT ALL APPLICANTS FAIRLY

The mortgage process is rife with opportunities to take advantage of borrowers. As the plethora of federal regulations shows, many lenders have used—and continue to use—illegal and unethical practices to mislead and cheat applicants for the sake of increasing profits. It is up to each individual mortgage professional to always practice ethical behavior. Some basic tenets are: treat each applicant fairly and equally, be open and honest about products and terms, don't try to take advantage of anyone, and always safeguard applicants' personal financial information. Lenders should always adhere to fair lending laws, not only the letter of the law but the intent as well. Lenders should avoid doing business with unethical third-party providers, especially those that violate lending laws. Practicing honesty, integrity, and professional conduct with each applicant is not only law but necessary to the success of any mortgage professional.

FRAUD DETECTION

ASSET FRAUD

Asset fraud in a mortgage transaction typically occurs when borrowers falsify their ownership of assets to improve their mortgage application. On every standard Form 1003 mortgage application, the borrowers are asked to calculate their net worth, listing all of their assets and liabilities. Having a strong net worth can improve a mortgage application. One of the ways a borrower might commit fraud in this area is to inflate the value of investments. Because documentation of this type of investment is required, some borrowers have been known to falsify their investment statements. Borrowers' motivation to commit fraud might be to bolster a poor application or attempt to borrow more than they are qualified for. Freddie Mac classifies this type of fraud as fraud for housing. According to Freddie Mac, mortgage fraud is one of the fastest-growing crimes in the United States. Two other common fraud schemes are fraud for profit, often perpetrated by those working in the mortgage industry, and fraud for criminal enterprise, perpetrated by criminal networks for large gains.

APPLICATION RED FLAGS

Mortgage fraud comes in all shapes and sizes and is perpetrated by lenders and consumers. Basically, mortgage fraud is the misrepresentation of information on an application with the aim of obtaining loan funds. Some common red flags on a mortgage application are:

- Significant changes on an application, including use of white-out, more than one font, "squeezed-in" numbers, and other alterations
- Inconsistencies in names, Social Security numbers, addresses, and phone numbers
- An unsigned or undated application
- Use of PO box numbers
- Same phone number for applicant and employer
- An application for a cash-out refinance on a recently acquired property
- A loan for a refinance without the applicant living in the subject property
- The applicant purchasing a second home in close proximity to a current home
- The applicant downsizing but retaining the current home as a rental
- The applicant buying a second home or investment without owning his or her current home

Red flags are inconsistencies that common sense suggests will need further investigation.

VERIFYING LOAN APPLICATION INFORMATION

A mortgage is a potentially risky endeavor, so lenders will naturally attempt to verify anything a borrower states on his or her application. Some of the most common things that lenders verify are income, employment, assets, liabilities, and credit history. The most common ways to verify income are to ask a borrower to submit pay stubs, tax returns, and W-2s for review. Employment is usually verified by contacting a borrower's employer and verifying that he or she works there, the length of employment, and title and duties. A lender will verify assets by asking borrowers to submit investment and bank statements and other documents that prove ownership of assets. Liabilities can be proved in a similar fashion, as well as by pulling a borrower's credit report to make sure it matches with what the borrower has stated on his or her application. Borrowers must also provide supporting documentation for unusual or large deposits.

OCCUPANCY FRAUD

Occupancy fraud occurs when a mortgage applicant lies about whether the residence will be his or her primary home. It is a common form of mortgage fraud because most lenders charge lower interest rates for mortgages on primary residences than they do on secondary or investment properties. Lenders see primary residences as less risky than secondary or investment properties because primary homeowners are more attached to their homes and do not want to lose them. A second home or an investment property is less valuable to owners than a primary home, so in reality they will not work as hard to keep them or maintain them, making them riskier in the eyes of lenders. Occupancy fraud has become particularly problematic with the popularity of flipping houses. If lenders discover occupancy fraud, they can force the homeowner to repay the entire loan immediately. If the borrower cannot or refuses, lenders will foreclose.

INCOME FRAUD

Income fraud is another form of mortgage fraud whereby applicants inflate income to be approved for a loan. The prevalence of income fraud has been on the rise since the subprime mortgage crisis of 2007. After the mortgage meltdown, lawmakers forced lenders to prove that they could afford their loans. There are now strict limits on how much debt borrowers are allowed to carry compared to income. To qualify, more applicants are boosting their income figures. More applications are being done electronically as well, exacerbating income fraud. Some of the ways applicants commit income fraud are by making fake pay stubs or faking employment with the help of fraudulent services that act as the borrower's employer when banks call to verify employment. This type of mortgage fraud is more prevalent with purchase applications than for refinances.

EMPLOYMENT FRAUD

Another form of mortgage fraud on the rise since 2007 is employment fraud. Lenders and government organizations are reporting an increase in the number of applications in which borrowers are faking their employment histories. Some of these schemes are sophisticated. In December 2018, Fannie Mae issued a warning in California to lenders, alerting them to an increase in employment fraud. According to Fannie Mae, some red flags to watch out for are third-party or broker-originated loans, employment and salaries that don't jibe with applicants' ages, short time periods listed for employers on applicant job histories, previous employment listed as "student," suspicious pay stubs that don't include deductions for retirement or medical benefits, as well as large and unsubstantiated gifts made to borrowers. Mortgage fraud is often prosecuted in federal courts as bank fraud, wire fraud, mail fraud, and money laundering, and carries penalties of imprisonment for up to 30 years.

ADVERTISING

SCENARIOS WHERE INFORMATION IS MISLEADING WITHIN AN ADVERTISEMENT

Deceptive mortgage ads often make claims such as a low fixed rate or very low rates, low payments, teaser rates, or they may be lookalikes that try to make consumers believe they are affiliated with the federal government or reputable mortgage firms. Sometimes companies advertise fixed rates that are fixed for only a short time, not for the entire length of the mortgage term. Some ads talk about very low rates. Again, reading the fine print, a borrower might see that this very low rate is introductory, lasting only a short time. Some ads boast very low payments; however, these payments could be for interest-only loans, a product that is right for only select borrowers with specific circumstances and borrowing needs. Teaser rates might not be advertised as such in the main body of the ad but spelled out as much higher in the fine print. Teaser rates are used to lure unsuspecting borrowers. Ads might also convey an association with federal government agencies or other reputable mortgage companies to bolster legitimacy when in fact no association or relationship exists.

BAIT-AND-SWITCH SCENARIOS

One of the most common bait-and-switch scenarios is luring potential borrowers with teaser mortgage rates, then informing the borrower that the actual rate is much higher. Bait and switch is considered a form of fraud. An example might be a bank advertising a mortgage loan at a low rate of three percent. When the borrower arrives at the bank to inquire about this offer, the mortgage officer instead attempts to sell him or her a mortgage with a rate of seven percent. The bait is the low three percent offer, which was never actually available, and the switch is the seven percent deal, which is much more profitable for the bank. With federal regulations that limit how much fees and charges can change between a borrower receiving a Loan Estimate and the Closing Disclosure, part of the thinking is to protect borrowers against bait and switch.

LAWFUL ADVERTISING

The Truth in Lending Act (TILA) says that an advertisement must state only the actual terms that are available and will be offered to a borrower. Ads should clearly and conspicuously state the following: any charge that is considered a finance charge under TILA, rates expressed as an annual percentage rate (APR), and membership or participation fees that might be charged. Additional disclosures are required for advertising home equity loans. For a home equity loan, the ad must state any annual fees or fees imposed to implement the loan and the APR. Because some home equity loans have variable rates, the advertisement must state the maximum rate the lender could impose.

Advertisements must clearly state the terms for promotional rates, including the term of the discounted rate and the APR. If a balloon payment may happen as a result of any promotional term, the ad must clearly state this probability, even if such an occurrence is unlikely. Promises of the deductibility of interest for tax purposes must not be misleading.

Lenders are prohibited from using any misleading words or phrases in advertisements. An example of a misleading ad would be one that promises "free money" or uses any other similar concepts or phrases.

TYPES OF ADVERTISEMENTS THAT ARE SUBJECT TO FEDERAL REGULATIONS

Virtually any type of advertisement for a federally covered mortgage loan needs to meet certain minimum standards established by federal laws. This includes ads placed in newspapers, magazines, television, radio, the internet, billboards, direct mail, email, text messages, or other methods. The Federal Trade Commission has prosecuted many mortgage companies and individuals for violating federal advertising rules. Some of the most common deceptive practices in advertising are offering terms and conditions that are not actually available to borrowers, offering low payments and low rates that actually increase substantially soon after the repayment period begins, offering amortizing loans when actually only principal is being paid, misrepresenting balloon payments and prepayment penalties, failure to disclose loan fees and closing costs, promising preapprovals that are not actually available, making false claims about being a national mortgage lender, and packaging loans with other products such as insurance without the required disclosures.

PREDATORY LENDING AND STEERING

STEERING

Steering is the practice by mortgage lenders of selling mortgages to consumers that are the most profitable for the bank and not necessarily the best mortgage for the borrower. The term "steering" is also used to describe a practice by real estate brokers of directing buyers to or away from certain neighborhoods based on the neighborhood's racial makeup. Federal regulations prohibit both practices. The Consumer Financial Protection Bureau (CFPB) has issued rules that prohibit lenders from steering borrowers into risky or pricey loans. The rules ban certain incentives that were once paid to unscrupulous originators before the subprime mortgage crisis. The rules prohibit compensation that varies with loan terms. Also, originators cannot be paid more if the consumer agrees to work with certain companies affiliated with the bank or lending institution—for example, title companies or appraisers. The rules also prohibit the originator from getting paid twice, once by the consumer and once by the employer for the same mortgage.

Ethical Behavior Related to Loan Origination Activities

FINANCIAL RESPONSIBILITY

FEES THAT MAY NOT INCREASE DUE TO CHANGED CIRCUMSTANCES

There are some fees that lenders have complete control over and therefore may not increase from the Loan Estimate to the Closing Disclosure without violating TILA-RESPA Integrated Disclosure (TRID) rules. However, if one of the triggering events covered under TRID occurs, these fees can be increased by any amount. The zero-tolerance fees are: fees paid to the lender or mortgage broker or an affiliate of each for a required service, such as origination fees; fees for required services that borrowers are not allowed to shop for when the provider is not affiliated with the lender or the broker; and transfer taxes, which are set at a fixed amount according to the laws of communities where the property is situated. The first two are examples of fees that the lender controls and that are usually standardized based on loan amounts and set rates for services rendered.

SPLITTING FEES

Fee splitting occurs in a real estate deal when someone receives something of value that he or she did not earn. **Fee splitting** is similar to a kickback. An example would be a mortgage lending officer telling a real estate agent that he or she will split the origination fee with the agent in exchange for mortgage referrals. The agent has received compensation while providing nominal work. This is another instance where the mortgage loan originator (MLO) might increase the origination fee the borrower pays to recoup the full commission. In a real estate deal, the Real Estate Settlement Procedures Act (RESPA) prohibits payments or receiving anything of value without actually performing required work. Allowable compensation is fees, salary, and commissions for services that were actually rendered as part of a real estate deal. RESPA expressly prohibits splitting fees. RESPA also expressly prohibits accepting, receiving, or splitting fees in exchange for settlement services.

MORTGAGE COMPANY COMPLIANCE

ACCEPTABLE PRACTICES REGARDING APPRAISALS

The most important practice around appraisals is ensuring appraiser independence, ensuring that an appraiser can do his or her job without any pressure or influence from outside parties that might affect the objectivity of the appraisal. All appraisers must be licensed or certified by the state where the property is located. It is unethical and illegal for anyone—lender, seller, agent of the seller, anyone else, or any other third party—to influence or attempt to influence the integrity, objectivity, or result of any appraisal through means of coercion, bribery, collusion, or any other manner. It is expressly forbidden to ask an appraiser to provide a predetermined or desired valuation in an appraisal report. Lenders must also make appraisal copies available to the borrower no less than three days prior to closing. The copy shall be provided at no cost to the borrower.

RELATIONSHIPS WITH CONSUMERS

ETHICAL HANDLING OF A CUSTOMER'S PERSONAL INFORMATION

Confidentiality is important in maintaining a mortgage loan originator's (MLO's) and a lender's relationships with customers and the company's overall reputation. Failure to maintain a good reputation could be detrimental to an MLO and a lender's ability to survive in the competitive mortgage industry. Lenders have a strict duty to protect a borrower's confidentiality. When completing a mortgage application, a borrower is revealing his or her most private financial details and information. If any of this information falls into the wrong hands, through either omission or overt violations of confidentiality, it could be disastrous to the borrower's finances. It is illegal, as well as a breach of ethics, to fail to protect a borrower's confidentiality. The National Association of

Mortgage Brokers maintains a Code of Ethics that all MLOs should become familiar with, especially regarding confidentiality. Also, confidentiality and the safeguarding of consumer information are items the Consumer Financial Protection Bureau (CFPB) regularly examines when it audits financial institutions.

PERMISSIBLE REASONS FOR REQUESTING A CREDIT REPORT

It is permissible to pull a consumer's credit when the consumer requests a loan from a creditor in relation to an employment application, in conjunction with a consumer's application for insurance, and when a government agency uses the report to grant licenses or other benefits when such licenses or benefits pertain to the applicant's financial responsibility or status. Courts can also request or subpoena credit reports. A consumer can also request his or her own report. Creditors are allowed to pull credit when the consumer has an existing debt with the creditor and the creditor needs to assess the consumer's future risk or likelihood of continuing to repay the obligation.

PROPER DISCLOSURES BY AN MLO IF THERE IS A POTENTIAL CONFLICT OF INTEREST

A mortgage loan originator (MLO) has a legal and ethical responsibility to disclose to borrowers any potential conflict of interest. A conflict of interest could arise in numerous ways: family ties among the lender, appraiser, title company, or real estate agent; a broker acting as an agent for the borrower and the lender; having business relationships with any party to the loan; equity or financial interests in a property being offered as collateral; and prior employment relationships and confidentiality or noncompete agreements. MLOs are expected to avoid even the appearance of a conflict of interest and never use their position for gain that could reflect unfavorably on the MLO or his or her employer. The Dodd-Frank Act explicitly prohibits institutions from engaging in unfair, deceptive, or abusive practices. An abusive act can be one that interferes with a consumer's ability to understand a mortgage deal or takes advantage of a consumer's ability to protect his or her own interests.

PERMISSIBLE ACTS AFTER DISCOVERING INCONSISTENT DEPOSITS IN A BORROWER'S BANK ACCOUNTS

If a lender sees a large deposit in a borrower's bank account, the lender is permitted to inquire about its origins because it could affect the borrower's application. Some deposits are obvious, like a tax refund check or employer direct deposit, but borrowers will have to explain other deposits that appear on statements as "ATM deposit" or just "deposit." Lenders care about these deposits because they could hurt a borrower's application. For example, a large deposit could come from a loan or cash advance from a credit card. These debts can hinder a borrower's ability to repay a mortgage. A borrower will have to qualify for a mortgage with these new debts included. Also, some mortgages do not allow borrowers to borrow any portion of the down payment. Borrowers will be asked to prove the origin of large deposits. For example, if a borrower sells a car and deposits cash into an account, he or she will need to prove the funds came from selling the car. Proof could be the ad used to sell the car, a sales receipt, and a Kelley Blue Book report of the car's value.

SCENARIOS INVOLVING A GIFT RECEIVED BY THE BORROWER

Gifting money for the down payment on a home purchase is allowed, but the gifts must be documented. For most first-time home buyers, the down payment is the highest hurdle to clear, and few buyers these days can come up with 20 percent without some help. For Federal Housing Administration (FHA) loans, the minimum down payment is 3.5 percent, and it is permissible for the entire 3.5 percent to be gifted. For Fannie Mae loans, if a buyer is paying down 20 percent or more, the entire amount can be gifted, but if the buyer is paying down less than 20 percent, the buyer must contribute something toward the down payment. Lenders will request written documentation of gifts, as well as statements or canceled checks proving the source of the gift. Gifts are not taxable to the receiver. Gift givers should consider gift tax limitations. In 2024, the limit was $18,000.

CYBERSECURITY SCENARIOS

Mortgage lenders collect a bounty of personal financial information from applicants: tax returns, pay stubs, driver's license information, credit reports, bills, and bank statements. Furthermore, personal financial information is shared among the many parties involved in a mortgage transaction, including settlement service providers, attorneys, and insurers. It is the lender's duty to safeguard this information, and many federal agencies and regulations (Consumer Financial Protection Bureau [CFPB], Federal Trade Commission [FTC], Bank Secrecy Act, Gramm-Leach-Bliley, and USA PATRIOT Act) have means to protect and share consumer information. Yet every year, millions of consumer mortgage records are compromised. And the numbers keep rising. Also, today's cyber criminals are sophisticated: hackers, members of organized crime, foreign nationals, and sometimes foreign governments. Criminals attack for a range of goals, from political and social agendas to identity theft and other profit schemes to the desire to steal intellectual property and information. Even the smallest mortgage companies are targeted and must take steps to safeguard their consumers' information.

TRUTH IN MARKETING AND ADVERTISING

The Truth in Lending rules require that mortgage advertising clearly state loan terms and conditions and that lenders advertise only terms and conditions that are likely to be available to a borrower by the time the loan closes. Ads must be truthful and not mislead consumers. Ads should not misrepresent material facts or make false promises. Some phrases that might be considered appropriate would be "no down payment," "easy monthly payments," "low down payment accepted," and "loans available at reduced rates." Some trigger terms in mortgage advertising require additional disclosure and should be avoided: the amount of a down payment stated either as a dollar amount or a percentage, the amount of any payment expressed as a dollar amount or percentage, the number of payments or period of payments, and a finance charge expressed in a dollar amount. When preparing advertisements, lenders should ask themselves if the average consumer would consider the ad to be fair and truthful.

BORROWER EDUCATION

Borrowers most commonly lie about income, employment, assets, debts, occupancy, and identity on mortgage applications. Most mortgage fraud committed by borrowers may seem innocuous—they fully intend to pay back the loan; they want to be approved; but it is still a crime. Still prevalent but less common are schemes by borrowers who aim to profit from illegal deals. Borrowers lie about and falsify income, assets, and liabilities because they feel like they will not be approved for a mortgage otherwise. Borrowers will also lie about how long they have been employed or exaggerate their employment titles or duties to improve their mortgage applications as well. Another common fraud is to mislead lenders about occupancy status. For example, a borrower trying to get a home equity loan on a second home might tell the lender it is a primary residence because loan rates for primary homes are typically lower than for secondary homes.

MLO Practice Test #1

Want to take this practice test in an online interactive format?
Check out the bonus page, which includes interactive practice questions and much more: **mometrix.com/bonus948/nmls**

1. Why would a subordination be required on a refinance?

    a. There is child support owed by the borrower.
    b. The mortgage has a prepayment penalty.
    c. There is an existing second mortgage secured against the property.
    d. An encroachment survey is needed.

2. A potential borrower makes $55,200 per year before taxes. He or she has a mortgage payment of $850 per month, a car payment of $325 per month, a student loan payment of $120 per month, and a car insurance payment of $110 per month. What is the total debt ratio?

    a. 18%
    b. 25%
    c. 28%
    d. 30%

3. The Consumer Financial Protection Bureau (CFPB) has the authority to perform an examination of all the following EXCEPT

    a. banks or savings associations regardless of the assets held.
    b. consumer mortgage companies
    c. credit unions with assets greater than $10 billion.
    d. payday lenders.

4. What is NOT a function of the Consumer Financial Protection Bureau (CFPB)?

    a. Financial education
    b. Provide funding to programs that prevent discrimination in the financial sector
    c. Taking complaints from consumers
    d. Enforcing laws that pertain to discrimination in the financial sector

5. Which income source cannot be considered in a loan review?

    a. Educational military benefits
    b. Part-time income
    c. Alimony and child support
    d. Annuity income

6. A borrower is purchasing a home for $400,000 with a 10% down payment. The lender is charging 1.75% in discount points. How much will that cost the borrower?

   a. $5,5400
   b. $5,600
   c. $6,300
   d. $7,000

7. The Federal Housing Finance Agency (FHFA) requires applications submitted to Fannie Mae and Freddie Mac to include unique identification numbers for all of the following EXCEPT

   a. the loan originator.
   b. the loan origination company.
   c. the appraiser.
   d. the underwriter.

8. What is the difference between a full title report and a preliminary title report?

   a. A preliminary title report is issued prior to closing, and the full title report is issued after closing.
   b. A preliminary title report is required on purchases, and a full title report is required on refinances.
   c. A preliminary title report shows the current owner all current liens, and a full title report includes the same information plus all transfers of ownership over the last 30 years or more.
   d. A preliminary title report is only required on cash-only transactions, and a full title report is only requested on transactions that include a mortgage.

9. On an adjustable-rate mortgage (ARM) with a cap of 2/2/5, what does the 5 represent?

   a. The maximum amount the rate can adjust during the life of the loan
   b. The initial term in years for the initial fixed rate
   c. The initial fixed rate
   d. The maximum rate the ARM can adjust to

10. What term would best describe if a mortgage loan originator informs an appraiser that they will remove them from their list of approved appraisers unless they give a certain value to a property?

   a. Negotiation
   b. Coercion
   c. Bargaining
   d. Redlining

11. Verification of deposit (VOD) Is an acceptable way to document and verify a borrower's assets. Which scenario could be construed as a fraudulent use of a VOD?

   a. The VOD is handwritten.
   b. The VOD is completed by a teller and not a bank manager.
   c. The VOD is hand delivered by the borrower.
   d. The VOD only lists the last four numbers of the account.

12. A loan servicer is required to send an initial notice to a borrower at least ___ days before it puts in effect force-placed insurance.

    a. 15
    b. 30
    c. 45
    d. 60

13. Which of these loan products is considered a qualified mortgage?

    a. Loans guaranteed by Fannie Mae and Freddie Mac
    b. Interest-only loans
    c. Loans with a negative amortization
    d. Loans with a balloon payment

14. What is the standard due date and grace period for a mortgage payment?

    a. Due on the first of the month with a 5-day grace period
    b. Due on the fifth of the month with a 5-day grace period
    c. Due on the first of the month with a 15-day grace period
    d. Due on the fifth of the month with a 15-day grace period

15. What is a primary purpose of the USA Patriot Act?

    a. To verify if a consumer is a US citizen
    b. To improve the mortgage process for active-duty military and veterans
    c. To prevent and punish terrorist acts in the United States and throughout the world
    d. To protect US businesses from foreign competitors.

16. What is the maximum penalty that can be assessed under the Consumer Financial Protection Act as of 2023?

    a. $6,813
    b. $34,065
    c. $454,801
    d. $1,362,567

17. Which loan program typically does NOT qualify as an assumable loan?

    a. Federal Housing Administration (FHA)
    b. Rural Development (RD)
    c. Conventional—Fannie Mae/Freddie Mac
    d. Department of Veterans Affairs (VA)

18. Upon request, who is allowed to be given information regarding a borrower's financial information?

    a. The listing agent/realtor
    b. The underwriter
    c. The selling agent/realtor
    d. The escrow officer

19. A licensed institution manages the employment record of their licensed mortgage loan originator (MLO) in the Nationwide Multistate Licensing System (NMLS). According to the NMLS the institution is able to do all of the following EXCEPT

    a.   confirm a pending employment record.
    b.   request a correction to a pending employment record.
    c.   reject a pending employment record.
    d.   terminate a pending employment record.

20. Which of these is NOT an acceptable asset that can be used for a borrower's reserves?

    a.   Checking account.
    b.   Certificate of deposit
    c.   Proceeds from an unsecured loan
    d.   The cash value of a life insurance policy

21. In what situation would a lender be suspicious of a gift being used for a down payment?

    a.   The gift is coming from two donors.
    b.   The gift is from the borrower's uncle.
    c.   The gift letter does not include the source of the gift.
    d.   The donor borrows the fund for the gift.

22. A borrower's initial loan estimate reflected a 1% discount point. However, 2 weeks prior to closing, the mortgage loan originator (MLO) locked the borrower's interest rate and needed to charge a 1.5% discount point to offer the same rate. If the MLO did not disclose this prior to closing, which would be a true statement regarding the increased fee?

    a.   The fee is allowed because the rate lock determines the amount of discount being charged.
    b.   No discount point can be charged because it changed from the amount that was initially disclosed.
    c.   The original 1% discount can be charged but not the additional 0.5%.
    d.   The additional 0.5% can be charged as a separate rate lock fee.

23. The Truth and Lending Act ensures all of the following EXCEPT

    a.   it gives guidance to a lender on whether they should grant a loan to a borrower.
    b.   it requires all lenders to have a uniform set of disclosures.
    c.   it provides borrowers with the right to rescind.
    d.   it provides minimum standards for most residential loans secured by a dwelling.

24. When using a conventional loan, what is the minimum required down payment on a second home (not a primary residence)?

    a.   20%
    b.   15%
    c.   10%
    d.   5%

25. To avoid steering a customer to a loan product that may give higher compensation to a mortgage loan originator (MLO), an MLO must provide multiple loan options for a borrower to review. These loan options must include all of the following EXCEPT

    a. the loan with the lowest interest rate.

    b. the loan with the lowest amount of origination or discount points.

    c. the loan with the shortest term.

    d. the loan with the lowest interest rate that does not have a prepayment penalty, interest-only payments, a negative amortization, or a balloon payment in the first 7 years of the loan.

26. What is the typical length of a construction loan?

    a. 6 months

    b. 1 year

    c. 18 months

    d. 2 years

27. A fraud alert can be triggered by each of the following EXCEPT

    a. when a consumer's credit report shows that he or she is a victim of fraud.

    b. when a consumer's credit report reflects that he or she has filed a criminal complaint pertaining to identify theft.

    c. when a consumer's credit report reflects that he or she is an active-duty military member.

    d. when a consumer's credit report shows that he or she is under investigation for committing fraud.

28. When a lender is offering a 7/1 adjustable-rate mortgage at 3%, what does the 7 represent?

    a. The maximum interest rate of the mortgage

    b. The base index rate

    c. The number of months before the rates adjusts

    d. The initial fixed term of the initial rate

29. What would be considered an example of redlining?

    a. Denying financial services based on a particular neighborhood

    b. Denying financial services based on a certain credit score

    c. Denying financial services based on a minimum income

    d. Denying financial services based on a lack of assets

30. Unless someone removes his or her name, how long does an individual's name remain on the national do-not call list?

    a. 5 years

    b. 7 years

    c. 10 years

    d. Indefinitely

31. What is the number of housing agencies that is required to be listed on the housing counseling disclosure?

    a. 3

    b. 5

    c. 10

    d. 12

32. The Consumer Financial Protection Bureau (CFPB) Loan Originator Rule includes all of the following EXCEPT

a. prohibiting compensation based on the terms of a mortgage.
b. providing consistent background check requirements.
c. providing information regarding loan terms offered to a borrower.
d. providing requirements regarding licensing and registration.

33. The note includes all of the following EXCEPT

a. the interest rate.
b. the monthly amount for taxes and insurance.
c. the payment due date.
d. the amount owed on the loan.

34. All of the following are an example of a finance charge EXCEPT

a. interest.
b. points.
c. a loan processing fee.
d. title insurance.

35. All of the following could be considered a red flag on a mortgage application EXCEPT

a. the borrower's signatures vary through the application.
b. the borrower has had multiple jobs over the last 2 years.
c. the documentation is blurry or seems to have been copied multiple times.
d. the number of years that a borrower has been on a job is not consistent with the borrower's age.

36. A borrower is purchasing a home for $350,000 that appraised for $375,000. He or she then put down $63,000 as down payment. What is the loan-to-value (LTV) ratio?

a. 76%
b. 82%
c. 24%
d. 18%

37. All of these are key business areas of the Department of Housing and Urban Development (HUD) EXCEPT

a. healthcare programs.
b. multifamily housing.
c. housing counseling.
d. providing oversight to commercial building standards.

38. What is the purpose of private mortgage insurance (PMI)?

a. To pay off the loan if the primary or co-borrower dies
b. To protect the borrower if he or she falls behind on payments
c. To protect the lender if a borrower defaults on the mortgage
d. To cover payments if a borrower is injured and cannot work

39. What is the margin on an adjustable-rate mortgage (ARM)?

    a. A fixed percentage rate that is added to a base rate to determine the total indexed interest rate of an ARM

    b. The difference between the initial fixed rate and the rate after it adjusts

    c. The amount of interest paid the first year of an ARM

    d. The interest portion of a payment on an ARM

40. If a mortgage loan originator (MLO) does not renew a Nationwide Multistate Licensing System (NMLS) license, after how many years will the Secure and Fair Enforcement for Mortgage Licensing (SAFE) MLO test results expire and he or she therefore will have to retake the test?

    a. 2 years

    b. 3 years

    c. 4 years

    d. 5 years

41. Mortgage Company A sent out a mailer to veterans and active-duty members of the armed services offering a special Department of Veterans Affairs (VA) loan product. The mailer claims to be from the VA and implies that it is a division of the VA. What is this mailer an example of?

    a. Lawful advertising

    b. Cosponsored advertising

    c. Military-sponsored advertising

    d. Misleading advertising

42. A mortgage loan originator (MLO) has taken an application for an owner-occupied property. The borrower has indicated that he or she now does not intend to occupy the property. If the MLO does not change the occupancy type of the subject property, what is this considered?

    a. A clerical error

    b. A benefit to the borrower

    c. Occupancy fraud

    d. Nonowner occupied

43. Which type of loan is exempt from Real Estate Settlement Procedures Act (RESPA)?

    a. A loan to finance a commercial warehouse

    b. A reverse mortgage

    c. A home equity line of credit

    d. A mortgage to purchase a single-family home

44. Unless there is a valid change of circumstance, which fee disclosed on the loan estimate cannot increase?

    a. Appraisal

    b. Recording

    c. Home inspection

    d. Prepaid interest

45. When a lender advertises a low interest rate for a product that is seldom used, and then encourages a borrower to go with a product that has a higher rate, what is this called?

- a. Bait and switch
- b. Salesmanship
- c. Rate inflation
- d. Product swap

46. If a lender discovers that a borrower will be leaving his or her current employer 2 weeks after the loan closing, how should the lender view the borrower's income?

- a. The income is considered valid because he or she was employed at the time of application.
- b. The income is considered valid because he or she was employed at the time of closing.
- c. The income can still be used to qualify as long as the lender has the employer omit that information from the verification of employment.
- d. The borrower's income cannot be used because of the knowledge that he or she is leaving the current employer.

47. When is an adverse action notice required?

- a. When an application is withdrawn
- b. When a counteroffer is extended, and the offer is accepted
- c. When a counteroffer is extended, and the offer is rejected
- d. When there is a change in the terms of the mortgage

48. Besides the standard disclosures that must be issued to a consumer once he or she has completed an application, what additional disclosure must be issued on a majority of adjustable-rate mortgages (ARMs)?

- a. The ARM booklet
- b. The types of ARMs pamphlet
- c. What you need to know about interest only, hybrid, and payment option ARMs
- d. The consumer handbook on ARMs

49. When a borrower is guided into a certain loan product that may have less favorable terms than another loan product, what is this an example of?

- a. Credit counseling
- b. Steering
- c. A high-cost mortgage
- d. A change of circumstance

50. What is the minimum age to qualify for a reverse mortgage?

- a. 55
- b. 60
- c. 62
- d. 65

51. What is NOT an acceptable term when a mortgage loan originator (MLO) asks a consumer about marital status?

- a. Single
- b. Married
- c. Unmarried
- d. Separated

52. Typically, what is the minimum down payment for a Federal Housing Administration (FHA) loan?

    a. 3.0%

    b. 3.5%

    c. 5.0%

    d. 5.5%

53. What is NOT a factor in determining Department of Veterans Affairs (VA) residual income?

    a. Monthly debt reported on a credit report

    b. The square footage of the property being purchased

    c. The amount paid monthly in income tax

    d. The amount paid monthly for auto insurance.

54. How soon does a loan estimate need to be issued to a consumer after a lender has received an application?

    a. 3 business days

    b. 3 calendar days

    c. 5 business days

    d. 7 calendar days

55. Which factor can be considered when evaluating a loan application?

    a. Immigration status

    b. National origin

    c. Pregnancy

    d. Marital status

56. When is a lender required to send a consumer a copy of their appraisal?

    a. 7 days before a loan closes

    b. 3 days before a loan closes

    c. 3 days after the report is completed

    d. After a consumer has paid for the appraisal

57. After 7 years a consumer report will no longer contain all of the following EXCEPT

    a. bankruptcy.

    b. paid taxes liens from the date of payment.

    c. accounts placed for collection.

    d. civil judgments (unless the statute of limitations is longer).

58. When a mortgage loan originator does any type of advertising, they must retain a copy of material used for how long?

    a. 6 months

    b. 12 months

    c. 24 months

    d. 36 months

59. To renew a state mortgage loan originator (MLO) license, the MLO must take a minimum of how many hours of continuing education?

   a. 5
   b. 8
   c. 10
   d. 15

60. All of the following are required to be covered by HOEPA EXCEPT

   a. refinances.
   b. reverse mortgages.
   c. closed-end home equity loans.
   d. purchase-money mortgages.

61. If a borrower works 40 hours a week and makes $21.00 per hour, what is the monthly income?

   a. $3,360
   b. $3,640
   c. $3,500
   d. $3,920

62. What law prohibits discrimination in a mortgage transaction?

   a. The Equal Credit Opportunity Act
   b. The US Patriot Act
   c. The Fair Credit Reporting Act
   d. Regulation N—Mortgage Acts and Practices

63. Once a complete application has been received, the loan estimate must be delivered or mailed to the borrower

   a. 3 calendar days after receipt of the application.
   b. 3 business days after receipt of the application.
   c. 7 business days after receipt of the application.
   d. 7 calendar days after receipt of the application.

64. What would be considered a cash-out refinance?

   a. Refinancing a first mortgage and a purchase-money second into one loan
   b. A renovation loan in which funds are held by a lender and are disbursed as renovations are completed
   c. A conventional loan refinance in which a borrower receives $1,000 back at closing
   d. A refinance in which the proceeds are used to pay off the existing mortgage and additional consumer debt

65. What would NOT be considered a loan origination fee?

   a. Application fee
   b. Processing fee
   c. Appraisal fee
   d. Administration fee

66. After three failed attempts of taking the Secure and Fair Enforcement for Mortgage Licensing (SAFE) mortgage loan originator (MLO) test, what is the waiting period before an applicant can retake the test?

a. 30 days
b. 60 days
c. 120 days
d. 180 days

67. A borrower's bank account reflects several large deposits that are substantially larger than the borrower's documented monthly income. What would be an acceptable path to include these deposits as part of the borrower's assets?

a. A letter from the borrower explaining the deposit
b. Deducting the deposit amount from the total balance shown in the bank account
c. Providing a copy of the deposit along with a letter from the borrower explaining the deposit
d. Prior bank statements showing similar deposits

68. Once an application is received, what is the time frame to inform a borrower of the right to receive an appraisal?

a. 3 business days
b. 5 business days
c. 7 business days
d. 14 business days

69. In mortgage lending, what is the definition of *capacity*?

a. A borrower's ability to repay a mortgage along with other debt
b. The change from a borrower's current housing payment to the new mortgage payment
c. The total amount of available assets for a down payment
d. The amount of rent needed on an investment property to offset the mortgage payment.

70. What is the maximum amount of flood insurance available under the National Flood Insurance Program?

a. $150,000
b. $250,000
c. $350,000
d. $450,000

71. A borrower makes $124,800 per year. The mortgage payment is $1,805 per month and does not include an escrow account. The annual property taxes are $2,400, and the homeowner's insurance premium is $900 per year. What is their housing ratio?

a. 17%
b. 20%
c. 22%
d. 24%

72. The initial escrow statement includes all of the following EXCEPT

a. the amount of the monthly mortgage payment.
b. the amount that is collected for homeowners association dues.
c. the portion of the monthly payment going into the escrow account.
d. the amount of reserves or cushion as determined by the loan servicer.

73. **What is NOT an example of a "change of circumstance"?**
    a. The need for flood insurance
    b. A change in the loan amount after the Good Faith Estimate has been issued
    c. A disaster
    d. A change in the borrower's monthly income

74. **The recording fee on a borrower's initial loan estimate was $120. When the closing disclosure was issued, the recording fee had changed to $150. If there was no valid change of circumstance, how much of the recording fee is the borrower required to pay?**
    a. $150
    b. $135
    c. $132
    d. $120

75. **How many years does the Consumer Financial Protection Bureau (CFPB) require a lender to retain records of compensation paid to a mortgage loan originator?**
    a. 2 years
    b. 3 years
    c. 5 years
    d. 7 years

76. **Which statement is NOT true regarding per diem interest?**
    a. It is the daily interest on a mortgage that is outside of the regular repayment schedule.
    b. It is a factor only on adjustable-rate mortgages.
    c. It is paid for at the mortgage closing.
    d. It can be a credit back to a borrower at closing.

77. **What is NOT considered a valid change of circumstance?**
    a. Expiration of the original loan estimate
    b. An interest rate lock expiring
    c. A final inspection fee based on the appraisal report
    d. A change in the amount of a borrower's down payment

78. **A consumer is purchasing a home for $250,000. He or she wants to have a first mortgage that is 80% of the purchase price and a purchase-money second mortgage for the maximum amount allowed. If the loan product chosen has a maximum combined loan to value (CLTV) of 95%, what would be the amount of the second mortgage?**
    a. $37,000
    b. $37,500
    c. $45,000
    d. $50,000

79. **Who is typically NOT required to have a Nationwide Multistate Licensing System and Registry (NMLS) license?**
    a. A loan assistant who takes an application and proposes different options of loan terms for a borrower to choose from
    b. An underwriter employed by a bank who reviews and approves loan applications
    c. A commercial loan officer who also provides residential real estate loans
    d. A loan processor who receives a commission on the loans he or she helps originate

80. What is the basic standard mortgage limit for a Federal Housing Administration (FHA)-insured loan on a single-family residence in 2024?

   a. $472,030
   b. $498,257
   c. $647,200
   d. $766,550

81. How many hours of prelicensing education is required prior to receiving a Nationwide Multistate Licensing System and Registry (NMLS) license?

   a. 5 hours
   b. 10 hours
   c. 20 hours
   d. 30 hours

82. What would be the interest-only payment on a $150,000 loan with an interest rate of 4.5%?

   a. $560.00
   b. $562.50
   c. $625.00
   d. $630.75

83. When can the Department of Veterans Affairs (VA) loan funding fee be waived?

   a. When there is a 5% down payment
   b. When the borrower is on active military duty at the time of application
   c. When the borrower is a retired veteran
   d. When the borrower is receiving monthly VA disability income

84. Which of these are considered prepaids at the mortgage closing or settlement?

   a. The appraisal
   b. The property taxes
   c. The title insurance
   d. The underwriting fee

85. A mortgage lender pays a realtor $500 for referring him or her a borrower. According to the Real Estate Settlement and Procedures Act (RESPA), what would this be called?

   a. A referral fee
   b. A gift
   c. A commission
   d. A kickback

86. What is one of the minimum standards for a mortgage established by the Dodd-Frank Act?

   a. A lender cannot offer a mortgage to a consumer unless he or she can reasonably determine that it can be repaid.
   b. No prepayment penalties are allowed on a mortgage.
   c. A system was established to track the transfer of servicing once it is sold to a subsequent loan servicer.
   d. Mortgage fraud will be investigated by the Federal Bureau of Investigation.

87. Which statement is NOT true regarding using a power of attorney on a mortgage transaction?

    a. They can be used on a purchase of a second home.
    b. They can be used on a cash-out refinance of an owner-occupied property.
    c. They can be used on a rate and term refinance of an investment property.
    d. They must be property specific.

88. Which of the following would disqualify someone from receiving a Nationwide Multistate Licensing System (NMLS) license?

    a. A misdemeanor in the last 10 years
    b. A felony in the last 10 years
    c. A felony in the last 7 years related to financial services
    d. A misdemeanor in the last 5 years related to financial services

89. If a borrower is paid hourly and works a different number of hours each week (not a standard 40 hours per week), what would be an acceptable way to calculate their monthly income?

    a. Average the last 3 months of income.
    b. Average the last 6 months of income.
    c. Average the year-to-date income.
    d. Average the year-to-date income along with prior years W2s.

90. If a borrower wishes to initiate the cancellation of private mortgage insurance (PMI), what is NOT considered a requirement?

    a. A good payment history
    b. A minimum credit score depending on the loan product
    c. Providing a written request to the loan servicer to remove the insurance
    d. Having met the requirements that were established by the lender

91. If a closing disclosure (CD) was issued to a borrower and signed on a Monday, what is the earliest day he or she would be able to close on the mortgage?

    a. Tuesday
    b. Wednesday
    c. Thursday
    d. Friday

92. Which answer is a false statement regarding subprime mortgages?

    a. They have higher interest rates than a standard mortgage.
    b. They require a large down payment.
    c. They are not regulated by the Consumer Financial Protection Bureau (CFPB).
    d. They require a borrower to take home buyer counseling.

93. A Good Faith Estimate is not issued until a complete application is received from a consumer. Which answer is NOT part of the list of information that qualifies as a received application?

    a. Consumer's Social Security number
    b. Consumer's assets
    c. Address of the property
    d. The mortgage loan amount sought

94. **A borrower has an active mortgage application with a scheduled closing. He or she applies for and gets a new auto loan 2 weeks prior to closing. What is the mortgage loan originator required to do based on this information?**
   a. Ask the borrower to provide the monthly payment and balance of the loan.
   b. Have the borrower provide an official statement from the creditor that has the balance and payment of the new loan.
   c. Because the loan was not shown on the initial credit report, it does not need to be disclosed.
   d. A new credit report needs to be requested, then if the new loan does not appear on the report, it does not need to be included in the borrower's debt ratio.

95. **What is the term used that gives someone the right to use a portion of another person's land for a specific purpose?**
   a. Warranty deed
   b. Easement
   c. Road maintenance agreement
   d. Homestead

96. **Typically, a mortgage loan servicer cannot start a foreclosure until the borrower is more than ____ days late on payments.**
   a. 60
   b. 90
   c. 120
   d. 180

97. **What approach is MOST often used to determine a property's value on a residential appraisal?**
   a. Cost approach
   b. Income approach
   c. Sales comparison/market approach
   d. Base value approach

98. **Who is NOT considered an acceptable gift donor on a conventional loan?**
   a. A close family friend
   b. A spouse
   c. A domestic partner
   d. A cousin

99. **What would be considered a red flag on a sales contract?**
   a. Personal property is listed on the contract.
   b. There are three borrowers on the contract.
   c. The buyer and seller are related.
   d. The closing date is 60 days from the date the offer was accepted.

100. **Unless there is a valid change of circumstance, what fee is subject to zero tolerance?**
   a. Property insurance premiums
   b. The loan origination fee
   c. Recording fees
   d. The settlement fee

101. A suspicious activity report (SAR) must be filed no later than _____ calendar days after an incident has caused a need for the report.

    a. 60
    b. 45
    c. 30
    d. 15

102. Prior to a consumer receiving and e-signing electronic loan disclosures, what must he or she do?

    a. Properly consent to receive e-disclosures
    b. Register an email address with the lender
    c. Receive training on e-disclosures
    d. Provide a copy of an actual signature

103. According to the Consumer Financial Protection Bureau (CFPB) general rule, how many years must a mortgage lender retain records pertaining to loan disclosures?

    a. 3 years
    b. 5 years
    c. 7 years
    d. 10 years

104. How many hours of continuing education per year are required for all state licensed mortgage loan originators?

    a. 4 hours
    b. 6 hours
    c. 8 hours
    d. 10 hours

105. Which description is true regarding discount points?

    a. A fee paid to a lender for a lower interest rate
    b. A fee paid to a lender for reduced closings costs
    c. A fee paid to a lender only on fixed-rate mortgages
    d. A fee paid to a lender only on adjustable-rate mortgages

106. What is NOT a requirement when purchasing a nonowner-occupied rental property?

    a. Additional information on the appraisal
    b. Asset reserves beyond the minimum required down payment
    c. A larger down payment than an owner-occupied property
    d. Prior landlord experience

107. What is considered an acceptable practice under the Real Estate Settlement Procedures Act (RESPA)?

    a. A home seller requires a home buyer to use a certain title company as a condition of the sale.
    b. A home inspector pays a referral fee to anyone who refers business.
    c. Requiring escrows accounts as a condition of the loan.
    d. If a borrower sends a "qualified written request" to his or her loan servicer concerning the serving of the loan, the servicer must provide a written acknowledgment within 45 business days of receipt of the request.

108. A borrower closed on a refinance of an owner-occupied property on a Tuesday, May 5. What day will the loan fund?

    a. Wednesday, May 6
    b. Thursday, May 7
    c. Friday, May 8.
    d. Monday, May 11

109. Title 47 of the US Code of Federal Regulations addresses telemarketing. What are the times that are allowed for a residence to be called?

    a. After 8 a.m. and before 9 p.m.
    b. After 7 a.m. and before 8 p.m.
    c. After 9 a.m. and before 10 p.m.
    d. After 7:30 a.m. and before 8:30 p.m.

110. Currently, what percentage of the loan amount is required as an up-front mortgage insurance premium (UMIP) on a Federal Housing Administration (FHA) loan?

    a. 1%
    b. 1.5%
    c. 1.75%
    d. 2%

111. What is the loan to value of a mortgage that had a purchase price of $425,000, an appraised value of $415,000, and a down payment of $63,950?

    a. 82%
    b. 84%
    c. 85%
    d. 87%

112. Which piece of information may NOT be omitted by an applicant on a mortgage application?

    a. Race
    b. Sex
    c. Ethnicity
    d. Social Security number

113. What type of property does a right of rescission apply to?

    a. A second home
    b. A nonowner-occupied duplex
    c. A principal residence
    d. A nonowner-occupied condominium

114. What scenario would cause a verification of deposit (VOD) to be an unacceptable source to verify an asset?

    a. The account has been open for only 3 months.
    b. The account average balance is substantially higher than the current balance.
    c. The account has a joint owner who is not on the loan.
    d. The current balance is substantially higher than the average balance.

115. A borrower is getting a mortgage for $175,000 with a loan to value of 95%. The mortgage insurance rate is 0.53%. What is the monthly mortgage insurance premium?

    a. $73.42
    b. $77.29
    c. $78.59
    d. $92.75

116. How frequently does a Nationwide Multistate Licensing System (NMLS) license need to be renewed?

    a. Once a year
    b. Once every 2 years
    c. Once every 3 years
    d. Once every 5 years

117. What is the minimum down payment for a United States Department of Agriculture Single Family Rural Development Loan (RD)?

    a. 0% (no down payment)
    b. 3%
    c. 3.5%
    d. 5%

118. On an owner-occupied property a seller may contribute what percentage of the purchase price to the buyer's closing costs if the buyer is using a conventional loan and is putting 5% down as a down payment?

    a. 2%
    b. 3%
    c. 5%
    d. 6%

119. What could handwritten pays stubs and W2s, not providing an employer's physical address, and providing only a cell phone number to verify employment be an example of?

    a. Income fraud
    b. A small employer
    c. A rural employer
    d. Tax evasion

120. If a borrower is purchasing a $210,000 home and is required to have a 5% down payment, what is the dollar amount of that down payment?

    a. $9,950
    b. $9,975
    c. $10,000
    d. $10,500

Answer Key and Explanations for Test #1

1. C: A subordination is required when a first mortgage is being refinanced and there is an existing second mortgage. The second mortgage lien holder agrees to stay in second lien position to the new loan that is created through the refinance. The second mortgage provider often will want to know the appraised value and dollar amount of the new loan. They are not required to approve a subordination agreement and can therefore limit a borrower's ability to refinance.

2. C: The three debts that would be used to calculate the debt ratio are the mortgage, car payment, and student loan. The auto insurance would not be included. The three debts add up to $1,295 per month. To determine the debt ratio, we divide $55,200 by 12 and then divide $1,295 by the result.

$$\frac{\$55,200}{12} = \$4,600$$

$$\frac{\$1,295}{\$4,600} = 28\%$$

Some loan programs look at a borrower's total debt ratio as well as the housing ratio (the mortgage payment divided by a borrower's month gross income) when determining risk. The debt ratio is one of the primary factors in evaluating risk in mortgage lending.

3. A: The Consumer Financial Protection Bureau (CFPB) can conduct an examination of banks, savings associations, and credit unions that have assets greater than $10 billion. Banks with assets less than $10 billion would not fall under this guideline. However, the law also states that the bureau can examine anyone who poses risks to consumers related to financial products or services. The bureau itself is allowed to define who that might be and thus could examine a smaller bank if it felt the need to do so. If an institution is going to be examined, they must be notified 30–60 days prior to the on-site visit. The examiner may request documents throughout the entire exam and interview employees. The CFPB also provides a report after the examination with an associated score. The range is 1–5, with 1 being the highest and 5 being the lowest.

4. B: The Consumer Financial Protection Bureau (CFPB) regulates the financial sector based on established laws. It enforces those laws when they are violated through the court system. This keeps financial institutions accountable for any violations. The CFPB provides consumers the ability to file a complaint against an institution. It also educates consumers so that they can make informed choices when purchasing or utilizing a financial product.

5. A: Educational military benefits will not continue after the borrower has finished his or her education and therefore cannot be considered a source of income. As long as an income source can be determined to be consistent and continue for a sufficient amount of time, it can be considered a source of income.

6. C: A 10% down payment for a $400,000 purchase price would require a loan amount of $360,000. To determine the cost of the discount points, multiply the loan amount by the discount point rate:

$$\$360,000 \times 0.0175 = \$6,300$$

This fee is included in the borrower's closing costs and can be paid by the seller if agreed upon in the purchase agreement.

7. D: The Federal Housing Finance Agency (FHFA) does not require applications submitted to Fannie Mae and Freddie Mac to be acknowledged with unique identifiers. The loan originator and loan origination company each have a unique identifier assigned by Nationwide Multistate Licensing System (NMLS). The appraiser and any associated appraisal supervisor are given a license number by the state they operate in. These registration numbers must be on all applications. If more than one loan originator works on a particular application, then the NMLS number of whoever signs the loan application is used.

8. C: A preliminary title report shows a property's current owner along with all of the current liens, judgments, and encumbrances. A preliminary title report will also show if there are any outstanding taxes against the property. The full title report will have all of the information that the preliminary report has but also shows the transfer of ownership. Typically, lenders will require what is called a 24-month chain of title. One of the reasons for this is to allow a lender to see if the current owner recently acquired the property at a discounted price and is selling the property at an overinflated value.

9. A: The caps on an adjustable-rate mortgage (ARM) are broken down into three categories. In this scenario, the first 2 is the maximum amount the interest rate can change the first time it adjusts. The second 2 is the maximum amount the rate can adjust each subsequent adjustment. Both of these adjustments are up or down. The 5 represent the maximum it can adjust over the life of the loan. If the initial rate was 3%, then the maximum rate it could go up to is 8%. The adjustments are based on the index that the ARM is tied to such as the London Interbank Offered Rate (LIBOR), Federal funds rate, or the prime rate.

10. B: It is a violation of the law to coerce or bribe an appraiser to base their value of a property on anything other than their professional research and assessment. Threatening to withhold business is an example of coercion. The Consumer Financial Protection Bureau enforces valuation independence when an appraiser is assigned to appraise a property. Violation of this regulation could result in an inaccurate value and fines to those involved with the coercive actions.

11. C: Verifications of deposit (VODs) are an appropriate and convenient method to verify a borrower's assets. Many lenders use a standardized form that can be filled out by the borrower's financial institution. A bank teller is an acceptable representative to fill out the form. The form can be handwritten, and for the sake of privacy, omitting all of the digits except the last four of the account number is an acceptable. Because the form can be handwritten, the borrower should not have any contact with the form. This is so he or she does not fraudulently fill out the form.

12. C: If a borrower allows the homeowner's insurance to lapse and does not purchase a new policy, a lender has the option to put forced-placed insurance coverage on the property. They must notify the borrower at least 45 days before the insurance goes into effect. A second notice is sent 30 days prior to the effective date, and a third notice is sent 15 days prior to the effective date. This insurance coverage is typically much more expensive than an average homeowner's insurance policy.

13. A: A qualified mortgage is a loan that has stable features and avoids riskier options. Fannie Mae, the Federal Housing Administration (FHA), the Department of Veterans Affairs (VA), and United States Department of Agriculture (USDA) loan are all qualified mortgages. To be a qualified mortgage certain requirements must be met so that a consumer might reasonably repay the loan.

Some of these requirements include allowing that only a certain portion of a consumer's income can go toward debt. It also puts limits on the amount of fees that can be charged.

14. C: A majority of mortgage payments are due on the first of the month and have a 15-day grace period. This means that they would be considered late if they were paid on the 16th of the month. Lenders will notify a borrower if he or she has gone beyond the grace period. They will also charge a late fee, which is typically 4–5% of the principal and interest payment of the mortgage. Lenders do not report a mortgage payment as being late until the borrower is more than 30 days late.

15. C: The Financial Crimes Enforcement Network website states the following regarding the Patriot Act: "The purpose of the USA PATRIOT Act is to deter and punish terrorist acts in the United States and around the world, to enhance law enforcement investigatory tools, and other purposes." Some of the other purposes include financial services providers to report potential money laundering and to help retrieve stolen assets.

16. D: As of January 15, 2023, the maximum penalty that can be assessed under the Consumer Financial Protection Act is $1,362,567. The penalties are based on three tiers. Each tier increases in the amount of penalty and is based on the severity of the violation. There have also historically been cost-of-living increases from the prior year's maximum penalty amount. The maximum for tier 1 is $5,781, tier 2 $28,906, and tier 3 is $1,156,242. These penalties are considered civil penalties as compared to criminal.

17. C: To assume a loan means that a lender transfers ownership of a mortgage to a different borrower. The new borrower would then have the same rate, payment, remaining balance, and remaining term of the mortgage that was assumed. Typically, conventional loans are not assumable. There are a few adjustable-rate mortgages that qualify for an assumption, but a majority of mortgages backed by Fannie Mae and Freddie Mac are not assumable. Federal Housing Administration (FHA), Department of Veterans Affairs (VA), and Rural Development (RD) loans are assumable. A potential borrower would have to qualify for the assumption similar to qualifying for a mortgage. An assumption is an attractive feature in a rising rate environment.

18. B: A borrower's financial privacy is of the utmost importance when completing a mortgage. A realtor or title company employee does not have the right to inquire about a borrower's personal financial information. A realtor may ask that a borrower provide a preapproval letter. However, the realtor cannot request specific information from a lender regarding the borrower's credit, income, or assets. For an underwriter to approve or deny a loan, they must review a borrower's financial information.

19. D: An institution can terminate a confirmed employment record, but it cannot terminate a pending employment record. When an employer hires a new mortgage loan originator (MLO), there are certain steps that must be taken so that the MLO has an active Nationwide Multistate Licensing System (NMLS) registration and license. This includes any associated payments that must be made, submitting fingerprints, and confirming employment by the employer.

20. C: Financial reserves are liquid assets that are available to a borrower after a loan has closed. They include funds in checking, savings, or money market account. They also include stocks, bonds, and mutual funds. Vested retirement accounts that are not restricted to be withdrawn only upon retirement along with the cash value of a whole life insurance policy are also acceptable reserves. Proceeds from an unsecured loan cannot be used as reserves. Reserves are sometimes needed to offset risk. Often a primary residence will not have a reserve requirement, whereas second homes and investment properties will.

21. C: A gift from a donor is an acceptable way for a borrower to cover a down payment and closing costs. Multiple donors, gifts from blood relatives, and a donor's borrowed funds are acceptable practices. However, the source of the gift must be adequately documented based on the particular loan program being used. For example, a copy of the check and a copy of the donor's bank statement could be required.

22. C: If a lender does not re-disclose the change in a discount point from the initial loan estimate within 3 days of making the change, the lender must pay the difference in discount points on the borrower's behalf. A discount point falls into a fee category that cannot change unless there is a valid change of circumstance. When a change of circumstance occurs, the lender can make any necessary changes to the fees being charged as long as they are disclosed properly and within 3 business days.

23. A: The Truth and Lending Act does not tell a lender whether to grant a loan to a borrower or how much interest it can charge. According to the CFBP "The Truth in Lending Act (TILA) is intended to ensure that credit terms are disclosed in a meaningful way so consumers can compare credit terms more readily and knowledgeably. Before its enactment, consumers were faced with a bewildering array of credit terms and rates. It was difficult to compare loans because they were seldom presented in the same format. Now, all creditors must use the same credit terminology and expressions of rates."

24. C: The minimum required down payment on a second home is 10%. On a primary owner-occupied transaction, the minimum is 3% if the buyer meets certain requirements (such as being a first-time home buyer), but it is generally 5%. On an investment property it is anywhere from 15–25% depending on the number of units.

25. C: Different terms of a loan amount do not need to be provided to a borrower unless the borrower requests them. Steering a borrower to a particular loan product for higher compensation is considered to be steering and is in violation of the Truth in Lending Act's regulation Z. Multiple rates with their associated origination or discount fees help a borrower make an informed decision when choosing a mortgage loan.

26. B: A typical construction loan is 1 year. A construction loan usually requires a minimum of 20% down, and they often will require only an interest only payment. They require the borrower to provide plans and a description of materials with their associated costs. Once the home is completed, a lender will pay off the construction loan with a traditional mortgage. This is considered a rate and term refinance because the borrower has an existing lien against the property. Construction loans are held by individual banks rather than sold on the secondary market. For this reason, terms and interest rates can vary from bank to bank.

27. D: Fraud alerts do not pertain to those who commit fraud but to victims of fraud. According to the Fair Reporting Credit Act a fraud alert "notifies all prospective users of a consumer report relating to the consumer that the consumer may be a victim of fraud, including identity theft, or is an active-duty military consumer, as applicable." A lender must verify additional information pertaining to the borrower if a fraud alert is triggered. They may ask for additional identification or ask the consumer specific information regarding their credit history.

28. D: The 7 represents the initial fixed term of the initial rate. In this scenario the initial rate of 3% would be fixed for 7 years before it would adjust. A majority of adjustable-rate mortgages have an initial fixed term and then adjust annually after the initial term. Historically the initial rate is lower than fixed-rate loans, especially the 30-year fixed rate.

29. A: Redlining is the denial of financial services (including a mortgage) based on the race or ethnicity of an area or neighborhood. A borrower's qualifications are not considered in making the final credit approval. The Community Reinvestment Act of 1977 made all redlining practices illegal. There is also a term that is called reverse redlining. This is the practice in which certain neighborhoods are targeted and are charged higher rates and fees based on the neighborhood. In both instances they are typically minority neighborhoods.

30. D: A consumer will remain on the national do-not call list indefinitely or until he or she requests that his or her name be removed from the list. If a solicitor contacts a consumer, and the consumer requests his or her name to be removed from the solicitors call list, the solicitor must document that they have removed the consumer's name and phone number from the list. A solicitor must also have their written policy on hand regarding how they maintain their do-not call list.

31. C: Regulation X requires that a housing counseling disclosure be issued with a consumer's initial disclosures. There must be 10 agencies listed. Providing a list of 10 agencies gives a consumer multiple options if he or she chooses to contact one of the agencies. It also ensures that there is fairness and diversity among the available agencies.

32. C: The Consumer Financial Protection Bureau (CFBP) Loan Originator Rule does not address the terms that are offered to a borrower. A large component of the rule pertains to compensation. Along with prohibiting compensation based on the terms of a mortgage, it prohibits compensation from both a consumer and a separate entity (such as a lender). It addresses bac ground checks and mandates that mortgage loan originators (MLOs) are licensed under the SAFE act. It also requires MLOs to meet any other federal or state licensing requirements.

33. B: The note is a legal document that obligates a borrower to repay the mortgage. This document includes the interest rate, the amount of the loan, the term of the loan, and the payment due dates. The note also includes where the payments need to be sent and the penalties for not make payments on time. The note does not include the monthly amount for property taxes and insurance.

34. D: According to 12 CFR 1026—TRUTH-IN-LENDING ACT (TILA—REG Z), the definition of a finance charge is "the cost of consumer credit as a dollar amount. It includes any charge payable directly or indirectly by the consumer and imposed directly or indirectly by the creditor as an incident to or a condition of the extension of credit."

35. B: Red flags on mortgage transactions are defined as anything that seems inconsistent or misleading on a mortgage application and its supporting documents. Varying signatures, blurry documents, and inconsistent timelines could all be considered red flags. A red flag does not always imply that fraud is being committed. Rather, it prompts a lender to further investigate the information provided. A borrower having multiple jobs over the last 2 years would not be considered a red flag.

36. B: A $63,000 down payment would establish a loan amount of $287,000. And $287,000 divided by $350,000 is a loan to value (LTV) of 82%. On a purchase the LTV is based on the lesser of the purchase price or appraised value. The LTV is based on the first mortgage only. Currently the only qualified mortgages that allow 100% LTV are Department of Veterans Affairs loans and Rural Development loans issued through the United States Department of Agriculture.

37. D: Typically, the state government where the commercial building is located oversees the standards of how it is built and maintained. The Department of Housing and Urban Development (HUD) deals primarily with single-family and multifamily residential dwellings. They also provide funding for healthcare facilities. HUD provides housing counseling and regulates real-estate transactions as well.

38. C: Private mortgage insurance (PMI) protects the lender if they have to foreclose on a property. Often, a lender will lose money on a foreclosed property, and the PMI will help offset some of that cost. PMI is required on conventional loans unless a borrower has a down payment of 20% or more. Sometimes a lender may offer a lower down payment without PMI. In this scenario the lender would offer a higher interest rate and pay for insurance through charging a higher rate. Federal Housing Administration (FHA) and Rural Development (RD) loans require PMI regardless of the amount of down payment. RD loans never allow it to be removed. If a borrower puts 10% or more down on an FHA loan, the mortgage insurance stays in place for 11 years. Otherwise, it remains for the entire term of the loan. On a conventional loan, a borrower can request the removal of PMI once the loan balance is 80% of the value of the home. When the loan amount reaches 78% of the value of the home, it will automatically be removed by the lender.

39. A: The margin is a fixed percentage rate that is added to a base or indexed rate, which creates a fully indexed rate on an adjustable-rate mortgage (ARM). This rate comes into play after the rate on the introductory term has been completed. The indexed rate may be based on the *Wall Street Journal* prime rate, the London Interbank Offered Rate (LIBOR), or a bank's own internal rate. The index rate may change often, but the margin is fixed and does not change throughout the life of the loan.

40. D: If a mortgage loan originator (MLO) does not renew a license for 5 consecutive years or more, he or she will have to retake the Secure and Fair Enforcement for Mortgage Licensing (SAFE) MLO test again to renew the license. This applies to those who have left the industry as well as those who are still attempting to originate loans. The Nationwide Multistate Licensing System (NMLS) will notify the individual or entity 180, 60, and 30 days before the test results will expire. This includes the federal component of the test along with any specific state component.

41. D: This scenario is an example of misleading advertising. The Department of Veterans Affairs (VA) does not solicit mortgages. Nor does it partner with individual mortgage companies to offer special products. Mortgage Company A implying that it is a division of the VA is misleading and not true. This type of practice could result in a large fine from the Consumer and Financial Protection Bureau.

42. C: The mortgage loan originator (MLO) is this scenario should have changed the occupancy type to an investment property. Not doing so would be considered occupancy fraud. Investment properties require larger down payments and have higher interest rates. This might lead an MLO or borrower to give false information to have more favorable loan terms. At the loan closing the borrower signs an acknowledgment of the occupancy type of the subject property. Misrepresenting the truth on that form is fraudulent.

43. A: Real Estate Settlement Procedures Act (RESPA) typically applies to any loan that is secured by a first or second lien on a residential property. The property may be one to four units, and the proceeds are used to purchase or pay off an existing lien. Temporary loans (such as a construction loan) and business loans do not fall in this category and are therefore exempt.

44. A: Closing costs are divided into three categories when determining whether they can increase from the amount disclosed on the initial loan estimate: costs that can change any amount, costs that can never increase, and costs that can increase no more than 10%. These rules do not apply if there is a valid change of circumstance. The appraisal fee is a fee that cannot change. A recording fee can increase up to 10%. A home inspection and prepaid interest can change by any amount.

45. A: This is a scenario of bait and switch. A common example of this would be a lender advertising the rate of an adjustable-rate mortgage in bold print but with little or no mention of the loan product itself. Only mentioning the rate and that it is a 30-year loan is emphasized to attract potential customers. Once the potential borrower has inquired regarding the interest rate, other products are mentioned that have higher rates than advertised. This is considered an illegal practice.

46. D: For income to be used in qualifying a borrower for a mortgage, it must be considered stable and likely to continue. If a lender discovers that a borrower's current income is not likely to continue, the proposed income cannot be used to qualify. If a borrower has proof of new job or if the borrower has confirmation of income as a result of retirement, the new income sources can be used if they are going to begin shortly after closing.

47. C: On a mortgage application, an adverse action is a negative action reported to a consumer regarding the denial of the credit application. If a complete or incomplete application has an adverse action taken, a notice must be issued. If a counteroffer is issued and is rejected, a notice must be issued as well. Accepted counteroffers, withdrawn applications, and applications that do not involve credit do not require an adverse action notice to be issued.

48. D: The consumer handbook on adjustable-rate mortgages (CHARM) booklet must be given to consumers with the initial loan disclosures on a majority of adjustable-rate mortgages (ARMs). The Consumer Financial Protection Bureau publishes this document. It goes over many of the details of an ARM such as initial rate and payment, margin, index, interest rate caps, and discounted rates. It also addresses different types of ARM products, including interest-only, hybrid and payment option ARMs.

49. B: Encouraging a borrower to get a less favorable loan than another loan product is steering. A loan officer may do this to earn a larger commission or to make the processing of the loan easier. The suggested loan product may be one that the borrower cannot afford as well. This is considered an illegal practice and is punishable under the Fair Housing Act. A realtor could also be accused of steering by guiding a client to purchase a home he or she cannot afford.

50. C: The minimum age for a reverse mortgage is 62. A reverse mortgage allows the borrower to pay off an existing mortgage, take out cash, and have the option to take future advances against the equity in the home. Additionally, the borrower is not required to make a monthly payment on the mortgage. He or she must continue to pay the property taxes and homeowner's insurance. The loan balance does increase over time as interest accrues; however, the borrower does not need to repay the loan as long as he or she is living in the home.

51. A: There are three options that an MLO can choose when identifying a consumer's marital status. A consumer is married, unmarried, or separated. You cannot ask someone if he or she is single, divorced, or widowed. The Equal Credit Opportunity Act prohibits any discrimination based on marital status.

52. B: For a majority of Federal Housing Administration (FHA) loans, the minimum down payment is 3.5%. There are a few exceptions to the rule. If a consumer's credit score is between 500 and 579, then the required down payment is 10%. Also, if there is an identity of interest (such as a landlord selling to a tenant), the required down payment is 15%.

53. D: Auto insurance is not a factor when determining residual income or the debt-to-income ratio. Monthly debt, the square footage of the home (used to calculate an estimate for utilities), and income tax with holdings are used to calculate residual income. The Department of Veterans Affairs (VA) provides a table that shows how much residual income (income that is left after all of the mentioned deductions) is required. The table is based on family size and which region of the country the home is located in.

54. A: The loan estimate must be issued within 3 business days of a lender receiving an application. This estimate includes the total closing costs, interest rate, and a breakdown of the monthly payment (including property taxes, insurance, and private mortgage insurance). The form also addresses any special features, such as a balloon payment or what a payment might change to on an adjustable-rate mortgage. This form is standard with all lenders, so it allows a borrower to compare what different lenders are offering.

55. A: Because an individual's immigration status can affect his or her ability to repay a loan, immigration status can be considered when reviewing the application. Income and credit history also are factors in determining whether to extend credit. A borrower's race, sex, religion, national origin, marital status, and childbearing should not be considered when evaluating an application.

56. B: A lender is required to send a copy of a consumer's appraisal 3 days before the loan closes. They should also send it as soon as possible after they receive the report. All consumers have a right to receive a free copy of the appraisal report.

57. A: A bankruptcy will typically remain on a consumer report for 10 years from the discharge date. Paid tax liens, collections, judgments, charge offs, and any conviction of a crime should not be included on the report. Delinquent student loan debt in some case can remain on a report for longer than 7 years.

58. C: According to regulation N, records of any advertising done regarding a mortgage product must be kept for 24 months. This includes copies of the actual material and/or records that provide evidence of the material that was presented. The specific names and details of each mortgage product advertised must also be a part of this record.

59. B: To renew a state mortgage loan originator (MLO) license, an MLO must take a minimum of eight hours of continuing education approved by the NMLS. The eight hours of continuing education must include: three hours of federal laws and regulations; two hours of ethics (including instruction on fraud), consumer protection, and fair lending; and two hours of training related to lending standards for the nontraditional mortgage product marketplace.

60. B: A majority of home mortgages is required to be covered by HOEPA. This includes owner-occupied, second home, and investment properties. HELOCS also require HOEPA coverage. Construction loans that finance the initial construction do not require coverage. Loans directly originated by the Housing Finance Agency and the US Department of Agriculture's 502 Direct Loan program do not require HOEPA coverage.

61. B: To calculate this borrower's monthly income based on a standard 40-hour work week you multiply $21.00 by 40 hours ($840). You then multiply $840 by 52 (number of weeks in a year), which gives you an annual income of $43,680. To determine the monthly income, divide $43,680 by 12, which is $3,640. Because not all months have 4 weeks, you must multiply the weekly income by the total amount of weeks in a year. The same answers can also be found by multiplying $21.00 by 2,080 and then dividing by 12.

62. A: The Equal Credit Opportunity Act (ECOA) prohibits discrimination when issuing credit. According to the Department of Justice this act "prohibits creditors from discriminating against credit applicants on the basis of race, color, religion, national origin, sex, marital status, age, because an applicant receives income from a public assistance program, or because an applicant has in good faith exercised any right under the Consumer Credit Protection Act." The Department of Justice can prosecute those who violate this law.

63. B: A lender must ensure that a loan estimate is delivered (including electronic delivery) to a borrower or placed in the mail to the borrower no later than the third business day after receipt of the borrower's application. Also, it should not be issued less than 7 days before the loan closing. Failure to follow this regulation can result in the lender paying for some of the borrower's loan fees.

64. D: A cash-out refinance is a loan in which the loan proceeds are given to the borrower for any purpose the borrower chooses. Most loan programs only allow a borrower to do a loan that is 80% of the appraised value of the home when doing a cash-out refinance. A rate and term refinance is a refinance in which only the existing balance is refinanced. Conventional loans allow up to $2,000 cash back. Anything above that would be considered a cash-out refinance. A renovation loan and loan that pays off a first mortgage and a purchase-money second mortgage is considered a rate and term refinance. A cash-out refinance typically has a slightly higher rate than a purchase or rate and term loan. This is because they are considered higher risk.

65. C: An appraisal fee is not considered a loan origination fee. Some lenders may view origination fees and discount points as the same thing because both can be calculated as a percentage of the loan amount. Recently the Consumer Financial Protection Bureau published the following statement regarding origination fees: "An origination fee is what the lender charges the borrower for making the mortgage loan. The origination fee may include processing the application, underwriting and funding the loan, and other administrative services. Origination fees generally can only increase under certain circumstances."

66. D: After three failed attempts of taking the Secure and Fair Enforcement for Mortgage Licensing (SAFE) mortgage loan originator (MLO) test an applicant must wait 180 days before retaking the test. After the first and second failed attempt, the waiting period is 30 days. After the 180-day waiting period, the same waiting periods apply for the subsequent first, second, and third attempts. The test must be paid for on each attempt.

67. C: The explanation of large deposits shown on a bank statement is important when reviewing a loan application. A large deposit is typically any deposit other than direct deposited income that is more than 50% of a borrower's monthly income. Ultimately, an underwriter has discretion on whether a large deposit needs to be addressed. A copy of the deposit along with an explanation from the borrower is acceptable documentation to address the deposit. If the deposit is cash, or if it is proceeds from an undisclosed loan, it could adversely affect the credit decision made by a lender.

68. A: The lender has 3 business days to notify a borrower of the right to receive a copy of the appraisal. This document is part of the initial disclosures given to a borrower once an application is received. This disclosure is signed by the borrower to acknowledge receipt. Once the lender receives the appraisal, they are required to share a copy of the report with the borrower as quickly as possible.

69. A: In mortgage lending *capacity* is the borrower's ability to repay the mortgage and all other debt. This is analyzed and determined by evaluating two different ratios. The first is the housing ratio. This ratio is calculated by dividing the total mortgage payment by the monthly gross income.

The second ratio is the total debt ratio. This ratio is determined by dividing a borrower's total debt (including the mortgage payment) and dividing it by the monthly gross income. Typically, lenders would like to see a housing ratio to be no more than 28–31% and the total debt ratio to not be higher than 39–41%. However, lenders will approve loans with higher ratios if there are factors that offset risk, such as good credit and a large down payment.

70. B: The maximum amount of flood insurance available under the National Flood Insurance Program is $250,000. Therefore, you could have more coverage on your regular homeowner's policy than you have through your flood insurance coverage. Fannie Mae, Freddie Mac, the Federal Housing Administration, the Department of Veterans Affairs, and the United States Department of Agriculture Rural Development program all require flood insurance if a dwelling is in the flood plain as determined by the Federal Emergency Management Agency (FEMA).

71. B: A borrowers housing ratio is determined by dividing the total monthly payment (principal, interest, taxes, and insurance) by their gross monthly income. In this scenario, the total monthly payment is $2,080, and the monthly gross income is $10,400.

$$\frac{\$2,080}{\$10,400} = 20\%$$

Homeowners association dues and flood insurance would also be included in a borrower's monthly payment. It is recommended that a borrower's housing ratio be 29% or lower, but a higher housing ratio will not automatically disqualify a borrower from getting a mortgage.

72. B: Homeowners association dues are not collected into the escrow account and are not a part of the monthly mortgage payment. The initial statement will have an itemization of the taxes, insurance, and mortgage insurance (if applicable) being placed into the escrow account. It will also have a schedule of anticipated disbursements for the next 12 months.

73. D: A change of circumstance includes emergencies, disasters, war, and acts of God. It also includes information that was disclosed on a Good Faith Estimate that is found to be incorrect. This may include the loan amount, fees, and the interest rate. Boundary disputes, the discovery that a property is located in a flood zone, or environmental issues can also be considered a change of circumstance.

A borrower's income, assets, or spelling of the name do not require a change of circumstance. In addition, information that was collected from the credit report prior to the Good Faith Estimate being issued is not a change of circumstance.

74. C: When addressing closing costs changing from what was initially disclosed on the loan estimate, the costs are dived into three categories: costs that can change any amount, costs that can never increase, and costs that can increase no more than 10%. These rules do not apply if there is a valid change of circumstance. The recording fee falls into the category of fees that can increase no more than 10%. Since 10% of $120 is $12, the total fee that would be allowed to be charged is $132. The lender would have to pay the difference.

75. B: A lender must retain records of the compensation paid to a mortgage loan originator (MLO) for 3 years from the time they paid the compensation. This includes payment from a creditor, a consumer, or any other third party. Also, any compensation agreement between a lender and MLO must be included in this record retention.

76. B: Per diem interest is the interest that is outside of the regular repayment period on all mortgages. Mortgage payments are on a schedule that pays the interest for the prior month. Therefore, the interest from the closing date until the end of the month needs to be accounted for. For example, if a borrower closes January 15, the first payment would be March 1. The interest from January 15 until January 31 is the per diem interest and is paid for as a part of the prepaid expenses. If a borrower closes on the first of the month, he or she has the option to have the first payment be the first day of the subsequent month. In this case 1 day of interest would be credited to the borrower.

77. B: A change of circumstance is a situation in which a new lender estimate is issued because of changes to fees that are being charged. A rate lock expiring does not result in an actual fee. If there is a fee for a new rate lock or a rate lock extension, that would be considered a change of circumstance. If a borrower requests a change, such as a lower down payment, which could result in a change in fees, that would also be considered a valid change of circumstance. Changes that affect the value of the subject property and the expiration of the loan estimate also are valid changes of circumstance.

78. B: If the maximum combined loan to value (CLTV) is 95%, and the first mortgage is 80% of the purchase price, then the second mortgage would be 15% of the purchase price, or $37,500. Purchase-money second mortgages typically are utilized to avoid private mortgage insurance because the first mortgage can remain at 80% of the purchase price. They usually have a higher rate than the first mortgage. First-time home buyers sometimes have the option of using a community second mortgage, which is a mortgage that is issued by a state or local government or a nonprofit agency. They can be not only used to finance the down payment but can also include the closing costs. The CLTV allowed can be up to 105% on a community second mortgage.

79. B: An underwriter typically does not need to have a Nationwide Multistate Licensing System and Registry (NMLS) license. According to the NMLS, the following would necessitate the need for an NMLS license:

1. An individual or entity that takes a residential mortgage loan application
2. An individual or entity that advertises the availability of a mortgage
3. An individual or entity that negotiates the terms of a mortgage and is compensated for it

Typically, it is a mortgage loan originator who fulfills these duties. However, a loan assistant or processor may participate in some of these job functions as well, which would require them to have an NMLS license.

80. B: The basic standard limit for an FHA-insured loan on a one- or single-family home in 2024 is $498,257. In 2023 this limit was $472,030. The limit is increased for multi-unit properties and for properties that are considered to be in a high-cost area ($1,149,825). The 2024 standard conventional conforming limit is $766,550.

81. C: According to the Secure and Fair Enforcement for Mortgage Licensing Act (SAFE Act), 20 hours of prelicensed education is required before being issued a Nationwide Multistate Licensing System and Registry (NMLS) license. Many states even require this before submitting an application for the license. The education must include: three hours of federal law; three hours of ethics (this must include education on fraud, fair lending, and ways that consumers are protected, 2 hours pertaining to nontraditional mortgages, and 12 hours of elective education on mortgage lending).

82. B: To calculate an interest-only payment, you must multiply the loan amount by the interest rate, and divide that number by 12.

$$\frac{\$150,000 \times 0.045}{12} = \$562.50$$

Interest-only payments are no longer available on loans that are backed by Fannie Mae or Freddie Mac. Also, you cannot have an interest-only payment on a Federal Housing Administration, Department of Veterans Affairs, or Rural Development loan. Interest-only payments are available on home equity lines of credit, in-house/portfolio bank loans, and nonconforming and jumbo loans. They are considered higher risk because the interest-only period of payments eventually ends, the original principal balance remains, and the new payment could be higher.

83. D: The Department of Veterans Affairs (VA) funding fee is waived when the borrower is a recipient of monthly VA disability income. This is regardless of the percentage of VA disability granted to the veteran. The VA funding fee is discounted when 5% is put down as a down payment. It is discounted even more when the down payment is 10% or more. However, it is not waived. The fee varies based on first time and subsequent use and whether the applicant was in the regular military or reserves.

84. B: Prepaids are costs that a borrower pays at the closing that are not yet due. These expenses are part of funding the escrow account. They include property taxes, homeowner's insurance, flood insurance, and private mortgage insurance. They can also include a Sanitary and Improvement District for the repair of roads and sewers.

85. D: A mortgage lender cannot pay a realtor because he or she referred a customer. This is an illegal practice and is considered a bribe or kickback. Not only does this include monetary compensation, but it also includes anything of value. It is considered that someone might receive more favorable treatment based on a kickback. This creates a lack of parity for the public at large.

86. A: The Dodd-Frank Act was put into law in July 2010. It brought major reform to the financial services industry. This act also brought about major reform in the mortgage industry as well. The reforms included minimum standards for a mortgage. Some of those minimum standards are caps on interest rates above the national average, restricting the amount of fees on late payments, and prohibiting balloon payments that could more than double the initial payment on a mortgage. The act also created stricter mortgage servicing regulations and instituted more regulation with the appraisal process. For example, an appraiser must be randomly selected from a pool of appraisers. There also must be minimal contact between the MLO and appraiser so as to not create undue influence. Mortgage modifications and high-cost mortgages are also addressed in this law.

87. B: A power of attorney allows another individual to sign mortgage documents on your behalf. The individual who is granted the power of attorney is called the attorney-in-fact. For a mortgage it is typically a limited power of attorney. It is usually property and transaction specific. Purchase and rate and term refinances are allowed to use a power of attorney. However, a borrower is not allowed to use a power of attorney on a cash-out refinance. Also, a borrower cannot have an employee of the lender be the attorney-in-fact.

88. C: Anyone who wishes to have a Nationwide Multistate Licensing System (NMLS) license must go through a criminal background check. The applicant must submit fingerprints, which are then processed by the Federal Bureau of Investigation. If the individual has had a felony related to financial services, he or she is not eligible to receive a NMLS license. This would include theft, bribery, and fraud. This is regardless of how long ago the offense occurred. Misdemeanors do not disqualify someone from receiving a license. Any nonfinancial-related felony will disqualify an applicant unless it is more than 7 years old.

89. D: When a borrower works different hours per week, receives bonuses, or works overtime, this income is called variable income. Those whose income is more than 25% commission are also in this category. Simply looking at recent or year-to-date income is not sufficient to determine an income trend. Year-to-date income average with prior year W2s is a good way to determine a borrower's income. If the income is declining, it may be considered unstable, and further analysis may be needed to determine what income can be used to qualify the borrower.

90. B: There is not a requirement that a borrower's credit be checked when requesting the removal of private mortgage insurance (PMI). A written request must be provided to the servicer to remove the insurance. There must be a good payment history, and the borrower must be current. Also, the requirements that were set up at the time of origination must be met. For example, there must be some type of evidence that the property value has not decreased below the value at the time the loan was originated. Typically, the loan amount must be 80% of the value of the property. PMI can be canceled only on conventional loans.

91. C: A closing disclosure must be issued at least 3 business days prior to closing. It is not a requirement that it be signed; however, most lenders require it to be signed as proof of receipt. It can be hand delivered, electronically delivered, or mailed. If it is mailed, then three additional business days are added to the waiting period. If anything changes that causes the annual percentage rate (APR) to increase more than 0.125% during the waiting period, a new CD must be issued, and a borrower must wait an additional 3 business days from the time the new CD was issued.

92. C: Subprime mortgages are regulated by the Consumer Financial Protection Bureau (CFPB). They are considered to be a major contributor to the mortgage crisis of 2007–2008. They are still available, but they are not as prevalent. They are designed to provide a mortgage product to consumers that have poor credit. They have higher interest rates and require a larger down payment. They can have terms longer than 30 years, may have an interest-only payment feature, or be an adjustable-rate mortgage.

93. B: The consumer's assets are not an essential piece of the Good Faith Estimate. A Good Faith Estimate (Loan Estimate) must be provided to the consumer no later than three business days after the receipt of an application. An application is considered received when the consumer provides the following information: consumer's name, consumer's income, consumer's Social Security number to obtain a credit report, address of the property, estimate of the value of the property, and the mortgage loan amount sought.

94. B: Any undisclosed debt must be provided to a lender. This is applicable at the time of application, during the processing of the loan, and prior to the loan closing. A lender must be provided official documentation from the creditor so that the monthly payment can be included in the borrower's debt ratio. A lender may also request a credit supplement from the vendor that provided the credit report to verify the new debt information.

95. B: An easement gives someone the right to use a portion of another's persons land for a specific purpose. It is a legal document that is recorded and filed with the county clerk and recorder. One example of this is for a road that crosses over a piece of land to get to a different owner's property. This prevents the second owner mentioned from being landlocked. Utility companies may be granted an easement to access power lines that cross over multiple properties. A shared well between two neighbors would require an easement to grant the neighbor that does not have the well on his or her property access the well.

96. C: Typically, a loan servicer does not start the foreclosure process until a borrower is more than 120 days late. If a borrower is late on a payment, the servicer must attempt to contact a borrower no later than 36 days from the time the payment became past due. If a borrower is more than 45 days late, the servicer must provide options to try and assist the borrower to prevent foreclosure. This could include a loan modification to help bring the mortgage current. Foreclosure is when the lender takes back the home due to failure to make payments on the loan.

97. C: The sales comparison or market approach is the most often used when determining value on an appraisal. This approach uses comparable properties that have sold in the vicinity of the subject property. Most lenders will require comparable properties that have sold within the last 6 months. However, exceptions can be made to extend that time period to 1 year. The income approach bases the value of the property off the income it produces. The cost approach evaluates the cost to build (including the land value) the property to determine its value.

98. A: A gift is a monetary gift that a donor gives to a borrower to cover down payment and closing costs. Acceptable gift donors include any relative by blood, marriage, or adoption. They also include a fiancé or domestic partner. A friend is not an acceptable donor on a conventional loan. Also, a builder, real estate agent, or developer cannot give a gift to the borrower for the down payment. In some instances, they may be able to contribute to closing costs if they meet the requirements set for allowable contributions by an interested party to the transaction.

99. C: When a buyer and seller are related, a lender must do a thorough review of the application. This is considered a non-arm's length transaction and is a higher-risk loan. A red flag does not necessarily mean that fraud is being committed, but rather there is a greater likelihood of fraud to happen as compared to the seller not being related to the buyer. A seller and buyer with an established relationship could inflate the price so that the lender has a loan that is over the true value of a property. Personal property, multiple borrowers, and extended closing dates may need some justification but do not necessarily constitute a red flag.

100. B: Unless there is a valid change of circumstance, there is zero tolerance to change a fee disclosed on the lender estimate that is paid directly to the lender. A valid change of circumstance such as a change in the estimated appraised value, a change in the initial down payment, or a change in the purchase price would allow a lender to issue a new lender estimate with updated fees. Fees that are part of the escrow account are not subject to this rule. Fees that are paid to a third party in which a borrower did not have the opportunity to select the party can change, as long as the cumulative amount of those fees does not go up by 10%.

101. C: A suspicious activity report (SAR) must be filed no later than 30 calendar days after the detection of a suspicious activity. Some examples of suspicious activity could be large and irregular cash deposits, irregular incoming wires, and hacking into a financial institution's server. This report primarily pertains to acts of money laundering and fraud. The report is filed with the Financial Crimes Enforcement Network. Financial institutions and their employees are not allowed to notify those individuals accused of the suspicious activity.

102. A: A consumer must properly consent to receive electronic records. He or she must be provided with information regarding the rights to receive the same information in a paper form as well. He or she must also be given information that clarifies that the electronic record being provided only pertains to the specific transaction and that they can withdraw consent at any time.

In addition, a consumer must be notified of the specific hardware or software that may be needed to receive electronic disclosures.

103. A: A mortgage lender must keep records for a minimum of 3 years. However, a state may require a longer period of time based on its own regulations. The records to be retained include a majority of the disclosures associated with a loan application. There are a few exceptions. For example, a closing disclosure must be retained for at least 5 years. The Consumer Financial Protection Bureau (CFBP) has the right to request a copy of these disclosures.

104. C: State licensed mortgage loan originators are required to take 8 hours of continuing education annually. In most states it is required to be completed by December 31. The National Mortgage Licensing System and Registry monitors this in accordance with the Secure and Fair Enforcement for Mortgage Licensing Act (SAFE Act). The act requires 3 hours on federal mortgage requirements, 2 hours on ethical practices (this includes fair lending, consumer protection, and fraud), 2 hours on nontraditional mortgage products, and 1 hour of elective credits pertaining to mortgage origination.

105. A: A discount point is a fee that is paid directly to a lender for a reduced interest rate. One point is equal to 1% of the loan amount. The amount needed to purchase a lower interest rate varies and depends on the posted rates for that day. This is also known as buying down the rate. A consumer should evaluate the time it takes to recoup the cost of the discount point based on the monthly savings gained with a lower interest rate.

106. D: Prior landlord experience is not required when purchasing a nonowner-occupied rental property. Fannie Mae decision engine, Desktop Underwriter (DU), Freddie Mac's decision engine, and Loan Prospector (LP) will give the MLO feedback on what the required amount of reserves are based on the risk of the transaction. The required reserves are typically 2–6 months' worth of payments. The appraisal will also require a rent schedule, an operating income statement, or both. The down payment amount is also higher on an investment property. It is anywhere from 15–25% depending on the number of units.

107. D: Real Estate Settlement Procedures Act (RESPA) limits the amount of money a lender may require the borrower to hold in an escrow account for payment of taxes, hazard insurance, and other charges related to the property. RESPA does not require lenders to impose an escrow account on borrowers; however, certain government loan programs or lenders may require escrow accounts as a condition of the loan.

108. D: On a refinance of an owner-occupied property, there is 3-day right of rescission period before a loan funds—Sundays do not count. Saturdays can be included in the 3 days, but because most title companies and county clerk and recorders are closed on Saturday, a loan typically will not fund on a Saturday. When the proceeds of a loan are paid to the seller, disbursed to pay off an existing lien, or given to a borrower, that is considered a funded loan. The right of rescission gives the borrower the option to reconsider completing the loan even after he or she has signed all of the closing documents. Once the clock starts, the borrow has until midnight three days later to cancel the contract. In this scenario, midnight three days later would land on Friday night, resulting in the loan funding on Monday, May 11. The right of recission is not applicable to home purchases or any transaction involving a second home or investment property.

109. A: A residence that has not opted to be on the do-not call list may not be contacted before 8 a.m. or after 9 p.m. This includes the delivery of prerecorded information as well. If a consumer gives permission to be called outside of these hours, it is not a violation by the telemarketer to do so. Also, if a call is made in error or the telemarketer has a personal relationship with the consumer, it is not a violation of the regulation.

110. C: The Federal Housing Administration (FHA) currently requires 1.75% of the loan amount as an up-front mortgage insurance premium. This is in addition to the monthly mortgage insurance that is required on an FHA loan. This premium is allowed to be financed into the loan and does not affect the loan-to-value or combined loan-to-value requirements. The premiums are collected by the Department of Housing and Urban Development and are used to offset the losses due to foreclosures and other mortgage deficiencies (such as a short sale).

111. D: The loan to value is calculated by dividing the loan amount by the lesser of the appraised value or purchase price.

$$\$425,000 - \$63,950 = \$361,050$$

$$\frac{\$361,050}{\$415,000} = 87\%$$

Some borrowers may think that the loan to value would improve if the appraised value is higher than the purchase price. However, the loan to value is based on the purchase price, and the benefit of the higher value is not passed onto the loan-to-value ratio.

112. D: A Social Security number must be provided on a mortgage application so that a credit report can be ordered. According to the Home Mortgage Disclosure Act an applicant does not need to provide information regarding race, sex, or ethnicity. If an application is taken in person, this information may be input based on a visual observation and surname. If the application is taken over the phone, by mail, or on the internet, the data does not need to be provided.

113. C: The right of rescission applies only to a refinance of a principal residence. This law is covered under the Truth and Lending Act. It allows a consumer to cancel a transaction within 3 days after a loan closing. It is applicable regardless if it the property has one to four units.

114. D: A verification of deposit (VOD) is an acceptable source to verify an account balance of an asset. Generally, a VOD form is provided to a financial institution to be completed. The information on this form includes account numbers, account owners, the date the account was opened, the current balance, and the average balance. The account must have been opened for at least 2 months so that an average balance may be determined. If the current balance is substantially higher than the average balance, then the VOD cannot be used, and 60 days' history of the account would need to be provided. The difference in the current balance and average balance would lead an underwriter to question if there was a large deposit that needs to be accounted for.

115. B: Private mortgage insurance is calculated by multiplying the loan by the mortgage insurance rate and then dividing that amount by 12.

$$\$175,000 \times 0.0053 = \$927.50$$

$$\frac{\$927.50}{12} = \$77.29$$

The premium is based on an annual rate, so that is why you must divide it by 12 to determine a monthly rate. There are multiple factors that determine the rate. They include FICO score, debt-to-income ratio, loan to value, occupancy type, building type, and the term of the loan. Mortgage insurance premiums are higher on loans that are considered higher risk.

116. A: A Nationwide Multistate Licensing System (NMLS) license must be renewed once a year. The renewal period begins November 1 and ends December 31 each year. Both individuals and institutions must participate in renewing their respective licenses. This is done directly through the NMLS website. If the renewal is not done prior to December 31, the participant is placed in an inactive status. An additional fee must be paid to reactivate the NMLS license status.

117. A: Rural development (RD) loans do not require a down payment. They are designed to help promote home ownership in rural communities. Only certain areas within the United States are eligible for RD financing. Also, there are income limits for those who want to use this program. The income limits are based on the median income in the area and family size. RD loans have stricter underwriting guidelines than a Federal Housing Administration (FHA) or Department of Veterans Affairs (VA) loan. For example, typically the maximum debt-to-income ratio is 43%. The property also cannot be an income-producing farm or ranch.

118. B: The maximum contribution from a seller in this scenario is 3%. The amount that a seller may contribute to a buyer's closing costs on a conventional loan depends on the occupancy and the amount of down payment. For example, if a borrower puts 10% down (on a primary or second home), the seller can contribute 6% of the purchase price toward the borrower's closing costs. The maximum seller concession on an investment property is 2% of the purchase price regardless of the amount of the down payment.

119. A: This scenario is an example of possible income fraud. Borrowers could write the pay stubs and W2s themselves. Also, a potential borrower could establish a cell phone number and PO box exclusively for a nonexistent business. One way a lender could verify the legitimacy of the borrower's income would be to request W2 transcripts from the Internal Revenue Service to see if they have been provided over the past 2 years.

120. D: To calculate the down payment, multiply the loan amount by the percentage of required down payment: $210,000 \times 0.05 = $10,500$. Minimum required down payments vary depending on the loan product or program. For conventional conforming mortgages the standard minimum down payment on an owner-occupied property is 5%. However, it is 3% for first-time home buyers. A Federal Housing Administration (FHA) loan require 3.5%. Department of Veterans Affairs (VA) and Rural Development (RD) loans do not require a minimum down payment.

MLO Practice Test #2

1. Bob is a borrower who received a Loan Estimate (LE) that disclosed a title insurance fee of $500. However, on the Closing Disclosure (CD), Bob notices that the final amount for the fee is $540. Which of the following is most true about the increased amount of this fee?

   a.   This fee can increase, but it has exceeded the allowable tolerance.
   b.   None of the fees on the LE can change in the CD.
   c.   This type of fee cannot increase at all.
   d.   This fee can increase, and it is within the allowable tolerance.

2. What is the MAIN benefit of having an escrow account for homeowners?

   a.   Assurance that insurance premiums are always paid on time
   b.   Easier management of mortgage payments
   c.   Protection against foreclosure due to unpaid taxes
   d.   The ability to pay property taxes in a lump sum

3. Which federal regulation requires financial institutions and creditors to establish written identity theft prevention programs.

   a.   Bank Secrecy Act/Anti-Money Laundering (BSA/AML)
   b.   Federal Trade Commission Red Flags rule
   c.   Mortgage Acts and Practices—Advertising
   d.   Homeowners Protection Act

4. What is the primary function of the Department of Housing and Urban Development (HUD) in relation to affordable housing programs?

   a.   Awarding grants and subsidies to support affordable housing initiatives
   b.   Providing direct loans to low-income homebuyers
   c.   Regulating mortgage interest rates for affordable housing loans
   d.   Overseeing credit reporting agencies and credit scoring models

5. What does the NMLS stand for in the mortgage industry?

   a.   National Mortgage Lenders System
   b.   Nationwide Multistate Licensing System
   c.   National Mortgage Licensing System
   d.   Nationwide Mortgage Lenders Service

6. What is a significant risk associated with taking out a home equity line of credit (HELOC)?

   a.   If you default on your HELOC payments, you may lose your home.
   b.   HELOCs often have higher interest rates compared to other loan options.
   c.   Using a HELOC could negatively impact your credit score.
   d.   HELOCs require large up-front costs, making them less appealing.

149

7. Under the Real Estate Settlement Procedures Act (RESPA), Regulation X requires that borrowers receive which disclosure to help them understand the costs and terms of their mortgage loan before closing?

a. Closing Disclosure
b. Good Faith Estimate
c. HUD-1 Settlement
d. Truth-in-Lending Disclosure

8. Which of the following advertising statements would be considered unethical and non-compliant?

a. "Get the lowest mortgage rates in town, guaranteed!"
b. "We have special connections with lenders that others don't have."
c. "No closing costs or fees for qualified borrowers."
d. "We can help you get approved for a mortgage, no matter your credit score."

9. Who can be an acceptable donor for a gift in a financial transaction?

a. Anyone who is a close friend of the borrower
b. A relative, a domestic partner, or a former relative of the borrower
c. An interested party involved in the transaction, such as a real estate agent
d. A financial institution providing grants to borrowers

10. Under Regulation Z, if an advertisement for credit states specific credit terms, what must it do?

a. It must state only those terms that are or will be arranged or offered by the creditor.
b. It must state both the actual and potential credit terms.
c. It must state all credit terms, including those not currently offered by the creditor.
d. It must state only those terms that will be offered in the future.

11. Which term refers to any claims, liens, or restrictions on a property's title that may impact its transferability?

a. Title insurance coverage
b. Easement
c. Encumbrances
d. Reconveyance

12. In the event of a mortgage default, what is the key difference between a mortgage and a deed of trust?

a. A mortgage requires a court order for foreclosure, while a deed of trust does not.
b. A mortgage is used for government-backed loans, while a deed of trust is used for conventional loans.
c. A mortgage provides more favorable terms to the borrower, while a deed of trust is more favorable to the lender.
d. A mortgage allows the borrower to sell the home independently, while a deed of trust requires lender involvement.

13. Which of the following is the purpose of Regulation B (Equal Credit Opportunity Act)?

a. To restrict access to credit for certain individuals
b. To ensure the availability of credit to creditworthy applicants without discrimination
c. To give priority to applications from protected groups
d. To provide lenders with additional information about applicants

14. What is the main purpose of Real Estate Settlement Procedures Act (RESPA) prohibitions?

a. To regulate mortgage interest rates
b. To ensure fair and non-discriminatory lending practices
c. To prohibit kickbacks and unearned fees in real estate transactions
d. To mandate borrowers to provide a detailed financial history

15. What information must a creditor include in the Equal Credit Opportunity Act (ECOA) notice provided to an applicant when adverse action is taken?

a. The specific reason(s) for adverse action and the applicant's right to request a statement of reasons within 60 days
b. A general notice of adverse action without listing specific reasons, allowing the applicant to inquire further if desired
c. The applicant's right to appeal the adverse action decision within 30 days
d. The applicant's number of loan inquiries

16. Which of the following scenarios represents a potential case of coercion in the mortgage lending process?

a. A borrower feeling pressured to accept unfavorable loan terms due to fear of consequences if they decline
b. A lender offering a special promotional interest rate for a limited time
c. Offering borrowers an incentive to submit their loan application quickly
d. A loan officer refusing to consider an application from a borrower with a disability

17. Which government agency offers flood insurance policies through the National Flood Insurance Program (NFIP)?

a. Federal Emergency Management Agency (FEMA)
b. Department of Housing and Urban Development (HUD)
c. Environmental Protection Agency (EPA)
d. Department of Homeland Security (DHS)

18. What is the primary function of Fannie Mae in the housing market?

a. Fannie Mae purchases mortgage loans made by lenders, which they then package into mortgage-backed securities.
b. Fannie Mae guarantees mortgage-backed securities to investors.
c. Fannie Mae originates mortgage loans directly to low-to-median income borrowers.
d. Fannie Mae invests in Low-Income Housing Tax Credit (LIHTC) properties.

19. Which of the following types of insurance is related to covering a borrower's personal belongings in case of property damage?

 a. Private Mortgage Insurance (PMI)
 b. Force-placed insurance
 c. Hazard insurance
 d. Government mortgage insurance

20. What differentiates subprime mortgages from prime mortgages?

 a. Subprime mortgages have higher interest rates and larger down payment requirements compared to prime mortgages.
 b. Prime mortgages are available to highly qualified borrowers, while subprime mortgages are for first-time homebuyers.
 c. Prime mortgages have more flexible terms and lower interest rates compared to subprime mortgages.
 d. Subprime mortgages are reserved for borrowers with good to excellent credit scores, while prime mortgages are available to borrowers with lower credit scores.

21. Which of the following requirements must mortgage loan originators (MLOs) meet under the Secure and Fair Enforcement for Mortgage Licensing (SAFE) Act?

 a. Provide fingerprints for an FBI criminal history background check
 b. Complete 20 hours of continuing education annually
 c. Maintain a real estate brokerage license
 d. Have a minimum credit score of 700

22. Which circumstances are considered "changed circumstances" under Regulation X?

 a. Changes in the borrower's employment status
 b. The borrower's request for a change in loan terms
 c. Acts of God, war, disaster, or other emergencies
 d. Changes in market interest rates

23. When should the notice of transfer of loan servicing be provided to the borrower?

 a. No less than 30 days before the effective date of the transfer
 b. No more than 30 days after the effective date of the transfer
 c. No less than 15 days before the effective date of the transfer
 d. No more than 15 days after the effective date of the transfer

24. What is the definition of "application" under Regulation X?

 a. The act of providing a borrower's financial information with the expectation of obtaining a credit decision for a federally related mortgage loan
 b. The process of evaluating a borrower's creditworthiness for any type of loan
 c. The completion of the loan origination process, including the signing of all necessary documents
 d. The appraisal of the property to determine its value for mortgage purposes

25. A mortgage loan originator (MLO) receives a credit report for a borrower but accidentally leaves it unattended on their desk overnight. What action should the MLO have taken to maintain security?

    a. Shred the credit report and dispose of it properly
    b. Inform the borrower about the incident and apologize
    c. Lock the credit report in a secure filing cabinet
    d. File the credit report in a publicly accessible area

26. Which federal law provides consumers the right to request a free copy of their credit report from each of the major credit reporting agencies once every 12 months?

    a. Dodd-Frank Act
    b. Electronic Signatures in Global and National Commerce Act (E-Sign Act)
    c. Bank Secrecy Act/Anti-Money Laundering (BSA/AML)
    d. Fair Credit Reporting Act (FCRA)

27. A borrower earns a gross monthly income of $6,000. Their total monthly debt payments, including the proposed mortgage, amount to $2,500. What is the borrower's Debt-to-Income (DTI) ratio? (Round to the nearest whole number)

    a. 25%
    b. 33%
    c. 42%
    d. 50%

28. A mortgage loan originator (MLO) receives a loan application from a borrower who recently lost their job. The MLO knows the borrower is unlikely to qualify for the loan but proceeds with the application anyway. Which ethical issue does this action represent?

    a. Coercion
    b. Redlining
    c. Predatory lending
    d. Kickbacks

29. In an assumable loan scenario, if the new borrower defaults on the loan, who is ultimately responsible for the debt?

    a. The original borrower who transferred the loan
    b. The new borrower who assumed the loan
    c. The lender who allowed the loan assumption
    d. The Federal Housing Administration (FHA) as the insurer of the loan

30. How does the Federal Housing Administration (FHA) benefit homebuyers through its mortgage insurance programs?

    a. It offers low-interest loans directly to homebuyers.
    b. It provides down payment assistance to qualified borrowers.
    c. It allows borrowers to purchase homes without a down payment.
    d. It protects lenders against losses, enabling them to offer more mortgages to homebuyers.

31. A buyer of a house with a sales price of $150,000 is paying a $15,000 down payment as well as two discount points and two points for loan origination fees. What is the total cost of the points?

    a. $3,850
    b. $4,250
    c. $5,400
    d. $6,850

32. What does a subordination clause in a mortgage do?

    a. It allows the homeowner to refinance the primary mortgage.
    b. It grants the lender the right to repossess the property in case of default.
    c. It prioritizes subordinate mortgages over the primary mortgage in case of default.
    d. It dictates the interest rate of the mortgage.

33. What is a balloon payment?

    a. A payment made at the beginning of the loan term
    b. A smaller-than-usual one-time payment at the end of the loan term
    c. A larger-than-usual one-time payment at the end of the loan term
    d. A payment made in equal installments throughout the loan term

34. If a borrower signs the promissory note on a mortgage refinance on a Thursday and then receives the Truth in Lending Act (TILA) disclosure document and two copies of the right to rescind notice on the same day, when does the right of rescission period end?

    a. Saturday midnight
    b. Monday midnight
    c. Sunday midnight
    d. Wednesday midnight

35. Which of the following terms in an advertisement triggers the requirement for additional disclosures under Regulation Z?

    a. The term "monthly payment"
    b. The term "APR"
    c. The term "finance charge"
    d. The term "number of payments"

36. What happens to the loan balance in a reverse mortgage over time?

    a. The loan balance decreases as monthly payments are made.
    b. The loan balance remains constant throughout the loan term.
    c. The loan balance is paid off in a lump sum after a certain period.
    d. The loan balance increases as interest and fees are added each month.

37. What is the maximum allowable debt-to-income (DTI) ratio for manually underwritten loans regarding Fannie Mae, considering the credit score and reserve requirements are met?

    a. 36 percent
    b. 45 percent
    c. 50 percent
    d. 55 percent

38. Which of the following is a potential risk associated with balloon mortgages?

a. Balloon mortgages often have higher interest rates compared to other loan products.

b. Balloon mortgages carry the risk of changes in property value that may affect the ability to refinance or sell the property.

c. Balloon mortgages are typically suitable for borrowers with stable and consistent income streams.

d. Balloon mortgages can lead to payment shock when the loan transitions from the initial fixed-rate period to the final payment at the end of the loan term.

39. In loan origination scenarios, what act is considered a "bait-and-switch" practice?

a. Advertising low-interest rates for a limited time

b. Offering a variety of loan options to borrowers

c. Promising cash incentives for loan applications

d. Changing loan terms after application without a valid reason

40. What is the purpose of Front-End debt-to-income (DTI) ratio in mortgage lending?

a. To determine the borrower's total monthly debt obligations

b. To assess the borrower's ability to make timely mortgage payments

c. To evaluate the borrower's creditworthiness based on their credit history

d. To calculate the maximum loan amount the borrower can qualify for

41. An appraiser is tasked with determining the value of a commercial building that generates rental income. Which appraisal approach is most likely to be used for this purpose?

a. Market approach

b. Cost approach

c. Income approach

d. Market data approach

42. As a mortgage loan originator (MLO), you are reviewing a borrower's credit report and notice a record of a foreclosure completed five years ago. The borrower is applying for a new conventional mortgage and had no extenuating circumstances that led to the foreclosure. What action should you take based on the waiting period requirements?

a. Proceed with the loan application without considering the foreclosure record

b. Inform the borrower that they must wait an additional year before applying for a new mortgage

c. Advise the borrower to wait for a total of seven years from the completion date of the foreclosure before applying

d. Seek legal advice before making any decisions related to the borrower's application

43. When must a creditor provide a copy of appraisals and other written valuations to a borrower?

a. At least 10 business days before consummation or account opening

b. Promptly upon completion, or three business days prior to consummation or account opening, whichever is earlier

c. Within 30 days after consummation or account opening

d. Only if the applicant requests the copies in writing after consummation or account opening

44. Michael is applying for a mortgage to purchase his first home. On his application, he claims to work as a senior manager at a well-known company and provides a salary figure that seems higher than the industry average for his position. However, during the verification process, the lender discovers that Michael's job title and income information do not align with the company's records. Which type of fraud best describes Michael's behavior?

    a. Asset fraud
    b. Income fraud
    c. Employment fraud
    d. Occupancy fraud

45. A mortgage loan originator (MLO) accidentally overcharges a borrower for an appraisal fee. What is the most appropriate course of action for the MLO to take?

    a. Refund the overcharged amount to the borrower
    b. Transfer the extra funds as a lender credit
    c. Offer the borrower a discount on future services
    d. Transfer the excess funds to the borrower's escrow account

46. Which type of credit plan is generally characterized by repeated transactions and the possibility of imposing a finance charge on an outstanding unpaid balance?

    a. Open-end credit plan
    b. Home equity plan
    c. Closed-end credit plan
    d. Mortgage transaction

47. What is the total monthly payment, including escrows, on a 30-year interest-only loan of $220,000, taxes of $1,500 per half-year, hazard insurance of $400 annually, $50 monthly mortgage insurance, and an interest rate of 5.5%? (Round to the nearest dollar amount)

    a. $1,231
    b. $1,285
    c. $1,342
    d. $1,413

48. Under what circumstance may less than two years of income history be acceptable for an applicant?

    a. When the applicant has a high credit score
    b. When the applicant's income source is verified through tax returns and W-2s
    c. When the applicant's income changed from hourly to salary income with the same employer
    d. When the applicant has recently graduated from college

49. Which of the following best describes the prohibited act of redlining in the context of ethical issues in the mortgage lending industry?

    a. Redlining refers to the practice of providing preferential treatment to borrowers based on their race, color, or national origin.
    b. Redlining involves denying or limiting access to credit or loan products to individuals based on their geographical location.
    c. Redlining occurs when mortgage lenders charge higher interest rates to borrowers with poor credit histories.
    d. Redlining refers to the practice of targeting borrowers with predatory lending practices to exploit their financial vulnerability.

50. A borrower is purchasing a home for $250,000. They are making a 20% down payment. How much is the down payment?

a. $10,000
b. $25,000
c. $50,000
d. $75,000

51. What is a power of attorney (POA) in a real estate transaction?

a. A legal document granting the lender the authority to foreclose on the property
b. A document that allows the borrower to transfer ownership of the property to another party
c. A legal document giving one person the power to legally bind another person in the transaction
d. A document provided by the title insurance company to protect the lender's interest

52. Which types of home loans are generally NOT assumable?

a. Home Equity Lines of Credit (HELOCs)
b. Loans insured by the Federal Housing Administration (FHA)
c. Loans backed by the Department of Veterans Affairs (VA) or United States Department of Agriculture (USDA)
d. Most conventional mortgages

53. Under the Equal Credit Opportunity Act (ECOA) and its regulations, which of the following statements accurately reflects the creditor's obligations and considerations regarding the marital status of loan applicants?

a. A creditor may treat joint applicants differently based on their marital status.
b. A creditor may require married applicants to provide additional information related to their marital status.
c. A creditor is prohibited from considering marital status in any aspect of a credit transaction.
d. A creditor is prohibited from lending to married applicants who were married in a different state.

54. What role does the Consumer Financial Protection Bureau (CFPB) play in addressing consumer complaints related to financial products and services?

a. The CFPB directly compensates consumers for their complaints and penalizes financial institutions without investigation.
b. The CFPB offers financial compensation to consumers who file valid complaints, but only after thorough investigation and review.
c. The CFPB provides free legal representation to consumers in court proceedings.
d. The CFPB processes complaints, works with companies to resolve issues, and publishes complaint data for public awareness.

55. An appraiser is hired to assess a property owned by their close relative. What should the appraiser do in this situation?

a. Decline the appraisal assignment to avoid a conflict of interest
b. Disclose the relationship and proceed with the appraisal
c. Conduct the appraisal but refrain from disclosing the relationship
d. Request a higher fee for the appraisal due to the conflict of interest

56. Jessica is in the process of obtaining a mortgage for her new home. She has received the Loan Estimate, which outlines the fees associated with the loan. Among these fees, which category of fees is subject to a zero-tolerance threshold?

a. Third-party service fees for required services that Jessica cannot shop for
b. Fees for required services that Jessica can shop for, and she selects a provider from the written list of service providers
c. Recording fees assessed by a government authority to record and index the loan and title documents
d. Fees for services not required by the creditor, which may be performed by an affiliate

57. What actions must a mortgage loan originator (MLO) take if a TILA-RESPA Integrated Disclosure (TRID) disclosure is incomplete or inaccurate?

a. Refuse to provide the loan to the borrower
b. Provide a revised disclosure to the borrower as soon as possible
c. Notify the Consumer Financial Protection Bureau (CFPB) immediately
d. Withdraw the loan application and start over

58. A borrower is purchasing a home for $200,000 and is making a $40,000 down payment. The house was appraised for $180,000. What is the loan-to-value (LTV) ratio for this mortgage? (Round to the nearest whole number)

a. 54%
b. 68%
c. 75%
d. 89%

59. Under what circumstances can a borrower extend their right of rescission timeline beyond the standard three-day period?

a. When the borrower wants to make changes to the loan terms
b. When the borrower never received the closing disclosure or the notice of right to rescind
c. When the borrower decides to switch lenders after signing the promissory note
d. When there is a title defect on the property

60. What is the primary purpose of the sponsorship requirement for mortgage loan originators (MLOs)?

a. To provide MLOs with additional mentorship and training
b. To hold employers accountable for the actions of their MLOs
c. To ensure MLOs have adequate pre-license education
d. To assess the creditworthiness of MLOs

61. Which mortgage market involves borrowers obtaining loans directly from lenders?

a. The primary mortgage market
b. The secondary mortgage market
c. Both the primary and secondary mortgage markets
d. Neither the primary nor the secondary mortgage market

62. Which entity is NOT typically required to have licensed mortgage loan originators (MLOs)?

   a. Mortgage brokerage firms
   b. Credit unions
   c. Mortgage servicing companies
   d. Mortgage lending subsidiaries of a bank

63. Which agency implements and enforces the Real Estate Settlement Procedures Act (RESPA) to ensure consumers receive disclosures and are protected from kickbacks and referral fees in real estate transactions?

   a. Federal Trade Commission (FTC)
   b. Department of Housing and Urban Development (HUD)
   c. Securities and Exchange Commission (SEC)
   d. Consumer Financial Protection Bureau (CFPB)

64. Why are jumbo loans considered riskier for lenders compared to conventional conforming loans?

   a. Jumbo loans have higher interest rates that can lead to payment fluctuations.
   b. Jumbo loans cannot be guaranteed by Fannie Mae and Freddie Mac.
   c. Jumbo loans require a larger down payment, increasing the risk of borrower default.
   d. Jumbo loans require less documentation from borrowers, making it challenging for lenders to assess their financial health accurately.

65. When must a lender, mortgage broker, or dealer provide a list of homeownership counseling organizations to a loan applicant?

   a. Within 30 days of the loan application submission
   b. Within one business day of receiving the loan application
   c. Within three business days of receiving the loan application or sufficient information to complete it
   d. Within seven business days of receiving the loan application

66. What is the definition of "adverse action" as it relates to Regulation B?

   a. A favorable change in terms of an account
   b. A refusal to grant credit in the amount or terms requested
   c. A termination of all accounts of a specific class of creditors
   d. An increase in the amount of credit available to an applicant

67. What is the recommended maximum debt-to-income (DTI) ratio for most conventional mortgage loans?

   a. 28 percent
   b. 36 percent
   c. 45 percent
   d. 50 percent

68. A mortgage loan originator (MLO) receives a referral fee from a title company for directing borrowers to their services. What must the MLO do with the referral fee?
   a. Keep the referral fee as additional income
   b. Use the referral fee to cover personal expenses
   c. Disclose the referral fee to the borrowers and give them the option to decline it
   d. Decline the referral fee

69. Which of the following scenarios presents the greatest potential for a case of occupancy fraud in the mortgage application process?
   a. A borrower providing documentation for their employment history and stable income
   b. A borrower planning to make a property their main residence
   c. A borrower intending to occupy the property but who inflates their assets on the mortgage application
   d. An applicant purchasing a second home in a vacation destination

70. Which of the following is NOT a feature of non-QM loans?
   a. Interest-only payments
   b. Negative amortization
   c. Fixed interest rates
   d. Balloon payments

71. How are discount points calculated in relation to the loan amount?
   a. Each point represents a fixed dollar amount, irrespective of the loan size.
   b. One point equals one percent of the loan amount.
   c. Discount points are set at a standard rate of 0.5 percent of the loan amount.
   d. The number of points depends on the borrower's credit history.

72. When will a borrower typically receive the Loan Estimate?
   a. On the day of the loan application
   b. Within 24 hours after filing the application
   c. No later than three business days after filing the application
   d. On the day of closing

73. What sets the maximum loan amounts for conforming loans?
   a. Fannie Mae or Freddie Mac
   b. The government
   c. The borrower's credit score
   d. The county where the property is located

74. How many times can an individual take the written test developed by the Nationwide Multistate Licensing System and Registry (NMLSR) to achieve a test score of at least 75 percent correct answers?
   a. Once
   b. Twice
   c. Three consecutive times
   d. Four consecutive times

75. Which of the following pieces of information is NOT required for a loan originator to collect from the borrower to issue a Good Faith Estimate (GFE), as per Regulation X?

   a. Name
   b. Monthly income
   c. Social Security number
   d. Employment history

76. John purchased a home for $200,000. His closing costs totaled 4% of the purchase price. However, the seller agreed to contribute 2% of the purchase price towards John's closing costs. How much cash did John need at closing to obtain his LTV of 85%?

   a. $25,600
   b. $32,000
   c. $34,000
   d. $38,800

77. A borrower initially qualified for a mortgage with a 5 percent down payment and an interest rate of 4.5 percent. However, the borrower's financial situation has changed, and they can now afford a higher down payment of 10 percent. They ask if this change would result in a lower interest rate. What should you do?

   a. Change the down payment and offer a lower interest rate
   b. Increase the interest rate to compensate for the higher down payment
   c. Inform the borrower that the change in down payment will not impact the interest rate
   d. Explain to the borrower that an increase in the down payment might lead to potential interest rate reduction

78. As a mortgage loan originator (MLO), you've had a long-standing working relationship with a local real estate agent. They refer many clients to you regularly. Recently, the agent has started offering you monetary gifts after each closed loan. What should you do?

   a. Politely accept the gifts as a gesture of appreciation for the referrals
   b. Accept the gifts but report them to your mortgage company's compliance officer
   c. Decline the gifts and inform the real estate agent that you cannot accept them
   d. Consult an attorney to determine the legality of accepting such gifts

79. How is the yield spread premium (YSP) calculated?

   a. The difference between the home's purchase price and the appraised value
   b. The difference between the buyer's down payment and the loan amount
   c. The difference between the par rate and the interest rate offered on the loan
   d. The difference between the origination fee and the closing costs

80. John purchased a property for $300,000 and obtained a mortgage loan of $270,000, all while having a monthly mortgage insurance payment. He has been making monthly payments on time, and he currently has a loan balance of $240,000. Based on this information, is John able to call his loan servicer and request to have the monthly mortgage insurance removed?

   a. Yes, because he has paid his monthly payments on time.
   b. Yes, because his loan amount is 80 percent or less of the original sales price.
   c. No, because his loan amount is not less than 78 percent of the original sales price.
   d. No, because you have to get a new appraisal to remove mortgage insurance.

81. An adjustable-rate mortgage (ARM) has an initial interest rate of 3.5%, a margin of 2%, and a lifetime cap of 6%. If the current index rate is 2.5%, what is the new interest rate when the ARM adjusts?

    a. 3.5%
    b. 4.5%
    c. 5.5%
    d. 6.0%

82. Which of the following is an advantage of a 15-year fixed-rate mortgage compared to a 30-year fixed-rate mortgage?

    a. 15-year mortgages are easier to qualify for in comparison to a 30-year fixed rate mortgage.
    b. 15-year mortgages have longer loan terms, providing more flexibility.
    c. 15-year mortgages result in significantly lower monthly payments.
    d. 15-year mortgages lead to greater interest savings over the life of the loan.

83. What is the primary function of the Consumer Financial Protection Bureau (CFPB)?

    a. Regulating the stock market and securities industry
    b. Ensuring the safety and soundness of banks and financial institutions
    c. Protecting consumers in the financial marketplace
    d. Enforcing antitrust laws to promote fair competition

84. Which of the following scenarios accurately describes redlining?

    a. Pressuring borrowers to accept unfavorable loan terms through threats or intimidation
    b. Targeting advertising efforts towards a specific neighborhood with high property values
    c. Offering mortgage products only to individuals with excellent credit scores
    d. Avoiding offering loan products to borrowers in a specific neighborhood because of its demographics

85. Under the Electronic Signatures in Global and National Commerce Act (E-Sign Act), which of the following documents is NOT eligible for electronic signatures?

    a. Loan applications
    b. Loan estimates
    c. Closing disclosure forms
    d. Notice of the right to rescind

86. During the loan application process, the borrower provides bank statements with suspicious activities and transactions that are inconsistent with their declared income. What should the mortgage loan originator (MLO) do?

    a. Ignore the suspicious activities, as they are not relevant to the loan application
    b. Advise the borrower to explain the suspicious activities and provide additional documentation
    c. Report the suspicious activities to the appropriate authorities without notifying the borrower
    d. Disregard the bank statements and focus only on verifying the borrower's employment history

87. A mortgage company offers a borrower an attractive interest rate during the application process. However, after a week, the company informs the borrower that the interest rate has increased. What must the mortgage company do in this scenario?

a. Explain that interest rates fluctuate regularly and are beyond their control
b. Inform the borrower of the increase and provide reasons for the change
c. Refund the borrower any fees already paid and cancel the application
d. Offer the borrower a discount on closing costs to compensate for the rate increase

88. Sarah is applying for a mortgage and works a part-time job at a retail store. She earns $15 per hour and works 25 hours per week. If she has no other sources of income, what is her estimated monthly qualifying income for the mortgage application?

a. $1,250
b. $1,625
c. $1,875
d. $2,000

89. Which of the following transactions would NOT be subject to Regulation Z?

a. A credit card account
b. A home-equity line of credit (HELOC)
c. A consumer loan with a fixed interest rate, payable in one installment
d. A mortgage transaction used to finance a principal dwelling

90. John and Sarah are a young couple looking to buy their first home. They both recently graduated from college and started their careers. While they have promising career prospects and anticipate significant salary increases in the coming years, their current income is relatively low. What type of loan is typically suitable for this type of borrower?

a. A jumbo mortgage
b. A Federal Housing Administration (FHA) loan
c. A Department of Veterans Affairs (VA) loan
d. A Graduated Payment Mortgage (GPM)

91. Which document legally binds the borrower to repay the mortgage and includes information on payment dates, interest, and consequences for missed payments?

a. Closing Disclosure
b. Deed of Trust
c. Promissory note
d. Initial Escrow Statement

92. What is the borrower's right to recission under the TILA-RESPA Integrated Disclosure (TRID) rule?

a. The right to cancel a mortgage loan application within three business days of receiving the Loan Estimate
b. The right to cancel a mortgage loan application within three business days of receiving the Closing Disclosure
c. The right to cancel a mortgage loan within three business days after loan consummation
d. The right to cancel a mortgage loan within seven business days after loan consummation

93. Which of the following fees is NOT typically included in the origination fee charged by the lender?

    a. Credit check fee
    b. Appraisal fee
    c. Underwriting fee
    d. Mortgage insurance premium

94. What happens if a borrower rescinds their mortgage within the three-day rescission period?

    a. The lender has 30 days to cancel the loan process and refund all fees.
    b. The lender has 20 days to cancel the loan process and refund all fees.
    c. The lender has 10 days to cancel the loan process and refund all fees.
    d. The lender has five days to cancel the loan process and refund all fees.

95. What is the main advantage of using a Purchase-Money Second Mortgage?

    a. It provides a secure fixed interest rate for a longer term than the first mortgage.
    b. It allows the buyer to avoid Private Mortgage Insurance (PMI) on loans with a loan-to-value (LTV) greater than 80 percent.
    c. It typically has lower note rates compared to standard second loans.
    d. It is financed by the same lender as the first mortgage, streamlining the application process.

96. What type of loan is exempted from Real Estate Settlement Procedures Act (RESPA) requirements based on its purpose?

    a. Loans secured by vacant or unimproved property
    b. Loans used for the construction of residential properties
    c. Business purpose loans, primarily for commercial or agricultural purposes
    d. Loans subject to prepayment penalties

97. A mortgage loan originator (MLO) works for a lender and has a personal financial interest in a real estate company. The MLO encourages borrowers to use the services of that real estate company to buy properties. What ethical issue does this situation present?

    a. Kickbacks
    b. Coercion
    c. Predatory lending and steering
    d. Appraiser conflict of interest

98. How far in advance of the loan closing must lenders provide borrowers with the "Know Before You Owe" closing disclosure?

    a. At least three business days before the closing
    b. At least 24 hours before the closing
    c. On the same day as the closing
    d. Any time before the closing

99. What does the interest rate on an Adjustable Rate Mortgage (ARM) consist of?

    a. The initial principal amount borrowed and the interest added each month
    b. The monthly principal and interest payment made by the borrower
    c. The total interest paid over the life of the loan
    d. The index, which reflects trends in the overall economy, and the margin added by the lender

100. A mortgage lender runs an advertisement with a low-interest rate promotion but fails to disclose certain terms and conditions. What act is the lender potentially violating?

    a. Federal regulation
    b. Misleading information
    c. Due diligence review
    d. "Unfair, deceptive, or abusive acts"

101. You notice irregularities in a borrower's financial documentation, including unreported income, unexplained deposits, and multiple credit applications in a short period. The borrower explains that the unreported income is from side jobs, and the deposits are gifts from family members. They also claim they were shopping for the best mortgage rate, leading to multiple credit applications. What should you do?

    a. Accept the borrower's explanation and proceed with the loan application
    b. Request additional documentation to verify the explanations provided
    c. Report the inconsistencies to your supervisor without further investigation
    d. Advise the borrower to submit a new loan application with accurate information

102. What is one objective of the Secure and Fair Enforcement for Mortgage Licensing (SAFE) Act concerning consumers?

    a. To eliminate the need for mortgage brokers
    b. To require mandatory credit counseling for all borrowers
    c. To provide consumers with information about mortgage loan originators' (MLOs) employment history and disciplinary actions
    d. To establish fixed interest rates for all mortgage loans

103. Under Regulation Z, when does the consummation of a credit transaction occur for a consumer who applies for a mortgage loan?

    a. At the time the consumer submits the mortgage application to the creditor
    b. On the date the creditor approves the consumer's mortgage application
    c. When the consumer signs the promissory note and becomes contractually obligated
    d. After the consumer makes the first mortgage payment

104. Under the Secure and Fair Enforcement for Mortgage Licensing (SAFE) Act for the Nationwide Multistate Licensing System (NMLS) exam, what is the waiting period for subsequent retests after an individual has failed three consecutive tests?

    a. 30 days
    b. 60 days
    c. 90 days
    d. Six months

105. What federal law requires financial institutions to assist U.S. government agencies in detecting and preventing money laundering activities?

    a. USA PATRIOT Act
    b. Dodd-Frank Act
    c. Electronic Signatures in Global and National Commerce Act (E-Sign Act)
    d. Gramm-Leach-Bliley Act (GLBA)

106. Which of the following transactions is NOT considered a finance charge under Regulation Z?

a. Interest on the credit amount
b. Transaction fees
c. Mortgage broker fees
d. Fees for unanticipated late payments

107. What is the purpose of the TILA-RESPA Integrated Disclosure (TRID) rule?

a. To regulate the interest rates on mortgage loans
b. To require lenders to provide a special information booklet to borrowers
c. To provide customers with clear information about their mortgage loan
d. To establish the maximum loan amount for a mortgage loan

108. How often does the NMLS require fingerprints and background checks for mortgage loan originators (MLOs)?

a. Once, during initial registration
b. Annually
c. Every five years
d. Every decade

109. Which of the following statements accurately describes fixed-rate mortgages as a mortgage loan product, considering their key characteristics and benefits?

a. Fixed-rate mortgages typically have higher interest rates compared to adjustable-rate mortgages, providing borrowers with stability and certainty in their monthly payments.
b. Fixed-rate mortgages offer borrowers the flexibility to adjust their interest rates periodically based on market fluctuations, minimizing the risk of interest rate increases.
c. Fixed-rate mortgages are suitable for short-term financing needs, usually with a loan term of five years or less, and often require lower down payments.
d. Fixed-rate mortgages allow borrowers to make interest-only payments for an initial period, providing more financial flexibility during the early years of the loan.

110. Which of the following is NOT typically included in a preliminary title report?

a. Recorded liens and encumbrances
b. Property tax assessment details
c. Easements and right-of-way information
d. Current market value of the property

111. What is the purpose of Regulation Z, also known as the Truth in Lending Act (TILA)?

a. To promote informed use of consumer credit by requiring disclosures about credit terms and costs
b. To regulate financial institutions' reform and enforcement
c. To regulate charges for consumer credit
d. To implement the Real Estate Settlement Procedures Act of 1974

112. Which of the following is NOT included in the limits set for a Qualified Mortgage (QM)?

a. Up-front points and fees charged by the lender
b. Charges for Federal Housing Administration (FHA) insurance premiums
c. The annual percentage rate (APR) for the loan
d. Balloon payments allowed under certain conditions for loans from small lenders

113. Under which regulation are financial institutions required to collect and report data about their mortgage lending activities to help identify potential discriminatory lending practices?

a. Home Mortgage Disclosure Act (HMDA)
b. Bank Secrecy Act/Anti-Money Laundering (BSA/AML)
c. Fair Credit Reporting Act (FCRA)/Fair and Accurate Credit Transactions Act (FACTA)
d. Dodd-Frank Act

114. What information is required to be included in the Loan Estimate provided to borrowers under the TILA-RESPA Integrated Disclosure (TRID) rule?

a. The borrower's credit score
b. An itemization of seller's closing cost
c. The related lender credit
d. The estimated interest rate

115. A borrower provides falsified income documents to a mortgage loan originator (MLO) during the loan application process. What should the MLO do upon discovering this information?

a. Proceed with the application but inform the underwriter about the falsified documents
b. Confront the borrower and insist on accurate documentation
c. Report the borrower to the authorities for providing false information
d. Withdraw the application and terminate all dealings with the borrower

116. What is the purpose of the Special Information Booklet?

a. To provide information about the lender's policies on credit reporting
b. To inform borrowers about their rights and responsibilities during the mortgage process
c. To explain the risks of taking out a mortgage loan
d. To list the contact information for various government agencies related to mortgages

117. What does the loan-to-value (LTV) ratio compare?

a. The amount of the mortgage with the down payment
b. The appraised value of the property with the down payment
c. The appraised value of the property with the total monthly costs
d. The amount of the mortgage with the appraised value of the property

118. To meet the pre-licensing education requirement for loan originators, an individual must complete at least how many hours of training on lending standards for the nontraditional mortgage product marketplace?

a. One hour
b. Two hours
c. Three hours
d. Four hours

119. What type of mortgages allow borrowers to defer payments of principal and, sometimes, interest?

a. Fixed-rate mortgages
b. Conventional mortgages
c. Nontraditional mortgages
d. Government-insured mortgages

120. Which of the following scenarios best reflects ethical behavior related to loan origination activities and financial responsibility in terms of permitted fees/compensation?

    a.   Mortgage loan originator (MLO) John charges borrowers an up-front fee for providing loan application assistance, which is non-refundable regardless of whether the loan is approved or funded.

    b.   MLO Jane discloses all fees and charges to borrowers up front, including origination fees, appraisal fees, and third-party fees, ensuring transparency and avoiding hidden costs.

    c.   MLO Mark receives a referral fee from a real estate agent for directing borrowers to their services without disclosing this arrangement to the borrowers.

    d.   MLO Sarah engages in fee splitting by sharing a portion of her commission with another MLO who referred a borrower to her, without the knowledge or consent of the borrower.

Answer Key and Explanations for Test #2

1. D: The increased amount of $540 for the title insurance fee on the Closing Disclosure (CD) indicates that the fee has changed from the Loan Estimate (LE). However, lenders are allowed a 10 percent tolerance for "good faith" estimates (e.g. recording fees and third-party service fees) between the LE and the CD.

In this scenario, the initial disclosure on the LE stated a title insurance fee of $500. The final amount on the CD is $540, which represents an increase of $40. Since $40 is less than 10 percent of $500, it falls within the permissible tolerance.

Therefore, the lender is within the allowable 10 percent tolerance for title service charges, and the additional $40 charge to Bob is considered acceptable under the TILA-RESPA Integrated Disclosures (TRID) rule.

2. A: The main benefit of having an escrow account for homeowners is the assurance that insurance premiums are always paid on time. The lender or mortgage servicer manages the account, using a portion of the monthly mortgage payment to pay property taxes and insurance when they are due. This prevents lapses in coverage, protects the homeowner's investment in the property, and ensures timely payments for insurance. Other benefits include easier management of mortgage payments and protecting against foreclosure due to unpaid taxes.

3. B: The primary objective of the Federal Trade Commission's Red Flags rule and programs is to identify, prevent, and reduce the impact of identity theft by recognizing and addressing potential warning signs or suspicious patterns of activity, or "red flags". The rule's purpose is to enhance security measures and protect individuals from falling victim to fraudulent practices related to identity theft.

4. A: The main focus of the Department of Housing and Urban Development (HUD) concerning affordable housing programs is to provide grants and subsidies. Although HUD does offer some direct lending programs for specific purposes, its primary role is not to offer direct loans to low-income homebuyers. Instead, it mainly supports affordable housing initiatives through grants and subsidies to organizations and developers.

HUD does not directly regulate mortgage interest rates for affordable housing loans. Interest rates are typically determined by the market and individual lenders, rather than by HUD. The oversight of credit reporting agencies and credit scoring models primarily falls under the jurisdiction of other federal agencies, such as the Consumer Financial Protection Bureau (CFPB) and the Federal Trade Commission (FTC).

5. B: NMLS stands for Nationwide Multistate Licensing System, which is a centralized registry used to track and regulate mortgage loan originators MLOs.

6. A: The home is used as collateral when taking on a home equity line of credit (HELOC), meaning that if you cannot make the payments, there is a risk of losing the home. This makes it crucial for borrowers to consider the potential consequences and ensure they can manage the loan responsibly.

7. B: Under the Real Estate Settlement Procedures Act (RESPA), Regulation X requires that lenders provide borrowers with a Good Faith Estimate (GFE), commonly replaced by the Loan Estimate

(LE). The GFE is a disclosure that outlines the estimated costs and terms associated with the mortgage loan. It must be provided to borrowers within three business days of the loan application. The GFE helps borrowers understand the approximate costs they will incur throughout the loan process, including the loan's interest rate, loan origination fees, appraisal fees, title charges, and other settlement costs. This information allows borrowers to compare loan offers from different lenders and make informed decisions about their mortgage loans.

8. A: Making guarantees or absolute statements about interest rates, such as "lowest mortgage rates guaranteed," can be misleading and unethical. Interest rates are subject to market fluctuations and borrower-specific factors, making such statements unrealistic. The other choices (B, C, and D) do not involve absolute guarantees and are generally compliant with truth in marketing and advertising standards.

9. B: Acceptable donors for a gift in a financial transaction include relatives, domestic partners, individuals engaged to marry the borrower and former relatives. These individuals share a familial relationship with the borrower and are allowed to provide gifts to assist with down payments or closing costs without being considered interested parties in the transaction.

10. A: In compliance with Regulation Z, credit advertisements must only include the terms that the creditor is currently offering or will offer. These advertisements must be accurate and free from any misleading information, ensuring that consumers receive truthful and reliable details about the available or forthcoming credit terms.

11. C: Encumbrances are any claims, liens, or restrictions on a property's title that may affect its transferability. They are essential to identify during the title search and are typically covered by title insurance to protect the buyer and lender from financial losses.

12. A: The primary distinction between a mortgage and a deed of trust is the process of foreclosure in the event of a mortgage default. While both serve as security instruments for loans, a mortgage generally requires a judicial foreclosure process. This entails the lender seeking a court order to initiate foreclosure proceedings, involving the filing of a lawsuit and obtaining a court judgment. In contrast, a deed of trust enables non-judicial foreclosure, wherein the lender can proceed with foreclosure without the need for a court order. Non-judicial foreclosure is typically a more streamlined process, often involving a trustee's sale or auction. This key distinction in foreclosure procedures significantly impacts the timeline and complexity of addressing default situations.

13. B: The purpose of Regulation B is to ensure the availability of credit to creditworthy applicants without discrimination based on race, color, religion, national origin, sex, marital status, or age. To achieve this, Regulation B prohibits creditors from discriminating against applicants based on these protected characteristics during the application and credit evaluation process. Regulation B guarantees that all individuals have an equal opportunity to obtain credit if they meet the creditworthiness criteria and other applicable requirements, without facing unfair or biased treatment. Additionally, Regulation B requires creditors to provide applicants with specific disclosures and notices, informing them of their rights and protections under the law, thereby enhancing transparency and fairness in the credit application process.

14. C: The Real Estate Settlement Procedures Act (RESPA) prohibits giving or receiving kickbacks, referral fees, or unearned fees in connection with real estate settlement services. It aims to protect consumers from being exploited in the homebuying and mortgage process.

15. A: When a creditor undertakes adverse action against an applicant, in accordance with the Equal Credit Opportunity Act (ECOA), it is obligated to furnish the applicant with an adverse action notice (AAN). This notice should encompass crucial details that inform the applicant about the grounds for the adverse action and their associated rights. This practice upholds openness and fairness in the lending process. The AAN should explicitly state the rationale behind the adverse action and duly apprise the applicant of their right to request an explanation within a period of 60 days. This provision empowers the applicant to comprehend the basis for the adverse action and potentially address any discrepancies or concerns that may have arisen. Additionally, if adverse action is implemented, as defined by the ECOA and Regulation B, the creditor is required to provide an AAN that discloses the factors contributing to the adverse action and, if a credit score was utilized, the key elements negatively impacting the score.

16. A: Coercion in the lending process refers to using threats or intimidation to force a borrower into accepting specific loan terms or engaging in a mortgage transaction. It is considered unethical and a prohibited act.

17. A: The Federal Emergency Management Agency (FEMA) is the government agency responsible for administering the National Flood Insurance Program (NFIP). The NFIP offers flood insurance policies to property owners in participating communities to help them recover from flood damages and mitigate future risks.

18. A: Fannie Mae does not directly originate mortgage loans for borrowers; instead, it collaborates with mortgage lenders and acquires the mortgage loans they originate. Once acquired, these loans are grouped into mortgage-backed securities, enhancing liquidity in the secondary mortgage market. This mechanism enables lenders to sustain their provision of mortgage loans to a wider audience, thereby broadening access to mortgage financing.

19. C: Hazard insurance, commonly referred to as homeowner's insurance, provides coverage for a borrower's personal belongings and property in the event of damage caused by hazards such as fire, theft, vandalism, or severe weather events. It is distinct from PMI, which safeguards the lender in the event of borrower default on the mortgage. Force-placed insurance refers to an insurance category that lenders can acquire and include in a borrower's mortgage payment when the borrower's existing insurance coverage lapses or is found to be inadequate. On the other hand, government mortgage insurance, like Federal Housing Administration (FHA) or Department of Veterans Affairs (VA) mortgage insurance, offers safeguards to lenders in situations of borrower loan default, but it does not extend coverage to a borrower's personal possessions or property damage.

20. A: Subprime mortgages differ significantly from prime mortgages in terms of borrower profile and structure. Subprime mortgages target borrowers with lower credit scores, resulting in higher interest rates, often exceeding 10 percent. Lenders typically demand a larger down payment, ranging from 25 percent to 35 percent, to offset the increased risk involved in lending to lower-credit-score borrowers.

On the other hand, prime mortgages cater to highly qualified borrowers with good to excellent credit scores. They may offer more flexible terms and lower interest rates, making them an appealing option for borrowers eligible for conventional loans. The key distinctions between these two mortgage types revolve around borrower qualifications and the associated loan terms and conditions.

21. A: Under the Secure and Fair Enforcement for Mortgage Licensing (SAFE) Act, mortgage loan originators (MLOs) must provide fingerprints for an FBI criminal history background check to ensure suitability for loan origination activities. MLOs are required to complete annual continuing education, but the required hours vary depending on the state of licensure. Typically, education includes three hours of federal law, two hours of ethics, two hours of nontraditional mortgage products, and one hour of electives and/or state-specific education.

It is important to note that while credit scores may be considered by some employers, the SAFE Act does not mandate a specific credit score requirement for MLOs.

22. C: According to Regulation X, changed circumstances include acts of God, war, disasters, or other emergencies that significantly impact the settlement cost information provided in the Good Faith Estimate (GFE). Examples can encompass unforeseen events such as natural disasters (e.g., earthquakes, hurricanes, or floods), civil unrest, or unforeseeable accidents. However, it is important to note that typical circumstances such as market fluctuations or personal situations (e.g., changes in personal finances or employment status) are not considered changed circumstances under Regulation X and would not qualify for a revised GFE. The regulation focuses on events beyond the control of the parties involved in the real estate transaction, affecting the settlement costs and triggering the need for a revised GFE.

23. C: The notice of transfer to the borrower should occur no less than 15 days before the effective date of the transfer of the servicing of the mortgage loan. This requirement is aimed at giving the borrower adequate time to prepare for the transfer of servicing and to become aware of the new servicer who will be handling their mortgage loan. By receiving the notice at least 15 days in advance, the borrower can make any necessary adjustments in their payment arrangements and address any concerns or questions they may have about the upcoming change.

24. A: Regulation X defines "application" as the borrower submitting financial information with the expectation of obtaining a credit decision for a federally related mortgage loan. This application includes specific components such as the borrower's name, monthly income, Social Security number, property address, estimate of the property value, mortgage loan amount sought, and any other information deemed necessary by the loan originator.

25. C: To maintain security and protect sensitive borrower information, the mortgage loan originator (MLO) should have stored the credit report in a secure location, such as a locked filing cabinet. Leaving it unattended in a publicly accessible area could risk unauthorized access to the report.

26. D: Under the FCRA, consumers have the right to receive a complimentary copy of their credit report from the three major credit reporting agencies (Equifax, Experian, and TransUnion) once every 12 months. This enables consumers to review their credit information and dispute any inaccuracies they may find.

27. C: To calculate the Debt-to-Income (DTI) ratio, divide the total monthly debt payments by the gross monthly income and multiply by 100 to express it as a percentage. In this case, the DTI ratio is ($2,500/$6,000) × 100 = 41.67%.

28. C: Predatory lending and steering involve practices that take advantage of vulnerable borrowers, often leading them into loans they cannot afford or do not understand. In this scenario, the mortgage loan originator's (MLO) action represents predatory lending since they knowingly proceed with a loan application for a borrower who is unlikely to qualify, putting the borrower at risk of entering into an unaffordable loan.

29. B: When a loan is assumed, the new borrower becomes fully responsible for the repayment of the debt and any default consequences, even though the original borrower may have transferred the loan. The new borrower is essentially taking on the loan "as is", with its remaining balance, interest rate, and terms.

By assuming the loan, the new borrower gains the benefit of the existing loan terms, which can be advantageous if the current interest rates are higher than the rate on the assumed loan. However, it is essential for the new borrower to fully understand the terms of the assumed loan and the potential risks involved. If the new borrower defaults on the loan, the lender can pursue collection actions, which may include foreclosure, to recover the outstanding debt. The original borrower, while no longer responsible for making payments, may still be affected if the new borrower defaults, as it could impact their credit history and financial standing.

30. D: The Federal Housing Administration (FHA) indirectly supports homebuyers through its mortgage insurance programs, offering insurance coverage to lenders. This insurance safeguards lenders in the event of borrower defaults, mitigating lenders' risks and empowering them to extend more mortgages to homebuyers. As a result, a greater number of homebuyers become eligible for loans and gain access to affordable financing options. However, it is important to note that the FHA does not directly provide low-interest loans, down payment assistance, or no-down-payment options to borrowers.

31. C: The points are calculated as a percentage of the total loan amount, not the sales price. The loan amount can be calculated by subtracting the down payment from the sales price: $150,000 (sales price) - $15,000 (down payment) = $135,000 (total loan amount). Each point costs the borrower 1% of the total loan amount, which is $135,000 × 0.02 = $2,700. Since there are 2 discount points and 2 points for loan origination fees, the total cost of the points is 4 × $2,700 = $5,400.

32. B: A subordination clause in a mortgage establishes the priority of the lender's lien above all other liens on the house. In the event of default, the lender with the subordination clause holds the right to reclaim the property and settle their loan's outstanding balance before addressing any other liens.

33. C: A balloon payment refers to a larger-than-usual one-time payment required at the conclusion of the loan term. Although it allows for reduced monthly payments during the loan, borrowers must be prepared for the significant lump sum payment when it becomes due. This payment can pose risks, especially if the borrower's financial situation has not improved as anticipated or if property values decrease. To safeguard borrowers from potential financial challenges upon the balloon payment's maturity, Qualified Mortgages (QMs) generally disallow balloon payments, with some exceptions.

34. B: The right of rescission period commences on the first business day after the borrower signs the promissory note and receives the Truth in Lending Act (TILA) disclosure document and the two copies of the right to rescind notice. The right of recission period is three business days. Saturdays are considered business days, while Sundays and holidays are not. Consequently, if the borrower signs the documents on Thursday, the first business day would be Friday, and the right of rescission period would extend until the end of the following Monday (midnight).

35. D: Regulation Z designates the term "number of payments" as a triggering term in credit advertisements. Whenever this term appears in an advertisement, additional disclosures become necessary to offer consumers a more comprehensive understanding of the credit terms being presented. These required disclosures entail specific information, including the downpayment amount or percentage, repayment terms, and any applicable finance charges. The objective of

Regulation Z is to foster transparency, enabling consumers to make informed decisions when evaluating different credit options.

36. D: In a reverse mortgage, the loan balance experiences an incremental rise over time, due to the accumulation of interest and associated fees that are added monthly. Unlike traditional mortgage scenarios, where monthly payments reduce the loan balance, a reverse mortgage functions inversely. As interest accrues and fees are compounded, the outstanding loan amount gradually increases. Consequently, this ongoing augmentation of the loan balance results in a decrease in home equity as the loan balance expands, potentially impacting the overall financial landscape for borrowers over the life of the loan. This unique characteristic of reverse mortgages underscores the importance of careful consideration and planning for individuals exploring this financial option.

37. B: Fannie Mae sets the maximum total DTI ratio at 36 percent of the borrower's stable monthly income for manually underwritten loans. However, this maximum can be surpassed, up to 45 percent, if the borrower meets the credit score and reserve requirements.

38. D: A balloon mortgage is a type of mortgage loan that features lower monthly payments for a fixed period, followed by a large "balloon" payment at the end of the loan term. This payment structure may provide borrowers with more affordable monthly payments during the initial phase of the loan. However, it is important to be aware of the potential risks associated with balloon mortgages. Failing to make the balloon payment at the end of the loan term can lead to financial difficulties or the need to refinance the loan. In some cases, it can even result in foreclosure.

39. D: A "bait-and-switch" practice in loan origination occurs when a lender changes the terms of the loan after the borrower has applied without a valid reason. This deceptive practice is prohibited and can lead to legal and regulatory consequences.

40. B: The Front-End debt-to-income (DTI) ratio focuses on the proposed mortgage payment only. It is used to assess the borrower's ability to make timely mortgage payments and manage mortgage-related expenses. The Back-End DTI ratio, on the other hand, considers all monthly debt obligations, including the proposed mortgage payment.

41. C: When appraising income-generating properties, such as commercial buildings that generate rental income, appraisers frequently employ the income approach. This approach takes into account the property's capacity to generate income over time, involving an analysis of rental income, operating expenses, and capitalization rates. While the other approaches (Market approach, Cost approach, and Market data approach) may be utilized in various appraisal scenarios, they are less relevant to the evaluation of income-producing properties.

42. C: The answer explanation should change to: C: According to mortgage company compliance regulations, a seven-year waiting period is generally required from the completion date of a foreclosure before a borrower can be eligible for a new conventional loan. Since the borrower's foreclosure was completed five years ago, they need to wait an additional two years before applying for a new mortgage. Extenuating circumstances could reduce the waiting period, but that is not applicable in this scenario. Proceeding with the loan application without considering the waiting period (choice A) or advising the borrower to wait for only one more year (choice B) would not be compliant with the waiting period requirements. Seeking legal advice (choice D) is unnecessary in this case since the waiting period is clearly defined by the regulations.

43. B: As per the Equal Credit Opportunity Act (ECOA), a creditor is required to furnish applicants with copies of all appraisals and other written valuations prepared concerning a credit application that will be secured by a first lien on a residential property. The creditor must provide the copy promptly upon completion, or at least three business days before the loan closing (for closed-end credit) or account opening (for open-end credit), whichever comes first. However, applicants have the option to waive the timing requirement and agree to receive the copy at or before the loan closing or account opening, except where prohibited by law. If the applicant provides such a waiver and the loan or account is not finalized, the creditor must provide the copies within 30 days of determining that the loan will not be closed, or the account will not be opened.

44. C: Michael is providing false information about his job status and income to secure a mortgage under false pretenses. This type of fraud involves misrepresenting details related to employment history, job title, and income to deceive the lender into offering more favorable loan terms than he would qualify for based on his true employment situation.

45. A: The mortgage loan originator (MLO) should promptly refund the amount overcharged to the borrower. Keeping the extra funds or transferring them to the MLO's personal account would be unethical and violates financial responsibility standards.

46. A: An open-end credit plan, as defined in Regulation Z, is a credit plan that allows consumers to make repeated transactions up to a certain credit limit. Unlike closed-end credit plans, which are typically used for a single purpose and have fixed repayment terms, open-end credit plans are more flexible. In an open-end credit plan, consumers can borrow, repay, and borrow again, up to the predetermined credit limit, without having to reapply for credit each time they need funds.

47. C: The interest-only payment is calculated by multiplying the loan amount of $220,000 by the annual interest rate of 5.5% and dividing by 12 monthly payments (($220,000 × .055)/12 = $1,008.33 per month). Next, the taxes are quoted per half-year, so this amount is divided by 6 and not 12 ($1,500/6 = $250 per month). The hazard insurance is quoted annually, so it must be divided by 12 ($400/12 = $33.33 per month). The mortgage insurance is quoted monthly ($50 per month). By adding these monthly amounts together, the total monthly payment is derived: $1,008.33 + $250 + $33.33 + $50 = $1,341.66 total monthly payment.

48. C: Less than two years of income history may be acceptable when the applicant provides sound justification, such as in cases where the applicant's compensation changed from hourly to salary income with the same employer in a similar job/position. In such situations, the Loan Originator may consider the income to be dependable and stable, even with less than two years of history. However, for most applicants, two years of income history is required to ensure a reasonable determination of income and financial stability.

49. B: Redlining is a prohibited act in the mortgage lending industry that involves denying or limiting access to credit or loan products based on the geographic location of individuals, such as specific neighborhoods or communities. It is considered unethical and discriminatory. Redlining was made illegal under the Fair Housing Act of 1968, which prohibits housing-related discrimination based on various factors. The practice of redlining perpetuates inequalities, contributes to neighborhood segregation, and hampers economic development. Laws and regulations aim to combat redlining and promote fair and equal access to housing and credit opportunities for all individuals.

50. C: Down payment = Purchase price × Down payment percentage. Down payment = $250,000 × 0.20 = $50,000.

51. C: A power of attorney (POA) is a legally binding document that authorizes a chosen individual, known as the agent, to act on behalf of and oversee various aspects of the real estate transaction, representing the borrower's interests and facilitating the completion of the transaction. This written authorization empowers the agent to carry out specific tasks and sign essential documents related to the transaction, such as the note and security instrument. The agent's actions under the POA are legally effective and enforceable, allowing them to streamline the transaction process, hold the borrower responsible, and work with the lender to complete the transaction successfully. It is important to note that a POA can play a vital role in ensuring the smooth execution of the real estate transaction and protecting the interests of all parties involved.

52. D: Most conventional home loans are generally not eligible for assumption. In contrast to Federal Housing Administration (FHA), Department of Veterans Affairs (VA), and United States Department of Agriculture (USDA) loans, which have specific conditions allowing for assumption, conventional mortgages typically do not permit the buyer to take over the seller's pre-existing mortgage arrangement.

Assumable loans refer to those that can be transferred from the seller to the buyer, enabling the buyer to adopt the existing loan terms. FHA, VA, and USDA loans might have particular criteria and qualifying factors that facilitate assumption. Conversely, conventional mortgages, which lack government backing, often include due-on-sale clauses mandating complete loan repayment upon property transfer. As a result, the opportunity for assumption is less prevalent with conventional mortgages compared to government-backed loan options.

53. C: The Equal Credit Opportunity Act (ECOA) and its regulations are in place to promote fairness and prevent discrimination in credit transactions. According to these regulations, creditors are explicitly forbidden from considering an applicant's marital status in any part of a credit transaction. A creditor cannot assess married and unmarried applicants differently, nor can they treat joint applicants differently based on their marital relationship. The ECOA ensures that all applicants are treated equally, regardless of their marital status, and prevents any discriminatory practices during the credit evaluation process.

54. D: The Consumer Financial Protection Bureau (CFPB) is committed to protecting consumers from unfair and deceptive practices in the financial marketplace. One of the essential functions of the CFPB is to handle and address consumer complaints related to financial products and services. The CFPB processes and reviews consumer complaints, contacting the companies involved to investigate and seek resolution. By working with financial institutions, the CFPB aims to address consumer grievances and prevent similar issues from recurring. Additionally, the CFPB publishes complaint data, making it publicly available to raise awareness about common consumer concerns and promote transparency in the financial industry.

55. A: To ensure the independence and objectivity of the valuation process, anyone involved must have no personal or financial interest in the property or transaction. This prevents potential compromises to the integrity of the valuation and helps maintain credibility and fairness in the process.

56. B: Fees for necessary services that consumers can compare and select from a provided list are classified under the zero-tolerance threshold. Within the zero-tolerance category, fees pertain to services under the creditor's control or those with accessible actual fee amounts. Creditors are required to provide precise and accurate information without any tolerance cushion. When consumers choose a service provider from the creditor's list, it is not considered shopping for that service. Any fee increase for such services from the Loan Estimate to the Closing Disclosure would constitute a violation of tolerance requirements.

57. B: Under the TILA-RESPA Integrated Disclosure (TRID) rule, it is crucial for mortgage loan originators (MLOs) and lenders to provide accurate and complete disclosures to borrowers. If the MLO becomes aware of any inaccuracies or omissions in the initial disclosure, they must take immediate action to provide a revised and corrected disclosure to the borrower. This revised disclosure should reflect the accurate and complete information related to loan terms, costs, and other important details. Providing the borrower with a revised disclosure as soon as possible helps to ensure that the borrower has the correct information and is fully informed before proceeding with the loan.

58. D: The loan-to-value (LTV) ratio is calculated by dividing the loan amount by the appraised value of the property and then multiplying by 100 to express it as a percentage.

LTV Ratio = (Loan Amount/Appraised Value) × 100. In this case: Loan Amount = $200,000 - $40,000 (down payment) = $160,000. Appraised Value = $180,000. Now, calculate the LTV ratio: LTV Ratio = ($160,000/$180,000) × 100 = 88.89%.

59. B: Certain circumstances may allow a borrower to extend their right of rescission timeline up to three years. If the borrower can prove that they never received the closing disclosure or two copies of the notice of right to rescind, or if these documents were inaccurate, they may have an extended rescission period.

60. B: The sponsorship requirement ensures that mortgage loan originators (MLOs) operate under the oversight of their employers, promoting ethical conduct and compliance. Employers are held accountable for their MLOs' actions, discouraging fraudulent practices and safeguarding consumers. This arrangement enhances regulatory control and, in many cases, encourages mentorship and professional growth for MLOs.

61. A: The primary mortgage market is where borrowers directly obtain mortgages from lenders, such as banks, credit unions, and online mortgage companies. This market involves the initial borrowing process, where homebuyers or refinancers work with lenders to secure a home, land, or business loan.

62. C: Mortgage servicing companies are responsible for collecting loan payments and managing escrow accounts. They do not generally originate loans, so they are not required to have licensed mortgage loan originators (MLOs).

63. D: The Consumer Financial Protection Bureau (CFPB) is the agency responsible for implementing and enforcing the Real Estate Settlement Procedures Act (RESPA). This regulatory framework aims to protect consumers from unethical practices, such as kickbacks and referral fees, in real estate transactions. The CFPB ensures that consumers receive transparent disclosures about settlement costs, allowing them to make informed decisions during the home buying process. Through its enforcement efforts, CFPB safeguards the interests of homebuyers and promotes fair and ethical practices within the real estate industry.

64. B: Lenders view jumbo loans as riskier due to their exceeding the maximum loan amounts established. Consequently, these loans are ineligible for government-sponsored enterprise guarantees, putting the lenders at risk of potential losses if a borrower defaults. In contrast, conventional conforming loans supported by these entities offer lenders a more secure investment. The absence of government backing is a significant factor contributing to the perception of jumbo loans as riskier for lenders.

65. C: Within three business days of receiving the loan application, or adequate information to complete it, a lender, mortgage broker, or dealer is required to furnish the loan applicant with a clear and conspicuous written list of homeownership counseling organizations. Here are a few homeownership counseling organizations that borrowers might find useful:

NeighborWorks America (www.neighborworks.org)

Housing and Urban Development (HUD) Approved Housing Counseling Agencies (www.hud.gov)

National Foundation for Credit Counseling (NFCC) (www.nfcc.org)

66. B: "Adverse action" refers to a refusal to grant credit in the amount or terms requested based on information in a borrower's credit report. This means that if a borrower applies for a loan or credit and the lender decides not to approve the application (or offers credit on less favorable terms than the borrower requested), then the lender's response is considered an adverse action. When an adverse action is taken, the lender must provide the borrower with a written notice explaining the reasons for the decision, including information about the credit reporting agency used to obtain the credit report and the borrower's right to obtain a free copy of the report. This requirement is part of the Equal Credit Opportunity Act (ECOA), which is implemented through Regulation B to protect consumers from discrimination in the credit application process. Providing borrowers with the reasons for the adverse action allows them to review their credit report, identify any inaccuracies or issues, and take steps to improve their creditworthiness in the future.

67. B: For most conventional mortgage loans, the suggested maximum debt-to-income (DTI) ratio is 36 percent. This implies that a borrower's overall monthly debt payments, inclusive of the proposed mortgage payment, should not surpass 36 percent of their gross monthly income. Nonetheless, certain government-backed loans may permit higher DTI ratios.

68. D: The mortgage loan originator (MLO) must decline the referral fee. Keeping the referral fee as personal income or using it for personal expenses would be a violation of financial responsibility standards.

69. D: Occupancy fraud takes place when a borrower deceitfully claims that they will occupy a property as their primary residence but intends to use it as an investment property or for rental income purposes. In this specific case, the purchase of a second home in a vacation destination has a high potential for occupancy fraud to obtain lower interest rates.

70. C: Non-QM loans are mortgages that fall outside the Consumer Financial Protection Bureau's (CFPB) criteria for qualified mortgages (QM). QMs are loans that adhere to the CFPB's "ability to repay" rule, typically featuring standard attributes like fixed interest rates. Conversely, non-QM loans offer greater flexibility and may incorporate riskier features, such as interest-only payments, negative amortization, and balloon payments, which are not commonly found in QM loans.

71. B: Discount points serve as a mortgage lending tool that permits borrowers to pay an up-front fee to lower their interest rate. The cost of each discount point is determined as a percentage of the loan amount.

For instance, a borrower taking out a $200,000 mortgage and choosing to pay one discount point would incur a cost of one percent of $200,000, which is $2,000. This $2,000 up-front payment would typically result in a reduction of the mortgage's interest rate, usually by approximately 0.25 percent to 0.50 percent, depending on the lender and prevailing market conditions.

Opting to pay discount points involves weighing up-front costs against long-term savings. By paying points, the borrower lowers the interest rate, subsequently reducing the monthly mortgage payments. This can lead to significant interest savings throughout the loan's duration. However, borrowers should carefully evaluate their financial situation and their anticipated length of stay in the property before deciding whether to pay discount points.

72. C: Borrowers typically receive the Loan Estimate as part of the TILA-RESPA Integrated Disclosure (TRID) no later than three days after filing an application for a loan. This disclosure combines the previous Truth-In-Lending Statement and the Good Faith Estimate, providing borrowers with essential information about the costs and risks of the mortgage.

73. B: The government sets the maximum loan amounts for conforming loans, while other rules for these loans are set by Fannie Mae or Freddie Mac.

74. C: An individual may take the written test developed by the Nationwide Multistate Licensing System and Registry (NMLSR) up to three consecutive times to achieve a test score of at least 75 percent correct answers. Each retest must occur at least 30 days after the preceding test. If the individual fails three consecutive tests, they must wait at least six months before taking the test again.

75. D: Per Regulation X, the required pieces of information for a loan originator to collect to issue a Good Faith Estimate (GFE) include the borrower's name, gross monthly income, Social Security number, property address, estimate of property value, and the mortgage loan amount requested. However, the borrower's employment history is not required until the loan has reached the underwriting stages.

76. C: Calculate the total closing costs: Closing Costs = 4% of the purchase price = (4 × $200,000)/100 = $8,000. Calculate the seller's contribution towards closing costs: Seller Contribution = 2% of the purchase price = (2 × $200,000)/100 = $4,000. Calculate the remaining closing costs to be paid by the borrower: Remaining Closing Costs = Closing Costs - Seller Contribution Remaining Closing Costs = $8,000 - $4,000 = $4,000. Calculate the desired loan amount (to achieve an LTV of 85%): Desired Loan Amount = 85% of the purchase price = (85 × $200,000)/100 = $170,000. Calculate the cash needed by the borrower at closing: Cash Needed = Purchase Price - Desired Loan Amount + Remaining Closing Costs Cash Needed = $200,000 - $170,000 + $4,000 = $34,000.

77. D: While changes in down payments typically do not directly impact interest rates, it is essential to inform the borrower that some lenders might offer rate adjustments based on down payment size. By suggesting that the borrower discusses the specifics with the lender, the mortgage loan originator (MLO) ensures that the borrower receives accurate and tailored information while maintaining ethical behavior.

78. C: Accepting monetary gifts from a real estate agent for referrals is considered fee splitting, which is generally prohibited in mortgage lending. In this scenario, you must decline such gifts (choice C) to avoid ethical and compliance violations. Choices A and B involve accepting the gifts, which would be unethical. Choice D is not necessary when the proper course of action is clear.

79. C: The yield spread premium (YSP) is determined by calculating the variance between the par rate (also referred to as the zero point rate) and the interest rate presented on the loan. It signifies the remuneration that the mortgage broker obtains for selling a higher interest rate to the borrower.

80. B: Removal of mortgage insurance can be requested when the balance of the mortgage is at 80 percent of the original purchase price but won't automatically happen until the balance reaches 78 percent. In this case, John's loan balance is 80 percent of the original purchase price, therefore he is eligible to request that the monthly mortgage insurance be removed.

81. B: New interest rate = Index rate + Margin = 2.5% + 2% = 4.5%. The lifetime cap of 6% is how much the maximum amount the interest rate could be but since 4.5% is less than the 6% cap that will be the new interest rate in this example.

82. D: A 15-year fixed-rate mortgage generally features lower interest rates compared to a 30-year mortgage. This leads to greater interest savings over the loan's lifetime due to its shorter amortization period. While the monthly payments for a 15-year mortgage may be higher, it proves to be a suitable choice for individuals seeking to build equity and repay their home loan swiftly.

83. C: While choices A, B, and D involve important functions within the realm of financial regulation and oversight, they do not specifically represent the main function of the Consumer Financial Protection Bureau (CFPB). The primary role of the CFPB is to safeguard consumers in the financial marketplace from unfair, deceptive, and abusive practices perpetrated by financial institutions and service providers. The CFPB achieves this by enforcing regulations that ensure transparent terms on loans and credit cards, investigating and addressing consumer complaints, monitoring credit reporting agencies for accuracy, and conducting supervisory examinations of financial entities to ensure compliance with consumer protection laws. Through these measures, the CFPB works to create a fair and accountable financial environment for consumers.

84. D: Redlining involves the discriminatory practice of denying or limiting access to mortgage products based on factors such as race, color, national origin, or other protected characteristics. The term "redlining" comes from the literal practice of drawing red lines on maps to delineate areas where loans or services would be withheld or restricted.

85. D: The "Notice of the right to rescind" is excluded from electronic signatures as per the E-Sign Act. This disclosure is issued to borrowers in specific loan transactions, apprising them of their right to cancel the loan within a designated timeframe after completion. Maintaining this notice in a conventional paper format ensures borrowers can readily review and comprehend their rights, upholding consumer protection and lending transparency.

86. B: As a part of fraud detection and prevention, the mortgage loan originator should not ignore suspicious activities in the bank statements. They should advise the borrower to explain these activities and provide additional documentation to support the source of the funds or transactions. This ensures transparency and helps in the proper assessment of the borrower's financial situation.

87. B: The mortgage company should inform the borrower of the interest rate increase and provide clear reasons for the change. This is required to maintain transparency and fairness in lending practices.

88. B: To calculate Sarah's estimated monthly qualifying income, we need to determine her gross monthly income from her hourly job. Calculate the Weekly Income: Weekly Income = Hourly Wage × Weekly Hours. Weekly Income = $15 × 25 = $375. Calculate the Estimated Monthly Income: Estimated Monthly Income = Weekly Income × Number of Weeks in a Year / 12. Estimated Monthly Income = ($375 × 52)/12 = $1,625.

89. C: A consumer loan with a fixed interest rate, payable in one installment, does not meet the conditions outlined in Regulation Z (more than four installments) and is, therefore, excluded from the regulation's coverage. Other choices, such as credit card accounts and mortgage transactions, typically involve multiple installments and would fall under the scope of Regulation Z.

90. D: A Graduated Payment Mortgage (GPM) is typically suitable for borrowers who expect their income to increase substantially in the future. GPMs start with lower initial payments that gradually increase over time. This structure allows borrowers with lower current income to afford homeownership while anticipating higher earnings in the future. As their income rises, borrowers can better manage the increasing mortgage payments over the life of the loan.

91. C: The promissory note is a legally binding document that obligates the borrower to repay the mortgage loan. It includes vital details such as the loan amount, interest rate, payment dates, and the terms and conditions of the loan. Through signing the promissory note, the borrower consents to the loan terms and acknowledges their commitment to making regular payments. It also delineates the repercussions for missed payments, which may involve penalties and the potential initiation of foreclosure proceedings by the lender.

92. C: The borrower has the right to rescind or cancel certain types of mortgage loans within three business days after loan consummation. This right applies to transactions where the mortgage is secured by the borrower's principal dwelling, and the loan is not used to purchase the property. It mainly applies to home equity loans, home equity lines of credit (HELOCs), and refinance loans.

Within the three-business-day rescission period, the borrower retains the freedom to cancel the loan for any reason by submitting written notice to the lender. Should the borrower exercise this right, the lender must refund any fees previously paid by the borrower and release the security interest in the property. It is crucial to bear in mind that not all mortgage transactions are subject to the rescission right, and it may not be applicable to purchase loans or loans obtained to acquire the borrower's primary residence.

93. D: The origination fee typically covers costs related to processing, underwriting, and documentation. Mortgage insurance premiums are separate fees paid for insuring the loan against default and are not part of the origination fee.

94. B: If a borrower rescinds their mortgage within the three-day rescission period, the lender has 20 days to cancel the loan process and refund all fees. The borrower will also have to return any funds received from the lender.

95. B: The main advantage of a Purchase-Money Second Mortgage is that it helps the buyer avoid paying Private Mortgage Insurance (PMI) on loans with a loan-to-value (LTV) greater than 80 percent, as the second mortgage makes up the difference in required funds to keep the first mortgage below the 80 percent LTV threshold.

96. C: The Real Estate Settlement Procedures Act (RESPA) is a federal law that aims to protect consumers in residential real estate transactions by providing them with certain disclosures and protections. However, not all types of loans are covered by RESPA. One category of loans that is exempt from RESPA requirements is business purpose loans (choice C). These loans are primarily intended for commercial or agricultural purposes, meaning they are used to finance business-related activities rather than for personal, family, or household purposes.

Loans secured by vacant or unimproved property (choice A) are not exempt from RESPA requirements. These loans, also known as lot loans, are typically used to purchase or refinance vacant land or unimproved properties.

Loans used for the construction of residential properties (choice B) are also not exempt from RESPA. These loans are specifically designed to finance the construction of residential homes and are subject to RESPA regulations.

Loans subject to prepayment penalties (choice D) are not automatically exempt from RESPA requirements. RESPA does not specifically address prepayment penalties, but it does regulate certain loan servicing practices, including the disclosure of fees and charges related to the loan.

97. A: This scenario represents a kickback or compensation situation, where the mortgage loan originator (MLO) is encouraging borrowers to use the services of a real estate company in which the MLO has a financial interest. This type of arrangement is prohibited, as it can create a conflict of interest and compromise the MLO's objectivity.

98. A: As part of the "Know Before You Owe" regulations, lenders are obligated to furnish borrowers with a comprehensive closing disclosure, detailing the final loan terms and associated costs. This disclosure must be provided to borrowers at least three business days prior to the scheduled loan closing. The three-day window offers borrowers sufficient time to thoroughly review the finalized loan terms and gain a clear understanding of all expenses related to the loan agreement before committing. Moreover, borrowers can utilize this period to compare the closing disclosure with the initial Loan Estimate received during the application process, ensuring consistency in the terms. By providing borrowers with this ample time frame, the "Know Before You Owe" rules aim to promote transparency and empower borrowers to make well-informed decisions about their mortgage transactions.

99. D: An Adjustable Rate Mortgage (ARM) is characterized by its variable interest rate, which is determined by the combination of an index and a margin. The index represents broader economic trends and influences interest rate fluctuations, while the margin is a constant value added to the index by the lender to cover their costs and profit. This dynamic combination results in periodic adjustments to the interest rate, making ARMs distinct from fixed-rate mortgages. The interest rate's variability is a key feature of ARMs, impacting borrowers' monthly payments and the overall cost of the loan over time.

100. D: The mortgage lender's failure to reveal specific terms and conditions alongside a low-interest rate promotion could potentially breach consumer protection regulations by engaging in "unfair, deceptive, or abusive acts" in advertising. This omission of essential information might mislead borrowers, highlighting the significance of transparent and complete disclosure in financial advertisements.

101. B: Ethical behavior requires mortgage loan originators (MLOs) to verify the accuracy of information provided by borrowers. Choice B reflects the appropriate course of action to ensure compliance and prevent fraudulent practices. Accepting the explanations without verification (choice A) or ignoring the irregularities (choice C) would not be ethical. Choice D is also incorrect because it suggests advising the borrower to submit a new loan application with accurate information. While encouraging accurate information is important, this option does not directly address the existing irregularities or provide a comprehensive solution to the situation.

102. C: The Secure and Fair Enforcement for Mortgage Licensing (SAFE) Act aims to enhance consumer protections by providing easily accessible information about mortgage loan originators' (MLOs) employment history and any publicly adjudicated disciplinary and enforcement actions. This empowers consumers to make informed decisions when engaging with MLOs and ensures transparency in the mortgage lending process. By offering information about the professional background and conduct of MLOs, the SAFE Act helps consumers avoid potential risks and promotes accountability within the mortgage industry.

103. C: The consummation of a credit transaction for a consumer who applies for a mortgage loan occurs when the consumer signs the promissory note and becomes contractually obligated to the terms of the loan. This moment is when the legal commitment to repay the loan is established and the credit transaction is considered consummated. It is important to note that consummation does not depend on the approval or funding of the loan by the creditor.

104. D: According to the Secure and Fair Enforcement for Mortgage Licensing (SAFE) Act exam rules, after failing three consecutive tests, an individual must wait for a period of at least six months before being eligible to take the test again. This waiting period allows the individual to reassess their knowledge, address any areas of weakness, and adequately prepare for the retake. It is important to adhere to the waiting period requirements to ensure a fair and thorough evaluation process.

105. A: The USA PATRIOT Act, a significant federal law aimed at countering terrorism and enhancing national security, amended the Bank Secrecy Act to require financial institutions to actively assist U.S. government agencies in detecting and preventing money laundering. This obligation entails reporting suspicious transactions and maintaining comprehensive records, while also necessitating the establishment of robust Anti-Money Laundering (AML) programs within financial institutions. These programs involve closely monitoring customer activities to identify potential signs of money laundering. By complying with the PATRIOT Act's requirements, financial institutions reinforce customer trust and play a pivotal role in maintaining the security of the global financial system. This is achieved through a proactive approach that deters illicit financial activities and contributes to the overall integrity of the financial sector.

106. D: Unanticipated late payment fees are excluded from being considered finance charges under Regulation Z. Finance charges are costs that a borrower must pay as a condition of obtaining credit, and they are typically imposed uniformly on both credit and cash transactions. However, fees for unanticipated late payments are not anticipated at the time the credit is extended and are not a condition for obtaining credit. These fees are specific to individual instances of late payment and are not imposed uniformly, making them exempt from the definition of finance charges. Regulation Z aims to provide clear guidelines on what constitutes a finance charge to ensure transparency and fairness in consumer credit transactions. By excluding unanticipated late payment fees, the regulation helps protect consumers from unexpected and potentially unfair charges that may arise in the event of delayed or missed payments.

107. C: The purpose of the TILA-RESPA Integrated Disclosure (TRID) rule is to combine certain disclosures that consumers receive in connection with applying for and closing on a mortgage loan under TILA and RESPA, streamlining the process and making it easier for consumers to understand loan terms and fees.

108. A: Mortgage loan originators (MLOs) are required to undergo fingerprinting and background checks once during the initial registration process in the NMLS. Fingerprinting and background check requirements may vary from state to state, but all MLOs are required to have fingerprinting and background checks performed for initial licensure.

109. A: Fixed-rate mortgages have a consistent interest rate throughout the loan term, offering stability and predictability in monthly payments. Unlike adjustable-rate mortgages, fixed-rate mortgages provide a constant amount of payment. They are popular due to their assurance of a steady rate, distinguishing them from adjustable-rate mortgages (choice B) that allow interest rate adjustments based on market fluctuations. While fixed-rate mortgages typically have higher interest rates, this is compensated for by the stability they offer. Options like balloon mortgages (choice D), short-term financing (choice C), or interest-only payments are associated with different loan products.

110. D: A preliminary title report provides information about the property's ownership history, recorded liens, encumbrances, easements, and other relevant details. The current market value of the property is not part of the title report. That is given during the appraisal.

111. A: Regulation Z, commonly known as the Truth in Lending Act (TILA), is designed to enhance consumer protection and foster transparency in credit transactions. Its main objective is to empower consumers by requiring lenders to provide clear and comprehensive disclosures about the terms and costs associated with credit offerings. This ensures that consumers can make well-informed decisions when borrowing money, understanding the true cost of credit, including interest rates, fees, and other relevant information. By promoting transparency and informed use of consumer credit, Regulation Z aims to create a fair and competitive credit market that prioritizes consumer interests and rights. This regulation plays a crucial role in safeguarding consumers from deceptive practices and ensuring that they have access to the necessary information to compare different credit options and choose the one that best suits their financial needs and capabilities.

112. B: A Qualified Mortgage (QM) imposes limitations on up-front points and fees (choice A) to safeguard borrowers. The annual percentage rate (APR) plays a vital role in a QM, offering borrowers a transparent view of the total loan expense, therefore Choice C is incorrect. Although balloon payments (Choice D) are typically restricted, small lenders have an exception under certain conditions. However, charges for Federal Housing Administration (FHA) insurance premiums (Choice B) are not subject to the QM restrictions, since they pertain to FHA-insured loans and are not imposed by the lender.

113. A: Under the Home Mortgage Disclosure Act (HMDA), specific financial institutions are obligated to gather, report, and reveal information concerning their mortgage lending activities. This data serves the purpose of monitoring and identifying potential instances of discriminatory lending practices and ensuring adherence to fair lending laws. The collected information is shared with regulators and the public to analyze trends and address any issues.

114. D: Under the TILA-RESPA Integrated Disclosure (TRID) rule, the Loan Estimate must contain the projected interest rate. This crucial information is intended to assist borrowers in comprehending the borrowing expenses, comparing loan offers, and evaluating the loan's affordability. By having access to the estimated interest rate, borrowers can approximate their monthly payments and make informed choices regarding various mortgage options available to them.

115. A: The mortgage loan originator (MLO) should inform the underwriter about the falsified documents so that they can take appropriate steps to verify the borrower's income accurately. An underwriter evaluates risk for loans or insurance. They decide approval, terms, and pricing based on applicants' financial profiles. Reporting the borrower to the authorities or terminating the application without notifying the underwriter would not be the MLO's responsibility.

116. B: The Special Information Booklet, also known as "Your Home Loan Toolkit", provides borrowers with information about their rights and responsibilities during the mortgage process, as well as tips and tools for shopping for a mortgage and understanding loan terms. The document is split into three main sections covering shopping and budgetary considerations for a mortgage, the closing process, and considerations to make after owning a home, such as payments, insurance, and refinancing.

117. D: The loan-to-value (LTV) ratio is a measure that compares the mortgage amount (the loan) to the appraised value of the property. This assessment assists mortgage lenders in evaluating the risk linked to the loan and deciding whether to extend credit to the borrower. Generally, a lower LTV ratio, achievable through a higher down payment, is viewed as less risky for lenders.

118. B: The individual must complete two hours of training on lending standards for the nontraditional mortgage product marketplace. The pre-licensing education for loan originators must include at least 20 hours of training, with specific requirements for federal law and regulations, ethics, and lending standards for the nontraditional mortgage product marketplace. This comprehensive education ensures that loan originators are well-equipped with the knowledge and understanding of key aspects in the mortgage industry, fostering responsible lending practices and consumer protection.

119. C: "Nontraditional mortgage products" offer borrowers the option to defer payments of principal and, in certain cases, interest. Such products encompass interest-only and payment option adjustable-rate mortgages (ARMs), which deviate from conventional mortgages with their standard payment structures. Nontraditional mortgages present distinctive risks due to their payment deferral attributes, setting them apart from fixed-rate mortgages, conventional mortgages, and government-insured mortgages.

120. B: Ethical behavior in loan origination activities and financial responsibility involves transparently disclosing all fees and charges to borrowers. mortgage loan originators (MLOs) should provide borrowers with a clear understanding of the costs associated with the loan and avoid hidden or undisclosed fees.

Choice A raises ethical concerns because it may impose a financial burden on borrowers without providing any guarantee of service or outcome.

Choice C is considered unethical because it lacks transparency and can undermine the borrowers' trust in the loan origination process. In addition, referral fees violate section 8 of the Real Estate Settlement Procedures Act (RESPA) and are illegal.

Choice D violates transparency and fairness principles. Fee splitting can create conflicts of interest and compromise the best interests of the borrower. This practice is also illegal, as outlined in section 8 of RESPA.

Transparency, disclosure, and avoiding hidden fees are essential aspects of ethical behavior in loan origination activities. By providing borrowers with clear and up-front information about fees and charges, MLOs can establish trust, ensure borrowers' understanding of the loan costs, and uphold ethical standards in the industry.

MLO Practice Test #3

1. A mortgage lender advertises "zero fees" for their loan products. However, upon closer inspection, borrowers find that certain fees are still charged but are rolled into the loan. Is this advertising statement permissible?

    a. Yes, it is permissible as long as the fees are included in the loan amount.
    b. No, it is impermissible, as it misrepresents the true cost of the loan.
    c. Yes, it is permissible because borrowers have the option to pay the fees up front.
    d. No, it is impermissible unless borrowers specifically request fee details.

2. Maria is looking to refinance her home, and she sees an online advertisement promising a remarkably low interest rate of 2.5% for a fixed-rate mortgage. However, when she contacts the lender, they inform her that the advertised rate is only available for a limited time and her actual rate will be substantially higher. What unethical practice does Maria experience with the lender?

    a. Redlining
    b. Bait-and-switch
    c. Collusion with competitors
    d. Discriminatory lending

3. Under what circumstances can a revised Loan Estimate be issued without violating accuracy tolerances?

    a. If the borrower's credit score improves
    b. If the property's appraised value increases
    c. When there is a valid change in circumstances that affects settlement charges
    d. Only at the borrower's request

4. In a loan secured by residential real estate, discrimination based on race, religion, gender, or other protected characteristics is prohibited by which federal law?

    a. RESPA
    b. Fair Housing Act
    c. TILA
    d. ECOA

5. HUD plays a significant role in:

    a. Enforcing community zoning laws
    b. Advancing America's home demands
    c. Homeownership taxation
    d. Regulating telecommunications

6. What does the term "straw buyer" refer to?

    a. A buyer who pays for a property in cash
    b. A person used to impersonate the real buyer in a transaction
    c. A buyer who qualifies for a mortgage based on their high income
    d. A real estate agent acting on behalf of a buyer

7. Purchase-money second mortgages are primarily used for:

a. Home purchases when the buyer cannot secure a primary mortgage
b. Refinancing existing mortgages
c. Funding home improvements
d. Leveraging equity for investment purposes

8. A mortgage company advertises loans with "no closing costs" but includes hidden fees that increase the overall loan amount. What term best characterizes this advertising practice?

a. Material misrepresentation
b. Occupancy fraud
c. Unfair, deceptive, or abusive advertising
d. Redlining

9. What government agency provides mortgage insurance for FHA loans?

a. Fannie Mae
b. Freddie Mac
c. HUD
d. VA

10. What is the purpose of the Closing Disclosure form under TRID?

a. To summarize the borrower's credit history
b. To provide an estimate of the property's market value
c. To outline the final loan terms and closing costs
d. To detail the borrower's income and expenses

11. Which of the following is NOT typically considered when evaluating a borrower's liabilities for mortgage qualification?

a. Credit card balances
b. Student loan payments
c. Monthly utility bills
d. Auto loans

12. What is a YSP?

a. A fee charged by lenders for processing loan applications
b. A penalty for early loan repayment
c. A tax incentive for borrowers who purchase energy-efficient homes
d. A payment made by lenders to brokers for originating loans with higher interest rates

13. ECOA requires creditors to notify applicants of credit decisions within what timeframe?

a. 7 days
b. 10 days
c. 30 days
d. 45 days

14. If an MLO's license becomes inactive, what must they do to reactivate it?

a. Nothing, it will automatically reactivate after a short grace period.
b. Pay late fees and continue to operate without any further action.
c. Submit a formal request for reactivation to the licensing authority.
d. Hire a legal representative to reinstate the license through a court process.

15. Which type of mortgage features a stable interest rate for the entire loan term?

    a. ARM
    b. Purchase-money second mortgage
    c. Fixed-rate mortgage
    d. Balloon mortgage

16. A borrower wants to buy a house that costs $300,000, and the lender requires a 20% down payment. How much is the down payment?

    a. $60,000
    b. $65,000
    c. $70,000
    d. $75,000

17. What is the primary advantage of a fixed-rate mortgage compared to an ARM?

    a. Lower initial monthly payments
    b. Potential for lower interest rates
    c. Consistent, predictable monthly payments
    d. Ability to make interest-only payments initially

18. Which of the following is NOT within the jurisdiction of the Consumer Financial Protection Bureau?

    a. Regulating credit card companies
    b. Enforcing fair lending laws
    c. Overseeing mortgage lenders
    d. Making credit decisions

19. Reverse mortgages are designed for:

    a. Young, first-time homebuyers
    b. Homeowners looking to make monthly payments
    c. Seniors who want to tap into their home equity without monthly payments
    d. Real estate investors

20. In which type of advertising must a mortgage lender include their NMLS unique identifier?

    a. Only in online advertisements
    b. Only in print advertisements
    c. Both online and print advertisements
    d. It is not required in any type of advertising

21. What happens at the point of "loan consummation," under TRID?

    a. The borrower submits a loan application
    b. The borrower signs the promissory note
    c. The borrower receives the Loan Estimate
    d. The borrower requests a closing extension

22. Under ECOA, what is a prohibited basis for discrimination in credit transactions?

  a. Age
  b. Educational background
  c. Primary language spoken
  d. Employment history

23. Which of the following is NOT a permitted fee for loan originators under federal regulations?

  a. Origination fee
  b. Appraisal fee
  c. Processing fee
  d. Up-front fee before loan estimate

24. A financial institution that originates and funds mortgage loans and often sells them on the secondary market is known as a:

  a. Third-party provider
  b. Primary market lender
  c. Conveyance agent
  d. Secondary market investor

25. What is the first step in the borrower application process?

  a. Verifying employment history
  b. Collecting financial documentation
  c. Accepting the borrower's application
  d. Offering/negotiating loan terms

26. Under RESPA, what is the maximum fine for a violation related to kickbacks and referral fees?

  a. $5,000
  b. $10,000
  c. $15,000
  d. $25,000

27. A mortgage broker receives a significant cash payment from a title company for referring borrowers exclusively to their services. What prohibited act does this situation represent?

  a. Kickbacks
  b. Steering
  c. Fair lending
  d. Appraiser conflict of interest

28. Who purchases title insurance for a real estate/mortgage transaction?

  a. The buyer
  b. The seller
  c. The real estate agent
  d. The title company

29. Mark and Susan are planning to build their dream home, and they need financing that allows them to fund the construction as it progresses. Which mortgage product should they explore to achieve this goal?

    a. Balloon mortgage
    b. Construction mortgage
    c. Interest-only mortgage
    d. Reverse mortgage

30. A loan originator discovers that a borrower has submitted mortgage applications to three different lenders within a short timeframe. What should the loan originator do?

    a. Contact the other lenders to coordinate efforts and streamline the approval process.
    b. Proceed with the loan application without notifying other lenders.
    c. Report the borrower to regulatory authorities for submitting multiple applications.
    d. Discourage the borrower from proceeding with the loan application.

31. Fannie Mae and Freddie Mac typically play a role in which type of mortgage program?

    a. Nonconforming
    b. Subprime mortgages
    c. Qualified Mortgages
    d. Non-qualified Mortgage

32. Which of the following is NOT a document typically filed for public record under the SAFE Act?

    a. Criminal background check
    b. Fingerprints
    c. NMLS unique identifier
    d. Business financial statements

33. What is the consequence of significant changes to loan terms after the Loan Estimate has been provided to the borrower under TRID?

    a. The borrower is required to pay a penalty fee
    b. The lender must provide a revised Loan Estimate and extend the waiting period
    c. The borrower's credit score is affected
    d. The lender is exempt from disclosing changes

34. What is the cooling-off period under TILA?

    a. The time frame during which borrowers can change their minds and cancel certain credit transactions
    b. The waiting period before a lender can approve a loan application
    c. The grace period for making late payments
    d. The period for disputing billing errors

35. When must MLOs notify NMLS of a change in their employment?

    a. Within the timeframe specified by their state's regulations, and only if they change employers within the same state
    b. Within 30 days, and only if they change employers outside the United States
    c. Within 30 days, and only if they are moving to a different state
    d. Within the timeframe specified by their state's regulations, including changing employers or moving to a different state

36. Which of the following statements accurately describes the concept of "disparate impact" in fair lending practices?

   a. Lenders intentionally discriminating against specific borrower groups
   b. Unintentional discrimination that results from neutral policies or practices
   c. Lenders providing equal access to credit for all borrowers
   d. Borrowers choosing loan products based on their preferences

37. During a loan origination process, a borrower asks the loan originator for guidance on selecting the right mortgage product. In this scenario, is the advice provided to the borrower solicited or unsolicited, and why?

   a. The advice is solicited because the borrower explicitly asked for guidance.
   b. The advice is solicited because the loan originator, as a professional, is expected to proactively provide guidance.
   c. The advice is unsolicited because the borrower's request for guidance was not made in writing.
   d. The advice is unsolicited because providing advice on mortgage products is not part of the loan originator's role.

38. When does government mortgage insurance typically terminate on an FHA loan with a 30-year term and a down payment of less than 10%?

   a. After 5 years and when the loan-to-value ratio reaches 78%
   b. After 11 years and when the loan-to-value ratio reaches 78%
   c. After 15 years and when the loan-to-value ratio reaches 78%
   d. It does not terminate; it lasts for the life of the loan

39. Which of the following is NOT typically covered by a standard flood insurance policy?

   a. Structural damage to the insured property
   b. Damage to personal belongings, such as furniture and clothing
   c. Loss of income due to business interruption caused by a flood
   d. Damage to vehicles parked on the insured property

40. A borrower receives a significant cash gift from a family member to cover their down payment. What is the appropriate action for the loan originator?

   a. Request the borrower to deposit the cash gift into their personal account and provide a bank statement.
   b. Inform the borrower that they can accept the cash gift without any further documentation since it's a family gift.
   c. Advise the borrower to return the cash gift and find an alternative down payment source.
   d. Document the gift, obtain a gift letter, and verify both the source of funds and the donor's relationship to the borrower.

41. The Homeowners Protection Act primarily relates to what topic?

   a. Privacy of consumer financial information
   b. Canceling private mortgage insurance (PMI)
   c. Reducing interest rates for homeowners
   d. Regulating mortgage brokers

42. What type of mortgage loans are exempt from Regulation X's requirements?

    a. Fixed-rate mortgage loans
    b. ARM loans
    c. Reverse mortgage loans
    d. Temporary mortgage loans

43. Section X and which section of RESPA prohibit kickbacks, fee-splitting, and unearned fees in real estate transactions?

    a. Section 4
    b. Section 6
    c. Section 8
    d. Section 10

44. What does "reverse redlining" refer to?

    a. Lending institutions unfairly favoring borrowers from specific neighborhoods
    b. A practice of targeting high-income borrowers for premium loan products
    c. Providing loans to borrowers with excellent credit histories
    d. Encouraging borrowers to refinance their existing mortgages

45. A borrower provides inconsistent income documentation, including several different pay stubs and income sources. What action should a loan originator take?

    a. Accept the income documentation as-is but increase the interest rate to account for the inconsistency.
    b. Suspend the loan application until the borrower can provide more-consistent income documentation.
    c. Accept the income documentation as-is but conduct additional credit checks.
    d. Advise the borrower to find a co-signer for the loan.

46. A buyer is purchasing a home for $300,000, and the estimated closing costs are 3% of the purchase price. Calculate the total closing costs.

    a. $90,000
    b. $9,000
    c. $900
    d. $90

47. Interest-only mortgages allow borrowers to:

    a. Make lower monthly payments by only paying interest for a specified period
    b. Lock in a fixed interest rate for the entire loan term
    c. Avoid making any payments until the end of the loan term
    d. Secure government-backed financing

48. What is the threshold for 10% tolerance service charges?

    a. Charges cannot exceed 10% of the loan amount
    b. Charges cannot exceed 10% of the property's appraised value
    c. Charges cannot exceed 10% of the estimated closing costs
    d. Charges cannot exceed 10% of the borrower's annual income

49. What is the penalty for a lender's failure to provide a TILA disclosure statement?

  a. A fine, imprisonment potential, and liability for damages to the borrower
  b. A warning letter
  c. Revocation of the lender's license
  d. Mandatory credit counseling for the borrower

50. What should mortgage lenders ensure when making claims about interest rates in their advertising?

  a. Interest rate claims must always be absolute and fixed.
  b. Interest rate claims should reflect the most recent market rates.
  c. Interest rate claims should be based on hypothetical scenarios.
  d. Interest rate claims should include detailed fine print.

51. What does "HELOC" stand for?

  a. High Equity Line of Credit
  b. Home Equity Loan Opportunity and Credit
  c. Home Equity Line of Credit
  d. High-Interest Loan Opportunity and Credit

52. The USA PATRIOT Act was enacted in response to which major event in US history?

  a. The Civil Rights movement
  b. The Watergate scandal
  c. The 9/11 terrorist attacks
  d. The Vietnam War protests

53. What is a distinguishing feature of an ARM?

  a. The interest rate remains constant throughout the loan term.
  b. The monthly payments increase or decrease based on prevailing interest rates.
  c. It is typically used for financing a second home.
  d. It is only available to first-time homebuyers.

54. Who is typically responsible for covering the cost of the appraisal fee?

  a. Borrower
  b. Lender
  c. Mortgage broker
  d. Seller

55. Which of the following is considered a liquid asset when assessing a borrower's financial situation for mortgage qualification?

  a. Retirement account
  b. Real estate property
  c. Collectible artwork
  d. Antique furniture

56. Which of the following fees is typically explained on the Closing Disclosure form as a part of the Prepaids section?

    a. Title insurance premium
    b. Property taxes
    c. Appraisal fee
    d. Loan origination fee

57. What is the maximum percentage of the down payment that can typically be gifted by a donor?

    a. 10%
    b. 25%
    c. 50%
    d. 100%

58. Which of the following documents is typically NOT required in a real estate closing?

    a. Promissory note
    b. Deed of trust or mortgage
    c. Purchase agreement
    d. Title insurance policy

59. A loan originator is also a part owner of a real estate company that occasionally refers clients to their own mortgage brokerage firm for financing. Does this situation represent a conflict of interest? Why or why not?

    a. Yes, it represents a conflict of interest because the loan originator may prioritize their real estate company's interests over the borrower's best interests.
    b. No, it is not a conflict of interest because owning multiple businesses in related industries is a common practice in the mortgage industry.
    c. Yes, it represents a conflict of interest, but disclosure is not necessary unless the borrower specifically asks about the loan originator's ownership.
    d. No, conflicts of interest only arise when the loan originator receives financial incentives from third parties.

60. Why is it essential for MLOs to obtain and use a unique identifier in their loan origination activities?

    a. To ensure compliance with state licensing requirements
    b. To accurately identify the MLO involved in the transaction and differentiate between individuals with similar names
    c. To track the MLO's personal finances and credit history for regulatory purposes
    d. To simplify the mortgage application process and reduce paperwork for consumers.

61. What does RESPA stand for?

    a. Real Estate Settlement Procedures Act
    b. Residential Equity and Security Protection Act
    c. Real Estate Services and Property Administration
    d. Regulation of Estate Settlement Procedures and Actions

62. Which of the following is NOT a right granted to borrowers under TILA?

a. The right to cancel certain credit transactions within three days
b. The right to dispute billing errors
c. The right to obtain a free credit report annually
d. The right to access credit counseling services

63. Which of the following best describes the primary purpose of the SAFE Act's requirement for background checks and fingerprinting of mortgage loan originators?

a. To ensure that loan originators have a clean credit history
b. To verify the applicant's immigration status
c. To assess the applicant's criminal history and financial responsibility
d. To determine the applicant's level of education

64. Under Regulation Z's Loan Originator rule, what is "dual compensation" in the mortgage industry?

a. Compensation provided to loan originators from both lenders and real estate agents
b. The simultaneous issuance of two mortgages for a single property
c. Compensation paid to loan originators based on the number of loans they originate
d. Payment of interest on two loans by a borrower

65. In the mortgage industry, what is a lien?

a. A fee paid to the mortgage broker
b. A legal claim or charge against a property that provides security for a loan
c. A type of mortgage insurance
d. A type of mortgage payment plan

66. What type of credit transactions are typically exempt from the requirements of ECOA?

a. Mortgage loans
b. Auto loans
c. Credit card applications
d. Commercial loans

67. What is accrued interest?

a. The fee paid by the lender to the borrower for accepting a higher interest rate
b. The interest that accumulates on a loan between the date of closing and the start of the first regular payment
c. A type of interest rate lock agreement
d. A fee charged by the mortgage broker

68. Which of the following is an example of a government-backed mortgage program?

a. Alt-A mortgage
b. Jumbo mortgage
c. USDA mortgage
d. Non-qualified Mortgage

69. Which party is primarily responsible for ensuring that the Loan Estimate and Closing Disclosure are accurate and compliant with TRID regulations?

    a. The real estate agent
    b. The mortgage broker
    c. The borrower
    d. The lender

70. The HUD-1 settlement statement itemizes the various fees associated with which type of real estate transaction?

    a. Fixed-rate mortgage
    b. HELOC
    c. Reverse mortgage
    d. Refinancing loan

71. Maria is a real estate investor and is looking to purchase a property that she intends to renovate and sell within a few years for a significant profit. Maria's goal is to minimize her monthly mortgage expenses during the renovation to maximize her potential profit margin upon sale. Which mortgage product would best suit Maria's investment strategy?

    a. Balloon mortgage
    b. Construction mortgage
    c. Interest-only mortgage
    d. Reverse mortgage

72. A borrower's annual income is $65,000. The expected PITI is $1,550. The borrower has a monthly recurring debt of $400. What are the borrower's front-end and back-end ratios?

    a. 36% and 29%, respectively
    b. 29% and 36%, respectively
    c. 63% and 92%, respectively
    d. 92% and 63%, respectively

73. Which financial term represents a reduction in the interest rate for the initial years of a mortgage loan?

    a. Discount points
    b. Finance charges
    c. Loan-to-value ratio
    d. 2-1 buy-down

74. What does the term "Temporary Authority to Originate" refer to in the mortgage industry?

    a. A short-term license for new MLOs
    b. The ability to originate loans while awaiting licensure
    c. A type of continuing education requirement
    d. Permission to work as an underwriter for a limited time

75. According to Regulation X, how many business days before closing must the borrower receive the Closing Disclosure?

    a.   1 business day
    b.   3 business days
    c.   5 business days
    d.   7 business days

76. What typically triggers a routine examination by a state regulatory authority for mortgage professionals and entities?

    a.   A consumer complaint about a specific mortgage transaction
    b.   A suspicion of violations based on the licensee's advertising practices
    c.   A yearly review as mandated by federal regulations
    d.   A requirement for all mortgage professionals regardless of compliance history

77. Which of the following is NOT one of the three primary approaches to property appraisal?

    a.   Market approach
    b.   Income approach
    c.   Credit approach
    d.   Cost approach

78. Under ECOA, how long must a creditor retain records related to credit applications?

    a.   24 months
    b.   25 months
    c.   26 months
    d.   27 months

79. Who typically provides homeownership counseling services to borrowers?

    a.   The lender's loan officers
    b.   Government agencies
    c.   The borrower's real estate agent
    d.   Private attorneys

80. Which mortgage program provides financing options for rural and eligible suburban homebuyers with favorable terms?

    a.   Alt-A mortgage
    b.   FHA
    c.   USDA
    d.   Non-qualified Mortgage

81. If the outstanding balance of a mortgage is $60,000, and the house is currently appraised at $180,000, what is the LTV ratio?

    a.   20.22%
    b.   33.33%
    c.   50.56%
    d.   75.78%

82. What term refers to the order in which loans were recorded, with the first recorded loan having the highest priority?

    a. Yield spread premium
    b. Rate lock agreement
    c. 2-1 buy-down
    d. Subordination

83. Which of the following is considered a conventional/conforming mortgage program?

    a. FHA
    b. VA
    c. USDA
    d. Fannie Mae

84. What is the purpose of obtaining a preliminary title report?

    a. To determine the current market value of the property
    b. To identify any potential issues with the property's title
    c. To assess the borrower's creditworthiness
    d. To estimate the borrower's ability to repay the loan

85. In what circumstances is the Consumer Financial Protection Bureau authorized to summon a loan originator or an individual possessing pertinent records for examination?

    a. Without any limitations
    b. When there are concerns about unlawful actions
    c. Upon request by the loan originator
    d. Annually for routine inspections

86. A young family with limited savings is seeking financial assistance to purchase their first home. What mortgage program should their loan officer recommend?

    a. Conventional/Conforming Mortgage
    b. FHA Mortgage
    c. Alt-A Mortgage
    d. ARM Mortgage

87. Which agency is responsible for investigating and addressing complaints related to consumer financial products and services?

    a. CFPB
    b. HUD
    c. IRS
    d. FTC

88. What is an Alt-A mortgage?

    a. A mortgage for borrowers with excellent credit scores
    b. A type of Non-qualified Mortgage with no income verification
    c. A government-backed mortgage program for rural properties
    d. A subprime mortgage program

89. What does "MIP" stand for?

    a. Mortgage interest premium
    b. Mortgage insurance premium
    c. Mortgage investment policy
    d. Mortgage interest payment

90. Under the Fair and Accurate Credit Transactions Act (FACTA), consumers have the right to request a free copy of their credit report at what interval?

    a. Every 6 months
    b. Once every 5 years
    c. Annually from each of the three major credit bureaus
    d. Only if and when they are denied a mortgage loan

91. Which federal agency is primarily responsible for enforcing regulations related to "unfair, deceptive, or abusive acts" in the consumer financial marketplace?

    a. FTC
    b. FDIC
    c. CFPB
    d. OCC

92. Which term describes a loan that allows a buyer to take over the seller's existing mortgage with the same terms and interest rate?

    a. APR
    b. Assumable loan
    c. Table funding
    d. Subordinate loans

93. Which entity is responsible for enforcing RESPA and its regulations, including Regulation X?

    a. FTC
    b. CFPB
    c. HUD
    d. Federal Reserve Board

94. When offering or negotiating loan terms, which of the following is permissible?

    a. Asking about the borrower's age
    b. Requesting information about the borrower's marital status
    c. Inquiring about the borrower's source of income
    d. Asking about the borrower's race or ethnicity

95. A buyer is purchasing a house with a 30-year fixed-rate mortgage of $250,000 at an annual interest rate of 4.5%. Calculate the monthly mortgage payment.

    a. $1,266.71
    b. $1,277.01
    c. $1,288.81
    d. $1,299.91

96. A mortgage company recently discovered a data breach in which borrowers' personal information, including sensitive financial data, has been exposed due to a security vulnerability. The breach has the potential to affect a significant number of borrowers. What is the most ethical course of action for the mortgage company to take in response to the data breach?

    a. Immediately inform all affected borrowers and relevant authorities about the breach.
    b. Delay notifying affected borrowers until authorities are involved.
    c. Offer affected borrowers a small compensation to mitigate any inconvenience caused by the breach.
    d. Notify all affected borrowers and provide mandatory compensation.

97. Which federal agency enforces compliance with ECOA?

    a. Federal Reserve System
    b. CFPB
    c. HUD
    d. FTC

98. Which of the following scenarios constitutes "taking a residential mortgage loan application"?

    a. A mortgage broker collects and sends borrower information to a lender but is not responsible for verifying it.
    b. A loan officer receives a loan application through the mail and forwards it to loan approval personnel.
    c. A loan officer assists a borrower in filling out a loan application by explaining its contents.
    d. A loan officer communicates directly with a borrower to mutually agree on prospective residential mortgage loan terms.

99. What does the APR represent, according to TILA rules?

    a. The total loan amount
    b. The interest rate charged on the loan
    c. The overall cost of the loan, including interest and certain fees
    d. The borrower's credit score

100. A borrower who is paid $32.50 per hour and works 40 hours per week is applying for a home loan. How much does the borrower make per month?

    a. $5,522.22
    b. $5,533.33
    c. $5,522.22
    d. $5,633.33

101. A borrower has a 15-year fixed-rate mortgage for $150,000 at an annual interest rate of 5%. What is the amount of interest the borrower will pay monthly?

    a. $610
    b. $620
    c. $625
    d. $650

102. Under what federal regulation are lenders required to disclose their affiliated business arrangements to borrowers?

    a. TILA
    b. HMDA
    c. RESPA
    d. ECOA

103. What is the primary purpose of the "three-day right of rescission" period in a mortgage transaction?

    a. To allow the borrower to cancel the loan without penalty
    b. To give the lender time to review the borrower's credit history
    c. To calculate the property's assessed value
    d. To determine the property's insurability

104. What is the penalty for lenders who fail to provide borrowers with the Closing Disclosure at least three business days before closing under "Know Before You Owe"?

    a. Lenders are required to refund all closing costs to the borrower.
    b. Lenders must extend the loan's interest rate lock period.
    c. Lenders may be subject to civil penalties and liability for damages.
    d. There is no penalty for lenders.

105. What is the term used to describe the practice of denying loans or insurance to specific neighborhoods based on racial demographics or economic factors?

    a. Discrimination
    b. Redlining
    c. Fair lending
    d. Coercion

106. A borrower submits a complaint regarding an unexpected fee on their loan estimate. The MLO investigates and finds that the fee was a legitimate charge. What should the MLO do next?

    a. Offer the borrower a discounted rate on the fee in question, provided they refer another potential borrower to the MLO's lending institution.
    b. Acknowledge the borrower's concern and explain the fee in detail.
    c. Inform the borrower that the fee will be waived to resolve the complaint.
    d. Refer the borrower to a competitor for an alternative loan estimate.

107. The Federal Trade Commission Red Flag rules primarily address what topic?

    a. Privacy of consumer financial information
    b. Reporting mortgage interest rates
    c. Detecting and preventing identity theft
    d. Mortgage loan origination procedures

108. Under TILA, what type of loans require the provision of a Truth in Lending disclosure statement?

    a. Business loans
    b. Mortgage loans
    c. Public utility loan
    d. Private student loans

109. Which term describes a mortgage lending practice in which lenders encourage borrowers to take on high-cost loans, often with excessive fees and terms?

   a. Fair lending
   b. Predatory lending
   c. Coercion
   d. Redlining

110. What is the monthly PMI cost of a $230,000 loan amount on a $350,000 home with a Fannie Mae coverage rate of 0.54%?

   a. $100.50
   b. $103.50
   c. $110.50
   d. $130.50

111. What is the term for an illegal practice where an individual or company receives payment for referring clients to a particular lender, real estate agent, or service provider?

   a. Compensation
   b. Kickback
   c. Fairness
   d. Redlining

112. What legal document grants someone the authority to act on behalf of another party in a mortgage transaction?

   a. Affidavit of title
   b. Deed of trust
   c. Power of attorney
   d. Title commitment

113. How long is the typical waiting period for retaking the SAFE MLO National Test?

   a. 7 days
   b. 30 days
   c. 90 days
   d. 180 days

114. What does "table funding" refer to?

   a. The act of providing lender credits to borrowers
   b. The transfer of a mortgage loan from one servicer to another
   c. A loan closing where funds are provided by the lender directly
   d. The practice of conveying property to a new owner

115. Which government-backed mortgage program is designed to assist eligible veterans and service members in obtaining home financing with favorable terms?

   a. FHA
   b. VA
   c. USDA
   d. Alt-A

116. Under which federal law are lenders required to report certain information about their mortgage lending activities, such as loan applications and originations, to regulatory agencies?

    a. HMDA
    b. FCRA
    c. BSA/AML
    d. GLBA

117. What does title insurance protect against in a mortgage transaction?

    a. Property tax assessments
    b. Changes in interest rates
    c. Undisclosed liens and title defects
    d. Homeowners association fees

118. When might a title binder be used in a real estate transaction?

    a. To bind the parties to the sale contract
    b. To secure a lower interest rate for the borrower
    c. To provide temporary insurance coverage until the title search is complete
    d. To guarantee a specific closing date

119. Which category of mortgages is associated with borrowers who may have lower credit scores or other risk factors and often includes adjustable-rate loans?

    a. Qualified Mortgages
    b. Non-qualified Mortgages
    c. Jumbo mortgages
    d. Subprime mortgages

120. Which of the following is NOT a permissible basis for a creditor to consider in evaluating creditworthiness under ECOA?

    a. Previous homeownership experience
    b. Number of children
    c. Income
    d. National origin

Answer Key and Explanations for Test #3

1. B: Advertising "zero fees" for loan products while still charging fees that are rolled into the loan is generally considered impermissible and misleading. Such advertising misrepresents the true cost of the loan to borrowers, as they may believe they are not incurring any fees when, in fact, they are paying them indirectly through the loan. This practice can be deceptive and may violate consumer protection regulations that require transparency in loan advertising.

2. B: "Bait-and-switch" is a deceptive marketing strategy where a business promotes an appealing offer to attract customers but later replaces it with a less favorable one when the customer shows interest.

3. C: A revised Loan Estimate can be issued without violating accuracy tolerances when there is a valid change in circumstances that affects settlement charges. Under TRID—the Truth in Lending Act (TILA) and Real Estate Settlement Procedures Act (RESPA) Integrated Disclosure—rules, certain changes in circumstances, such as changes in the borrower's financial information or unexpected events affecting the transaction, may allow for the issuance of a revised Loan Estimate. This ensures that borrowers have accurate and up-to-date information about their loan terms and settlement charges.

4. D: According to the Equal Credit opportunity Act (ECOA), discrimination based on race, color, religion, national origin, sex, marital status, age, or whether the borrower receives income from public assistance programs is specifically prohibited in credit transactions. ECOA ensures that all applicants for credit are treated fairly and without discrimination in the lending process.

5. B: The main role of the Department of Housing and Urban Development (HUD) is to address and promote affordable housing, community development, and urban revitalization. It manages various programs and initiatives aimed at improving housing conditions, assisting low-income individuals and families in accessing affordable housing, and supporting community development efforts. HUD also works to combat housing discrimination and promote fair housing practices.

6. B: A "straw buyer" is an individual who assumes the identity of the rightful property purchaser while representing another person or group participating in the fraudulent scheme. This subterfuge is employed to secure a mortgage using deceptive means.

7. A: Purchase-money second mortgages are typically used in scenarios where the buyer is unable to secure a primary (first) mortgage that covers the entire purchase price of the home. When a buyer lacks the down payment or doesn't qualify for a full mortgage amount, a second mortgage can be used to bridge the gap and facilitate the home purchase.

8. C: Advertising "no closing costs" but including hidden fees that increase the loan amount is a form of unfair, deceptive, and abusive advertising. It goes beyond mere misinformation. The practice is deceptive because it presents an incomplete and inaccurate picture to potential borrowers. It can lead borrowers to make decisions they might not have made if they had been fully informed about the true costs of the loan. This kind of advertising is considered unfair and potentially abusive because it can harm consumers by concealing crucial information and potentially trap them in unfavorable loan terms. Regulatory authorities often scrutinize and take action against such practices to protect consumers from deceptive advertising.

9. C: The US Department of Housing and Urban Development (HUD) offers mortgage insurance coverage for Federal Housing Administration (FHA) loans. These FHA loans are government-supported and assist individuals with limited down payment funds or lower credit scores in achieving homeownership. HUD administers and supervises the FHA program, extending insurance to lenders who originate FHA loans. This insurance serves as a safeguard for lenders in the event of borrower default.

10. C: The primary purpose of the Closing Disclosure form under TRID is to outline the final loan terms and closing costs for borrowers before they proceed with closing on the mortgage. This disclosure provides borrowers with essential information, such as the interest rate, monthly payments, closing costs, and the total cash required for closing. It allows borrowers to review and understand the financial aspects of the loan transaction in detail and ensures transparency in the closing process.

11. C: When appraising a borrower's liabilities to determine mortgage eligibility, the monthly utility bills, such as those for water, electricity, or gas, are not factored into the borrower's debt obligations. Instead, these utility bills are regarded as ongoing household expenses and are not seen as long-term debt commitments. Lenders focus on evaluating a borrower's existing debts and financial responsibilities that could potentially affect their capacity to meet mortgage payments.

12. D: The yield spread premium, or YSP, is a payment made by lenders to brokers for originating loans with higher interest rates. It previously served as compensation to mortgage brokers for selling an interest rate to a borrower that is above the lender's par rate for which the borrower qualifies. However, it is important to note that regulations have been introduced to govern YSPs and ensure that loan originator compensation practices are fair and transparent, protecting consumers from hidden fees. Additionally, rules prohibit loan originators from steering consumers toward loans that aren't in their best interest, preserving consumer choice and fairness in lending practices.

13. C: Upon acquiring all of the information typically used in the credit assessment process, the application is deemed finalized, and the creditor is obligated to inform the applicant of its credit decision within 30 days.

14. C: When a mortgage loan originator (MLO) allows their license to become inactive, they must submit a formal request to the licensing authority to reactivate it. This request may involve paying any required fees, meeting continuing education requirements, or fulfilling other conditions imposed by the state.

15. C: A fixed-rate mortgage maintains a stable, unchanging interest rate throughout the entire loan term, which can be advantageous for borrowers seeking predictability in their monthly payments.

16. A: The down payment is 20% of the house price. Convert the percentage to a decimal by dividing it by 100%, then multiply by the house price:

$$\text{Down payment} = \frac{20\%}{100\%} \times \$300{,}000 = \$60{,}000$$

17. C: The benefit of a fixed-rate mortgage compared to an adjustable-rate mortgage (ARM) is the stability and predictability it offers in terms of monthly payments. Borrowers can count on their monthly payments staying the same for the entire loan term, which simplifies budgeting and financial planning.

18. D: The Consumer Financial Protection Bureau (CFPB) safeguards consumers by supervising financial institutions and promoting fairness and transparency in the financial sector. The CFPB does not engage in credit decisions, such as approving or declining individual credit applications. These decisions are generally made by financial institutions or by consumers when they apply for credit. The CFPB's primary goal is to ensure that these decisions adhere to fair lending laws and regulations, rather than being directly involved in making credit decisions.

19. C: Reverse mortgages are financial products specifically designed to provide a source of income for homeowners aged 62 or older. They enable these homeowners to receive their home equity without the need to make monthly mortgage payments. Borrowers can access funds through options like receiving a lump sum, obtaining monthly payments, or establishing a line of credit. The interest on the loan and the loan itself are repaid when the borrower sells the home, moves out, or passes away.

20. C: A mortgage lender is obligated to provide their Nationwide Multistate Licensing System (NMLS) unique identifier, known as the NMLS ID, to consumers in all advertisements, regardless of whether the advertisement is published online or in print. It allows consumers to verify the lender's licensing and regulatory compliance.

21. B: Under TRID, loan consummation occurs when the borrower signs the promissory note, formalizing their commitment to the mortgage agreement. It is essential to understand that loan consummation and the closing of the mortgage transaction are separate events. Closing encompasses the entire transaction, while consummation specifically signifies the moment when the borrower becomes legally obligated to adhere to the mortgage terms by signing the promissory note.

22. A: The Federal Equal Credit Opportunity Act (ECOA) bars creditors from discriminating against credit applicants on grounds of race, color, religion, national origin, sex, marital status, and age. It is worth highlighting that while ECOA predominantly focuses on these specified factors, other federal and state laws and regulations may address discrimination in various contexts, including aspects like educational background, employment history, and primary language spoken.

23. D: Federal regulations prohibit loan originators from charging any up-front fees before providing the borrower with a Loan Estimate. The Loan Estimate is a key document that outlines the estimated costs of the loan, including fees. This prohibition ensures that borrowers receive essential information about the loan, including costs, before they are required to pay any fees.

24. B: Primary market lenders, which can include banks, credit unions, and mortgage brokers, are institutions that directly lend money to borrowers and originate mortgage loans. These lenders often sell these loans to investors on the secondary market.

25. C: The initial phase of the borrower application process entails receiving and acknowledging the borrower's application. This generally involves obtaining fundamental details from the borrower, such as their name, contact information, and the purpose of the loan. After accepting the application, the lender can then progress to subsequent steps in the mortgage application and approval process, including verifying employment history, gathering financial documentation, and presenting/negotiating loan terms.

26. B: The maximum penalty for a violation related to kickbacks and referral fees under RESPA is $10,000 and one year in jail. Kickbacks and referral fees involve giving money or incentives in exchange for referring business to a service provider. Kickbacks usually entail secret payments for customer referrals, like a real estate agent receiving money from a mortgage broker for client referrals. In contrast, referral fees are transparent compensation arrangements for referring customers to a service provider; they often involve direct payments or a percentage of the provider's fee. For instance, a title company might pay a real estate agent for recommending their services to homebuyers.

27. A: The Real Estate Settlement Procedures Act (RESPA) prohibits the payment of kickbacks or referral fees in exchange for the referral of settlement service business. While kickbacks may involve cash payments like in this scenario, they can also include non-monetary incentives, gifts, or any other form of compensation that is intended to induce referrals. These practices are illegal because they prioritize financial gain over consumers' genuine needs and harm fair competition.

28. A: Title insurance is a policy designed to shield both the buyer and their lender against possible title problems or complications that might emerge regarding the property's ownership history. As part of the closing costs, it is customary for the buyer to cover the expenses for both the lender's title insurance policy and their personal owner's title insurance policy. Although the seller may have certain title-related obligations, like furnishing a clean title, the responsibility for procuring title insurance predominantly rests with the buyer to guarantee the property's title is devoid of any defects.

29. B: A construction mortgage is designed to provide funds in stages as the construction of a new home progresses, making it the suitable choice for Mark and Susan's goal of building their dream home.

30. A: When a borrower submits mortgage applications to multiple lenders within a short timeframe, it is essential for the loan originator to take appropriate action while maintaining ethical standards and regulatory compliance. This allows for transparency, helps prevent any adverse impacts on the borrower's credit, and ensures that all parties involved are aware of the borrower's multiple applications, facilitating a smoother lending process.

31. C: Fannie Mae and Freddie Mac are government-sponsored entities with a crucial role in the secondary mortgage market. They purchase and securitize loans that meet the criteria for conforming loans, which typically align with the requirements for Qualified Mortgages (QMs). It is important to note that while many conventional loans technically fit the definition of non-QM loans, when people commonly refer to "conventional loans," they often mean conforming loans that do meet Fannie Mae and Freddie Mac's criteria for purchase and securitization.

32. D: Under the Secure and Fair Enforcement for Mortgage Licensing (SAFE) Act, mortgage loan originators (MLOs) are required to file various documents for public record, including their criminal background check results, fingerprints for identification, and Nationwide Multistate Licensing System (NMLS) unique identifier (NMLS ID). These documents are crucial for regulatory oversight and consumer protection. Business financial statements of the MLO are not required to be filed for public record under the SAFE Act. Business financial statements may be required by certain lenders or institutions as part of their internal due diligence processes, but they are not part of the public record.

33. B: According to TRID, if there are important changes to loan terms after the initial Loan Estimate has been given, the lender must supply a revised Loan Estimate to the borrower. In most cases, there is also a waiting period before closing, to give the borrower time to review these changes. This waiting period ensures that borrowers have enough time to grasp and evaluate the effects of significant alterations to the loan terms. TRID puts a strong emphasis on transparency and safeguarding borrowers throughout the lending process.

34. A: The cooling-off period under the Truth in Lending Act (TILA) is the 3 business days during which borrowers can change their minds and cancel certain credit transactions without incurring penalties or fees. This provision is intended to give borrowers an opportunity to reconsider their decisions and withdraw from specific credit agreements if they have second thoughts or find better terms elsewhere.

35. D: Mortgage loan originators (MLOs) must notify the Nationwide Multistate Licensing System (NMLS) of a change in their employment, regardless of state or country, within the timeframe specified by their state's regulations. It is important to note that while 30 days is a common notification window, some states may have different deadlines. This means that MLOs are legally obligated to follow the notification requirements as set forth by their specific state's regulatory authority. Compliance with these rules is crucial to avoid potential regulatory issues and to maintain licensing status. Therefore, MLOs should always be aware of and adhere to the notification timeframe prescribed by their state's regulatory authority to ensure that they are in full compliance with the law.

36. B: Disparate impact is when a lending policy or practice, even though it may appear neutral and non-discriminatory on the surface, ends up disproportionately affecting a particular group of people protected by fair lending laws, such as racial or ethnic minorities. The discrimination is unintentional, meaning that lenders may not have intended to discriminate, but the impact of their policies or practices results in unequal treatment. This concept is essential in fair lending regulations to identify and rectify discriminatory practices that may not be obvious but still have adverse effects on protected groups. These regulations focus on outcomes and statistical disparities rather than intentional discrimination.

37. A: The advice is solicited because the borrower explicitly asked for guidance on selecting the right mortgage product. Solicited advice is given in response to a specific inquiry or request from the borrower, while unsolicited advice is offered without the borrower explicitly seeking it.

38. D: For mortgages established between January 2001 and June 3, 2013, the mortgage insurance premium (MIP) automatically ceases once the borrower reaches a loan-to-value ratio of 78%. However, for borrowers who closed on or after June 3, 2013, MIP will end after 11 years, provided that they made a down payment equal to or exceeding 10%. In cases where the down payment was less than 10%, borrowers are obligated to continue paying MIP throughout the loan's entirety.

39. C: A standard flood insurance policy generally provides coverage for two main areas: (choice A) structural damage to the insured property and (choice B) damage to personal belongings like furniture and clothing, both resulting from a flood. Additionally, it may extend coverage to (choice D) damage incurred by vehicles parked on the insured property.

However, it is important to note that a standard flood insurance policy typically does not include protection for losses associated with (choice C) business interruption or income loss caused by a flood. Businesses seeking coverage for income loss due to unexpected events, such as floods, usually require a separate type of insurance known as business interruption insurance. Flood insurance policies primarily focus on safeguarding against property and contents damage and are not tailored to address business income loss.

40. D: The comprehensive approach of documenting the gift, obtaining a gift letter, and verifying the source of funds and the donor's relationship to the borrower is essential for regulatory compliance, ethical standards, and the overall integrity of the mortgage transaction. This approach safeguards the interests of all parties involved and ensures transparency throughout the lending process.

41. B: The Homeowners Protection Act, also known as the Private Mortgage Insurance Cancellation Act, primarily focuses on the discontinuation of private mortgage insurance (PMI). This legislation was established to outline the steps and standards for terminating or concluding PMI, providing homeowners with the opportunity to reduce their mortgage costs once certain requirements are fulfilled.

42. D: Regulation X includes exemptions for specific types of transactions in several different loan categories, including those designed primarily for business, commercial, or agricultural purposes. In addition, temporary loans such as construction loans are exempt, unless they possess certain characteristics, such as the potential for conversion to permanent financing by the same financial institution or being used to finance the transfer of title to the first user of the property.

43. C: Section 8 of RESPA and Regulation X specifically prohibit kickbacks, fee-splitting, and unearned fees in real estate transactions. Section 8 sets strict guidelines to deter the exchange of fees or anything of value among settlement service providers, such as lenders, real estate agents, and title companies, with the aim of safeguarding consumers' financial interests and maintaining the integrity of real estate transactions.

44. A: "Reverse redlining" is a term used to describe a discriminatory lending practice where financial institutions selectively target specific neighborhoods, often disadvantaged or minority communities, for financial products like loans or mortgages. In this practice, lenders may disproportionately offer high-cost or predatory loans to borrowers in these neighborhoods, exploiting their vulnerability. Unlike traditional "redlining," which involves denying services to certain neighborhoods, "reverse redlining" involves the unfair favoring of these neighborhoods, often leading to negative financial consequences for the affected borrowers.

45. B: When a borrower presents inconsistent income documentation, it is crucial for the loan originator to prioritize the accuracy and reliability of the borrower's income information. Suspension allows for proper verification and ensures that the loan decision is based on accurate financial information.

46. B: The purchase price is $300,000, and the estimated closing costs are 3% of the purchase price. Divide the percentage by 100% to get the decimal form, then multiply by the purchase price:

$$\text{Total closing costs} = \$300,000 \times 0.03 = \$9,000$$

47. A: Interest-only mortgages permit borrowers to make lower monthly payments for a set period by only covering the interest portion of the loan. During this initial period, borrowers are not required to make principal payments.

48. C: The threshold for 10% tolerance service charges refers to the limit on how much certain charges associated with a mortgage loan can exceed the estimated closing costs provided to the borrower on the Loan Estimate without triggering a violation of the Truth in Lending Act (TILA) and Real Estate Settlement Procedures Act (RESPA) Integrated Disclosure (TRID) rules. The 10% tolerance means that some charges, such as those for specific services provided by third-party providers (e.g., appraisals, credit reports), cannot exceed 10% above the amounts originally estimated on the Loan Estimate. If these charges exceed the 10% tolerance threshold, the lender may be required to refund the excess amount to the borrower.

49. A: Lenders who fail to provide a Truth in Lending Act (TILA) disclosure statement may face fines, potential imprisonment for severe violations, and possible liability for any damages suffered by the borrower due to non-compliance. TILA's purpose is to ensure transparency and consumer protection by mandating that lenders provide accurate and comprehensive disclosures about loan terms and costs.

50. B: When making claims about interest rates in their advertising, mortgage lenders should ensure that the interest rates they advertise reflect the most recent market rates. This is important for transparency and to provide borrowers with accurate and up-to-date information.

51. C: A "HELOC" is a "Home Equity Line of Credit," a common type of mortgage product that allows homeowners to access funds based on the equity in their homes. HELOCs often have low interest rates and potentially tax-deductible interest, and offer flexibility in borrowing and repayment.

52. C: The USA PATRIOT Act, short for "Uniting and Strengthening America by Providing Appropriate Tools Required to Intercept and Obstruct Terrorism Act," was enacted as a response to the terrorist attacks of September 11, 2001. The primary goal is to strengthen our national security and give law enforcement agencies better tools to fight terrorism. It brings in a wide range of measures that include surveillance, sharing intelligence, and efforts to counter terrorism that have implications for the mortgage industry.

53. B: An adjustable-rate mortgage (ARM) is defined by its feature that the interest rate can vary during the loan's duration, in response to shifts in a designated benchmark interest rate, such as the prime rate or the Secured Overnight Financing Rate (SOFR). Borrowers often opt for ARMs when they plan to sell or refinance their homes within a few years, as the initial lower interest rates lead to more manageable monthly payments during that period.

54. A: An appraisal is performed to establish the fair market value of the property being financed, and borrowers are typically responsible for covering this cost as part of the loan origination procedure.

55. A: When evaluating a borrower's financial position for mortgage eligibility, retirement accounts, including 401(k)s and IRAs, are typically categorized as liquid assets. Liquid assets are assets that can be readily converted into cash without a substantial loss in value. Retirement accounts fall into this category because they can be accessed under specific conditions, although early withdrawals may incur penalties or have tax implications.

56. B: The Prepaids section of a Closing Disclosure (CD) outlines expenses that the buyer is required to pay in advance at closing, including property taxes, homeowner's insurance, and mortgage insurance premiums. While the title insurance premium (choice A), appraisal fee (choice C), and loan origination fee (choice D) are important fees, they are not categorized as "Prepaids" on the CD form. Instead, they are listed in other sections of the CD that detail various closing costs.

57. D: A donor can gift the full down payment amount; in other words, up to 100% of the down payment. This means that borrowers can receive the entire down payment as a gift from a qualified donor, often a family member, without having to contribute their own funds for this purpose. This practice is widespread and enables individuals who may not have saved enough for a down payment to remain eligible for a mortgage. Nonetheless, it is important to note that the precise rules and criteria can differ from one lender or loan program to another. Therefore, borrowers should communicate with their lender to gain a clear understanding of the policies regarding gifted funds for their specific loan.

58. C: The purchase agreement represents a contractual agreement between the buyer and seller, delineating the terms and conditions governing the real estate transaction. While it plays a pivotal role in the negotiation and acceptance of the sale, it is generally formalized and completed prior to the actual closing.

59. A: In this scenario, the loan originator's dual role as a part-owner of a real estate company and a mortgage broker creates a potential conflict of interest. They may be inclined to steer clients toward their mortgage brokerage firm to benefit their real estate company, potentially at the expense of the borrower's best interests. Disclosing this conflict of interest is essential to maintain transparency and ensure borrowers can make informed decisions.

60. B: The Nationwide Multistate Licensing System (NMLS) unique identifier, often referred to as the NMLS ID, is assigned to each mortgage loan originator (MLO) to help accurately identify and distinguish between MLOs with similar names. This unique identifier serves multiple purposes, including appearing on the residential loan application and in all advertising to ensure that consumers can verify the identity of the MLO they are working with and the company that the MLO represents. This enhances transparency and accountability in the mortgage lending process.

61. A: RESPA stands for "Real Estate Settlement Procedures Act," which is the federal law governing real estate transactions and settlement procedures.

62. C: The Truth in Lending Act (TILA) primarily focuses on disclosure requirements and consumer protection in credit transactions, while free annual credit reports are governed by the Fair Credit Reporting Act (FCRA).

63. C: The background checks and fingerprinting required by the Secure and Fair Enforcement for Mortgage Licensing (SAFE) Act serve to assess the criminal history and financial responsibility of mortgage loan originators. This ensures consumer protection, risk mitigation, and regulatory compliance, and upholds public confidence in the mortgage industry.

64. A: The Loan Originator rule addresses "dual compensation," which is when loan originators receive compensation from both lenders and real estate agents or brokers involved in a mortgage transaction. This practice can create conflicts of interest because it might encourage loan originators to prioritize their own earnings over what is best for the borrower.

65. B: A lien is a legal claim or charge against a property that serves as security for a loan. It ensures that the lender has a claim on the property if the borrower fails to meet their loan obligations. If the debt is unpaid, the issuer of the lien can take possession of the property from the owner as part of the security arrangement.

66. D: Commercial loans are typically exempt from the requirements of the Equal Credit Opportunity Act (ECOA) because ECOA primarily focuses on protecting consumers in their personal credit transactions. Commercial loans, which are extended for business or commercial purposes, often involve different underwriting criteria, risk assessments, and business considerations than consumer loans.

67. B: Accrued interest is the interest that builds up on a loan from the date of closing, when the loan is issued, until the initiation of the initial regular loan payment. For example, if a mortgage closes on the 15th of the month, the first regular payment may not be due until the first of the following month, but interest will accrue on the loan during those two weeks. This accrued interest is typically included in the borrower's first payment.

68. C: A USDA mortgage is a government-backed program offered by the United States Department of Agriculture (USDA) to promote homeownership in rural areas, increase access to affordable housing, stimulate rural economic development, build stronger communities, and serve underserved populations in rural and designated suburban areas across the United States. USDA loans provide alternative financing options, including low to no down payment requirements, competitive interest rates, and flexible credit criteria.

69. D: The lender is primarily responsible for ensuring that the Loan Estimate and Closing Disclosure are accurate and compliant with TILA-RESPA Integrated Disclosure (TRID) regulations. This responsibility includes providing borrowers with the necessary disclosures, accurately calculating loan terms and closing costs, and complying with TRID's timing and content requirements. Lenders play a crucial role in ensuring that borrowers receive clear and transparent information about their mortgage transactions, aligning with the core purpose of TRID—to improve consumer understanding and transparency in the lending process.

70. C: The HUD-1 settlement statement includes a list of fees and credits to both buyer and seller in certain real estate transactions and loans, including reverse mortgages. Prior to October 3, 2015, a HUD-1 was provided at closing for most transactions. As of that date, for many transactions, including a traditional home sale with a fixed-rate mortgage, the HUD-1 was replaced by the Closing Disclosure, which contains more information, is easier to read, and is given to the buyer three days before closing so as to avoid any surprises. However, reverse mortgages are still accompanied by a HUD-1 settlement statement and a Truth-in-Lending disclosure. Refinancing loans are accompanied by a HUD-1A form, which is an abbreviated version of the HUD-1. Home equity lines of credit (HELOCs), manufactured housing loans not secured by real estate, and loans through certain homebuyer assistance programs are accompanied by a Truth-in-Lending statement but neither a HUD-1 settlement statement nor a Closing Disclosure.

71. A: A balloon mortgage is the ideal choice for Maria's investment strategy. Balloon mortgages offer lower initial monthly payments, which will assist her in managing her cash flow effectively during this period. The substantial final payment due at the end of the loan term aligns with her strategy to sell the property within a few years, using the proceeds from the sale to cover the final payment while potentially maximizing her profit margin.

72. B: Divide the annual income by 12 to determine the monthly income:

$$\$65,000 \div 12 = \$5,416.67$$

Divide the expected principal, interest, taxes, and insurance (PITI) by the monthly income to find the front-end ratio as a decimal, then multiply by 100% to determine the percentage:

$$\$1,550 \div \$5,416.67 = 0.29$$

$$0.29 \times 100\% = 29\%$$

To find the back-end ratio, add the PITI and reoccurring debt, then divide by the monthly income and multiply by 100%:

$$(\$1,550 + 400) \div \$5,416.67 = 0.36$$

$$0.36 \times 100\% = 36\%$$

73. D: The 2-1 buy-down is a strategy where the borrower or another party pays additional funds up front to reduce the interest rate for the initial years of the mortgage loan. This means that for the first two years, the interest rate is lower than the standard rate, providing borrowers with more affordable initial payments before the interest increases to the normal rate.

74. B: The Temporary Authority to Originate is a vital provision established under the Economic Growth, Regulatory Relief, and Consumer Protection Act. It grants individuals the opportunity to work as mortgage loan originators (MLOs) while their MLO license applications are being reviewed and processed. This provision helps facilitate the continuity of mortgage origination activities during the licensing application period, ensuring that consumers can access mortgage services without unnecessary delays.

75. B: Under the TILA-RESPA Integrated Disclosure (TRID) rule, borrowers are required to receive the Closing Disclosure at least three business days before the closing date. This allows borrowers sufficient time to review the final loan terms, interest rates, and closing costs to ensure they are accurate and to make informed decisions before proceeding with the closing. This three-business-day waiting period is intended to promote transparency and consumer protection in real estate transactions, ensuring that borrowers have time to understand the financial implications of the mortgage agreement.

76. C: Routine examinations are conducted on a yearly basis as part of proactive regulatory oversight. These examinations are mandated by federal regulations to ensure that licensed entities in the mortgage industry are continuously and consistently complying with the law. This regular, scheduled review helps identify any compliance issues, errors, or violations early on, allowing regulatory authorities to take appropriate actions, such as fines or corrective measures, if necessary, to maintain the integrity and legality of the mortgage industry.

77. C: Property appraisal relies on three primary approaches: the market approach, income approach, and cost approach. The market approach entails assessing the property's value by comparing it to recently sold similar properties within the same market. For income-producing properties, the income approach calculates the property's worth based on potential income and expected investor returns. Lastly, the cost approach determines value by estimating the cost to replace or reproduce the property, factoring in depreciation and obsolescence. These three methods serve as crucial tools in evaluating the value of real estate properties, each offering distinct insights into their financial worth.

78. B: Under the Equal Credit Opportunity Act (ECOA) and Regulation B, creditors are required to retain records related to credit applications for 25 months. This includes records such as application forms, credit reports, appraisal reports, and any other documents related to the application process. Keeping records for 25 months serves a crucial purpose: it empowers authorities to enforce ECOA's anti-discrimination rules and permits regulatory agencies to assess a creditor's lending practices to confirm that they are following the law.

79. B: Homeownership counseling services are typically offered by government-approved agencies and HUD-certified housing counselors. These professionals undergo specialized training and government certification to assist borrowers in assessing their financial situations, evaluating mortgage-related options, and creating a tailored plan to address mortgage challenges. These services aim to empower borrowers with knowledge about homeownership, mortgage terms, and foreclosure prevention.

80. C: The USDA mortgage program is designed to provide financing options for rural and eligible suburban homebuyers with favorable terms. It offers 100% financing (no down payment required) and competitive interest rates to support homeownership in eligible rural and suburban areas. This program is backed by the US Department of Agriculture.

81. B: To find the loan-to-value (LTV) ratio, divide the loan amount by the appraised value, then multiply by 100% to determine the percentage:

$$\text{LTV ratio} = \frac{\text{Loan amount}}{\text{Appraised value}} \times 100\%$$

$$\frac{\$60,000}{\$180,000} \times 100\% = 33.33\%$$

82. D: Subordination refers to the order in which loans or liens are recorded on a property's title. This practice establishes the priority of loans in the event of foreclosure or legal actions. The first loan recorded holds the highest priority, followed by subsequent loans recorded in the order they were obtained. This hierarchy ensures that the first recorded loan is paid off before the others in case of financial distress or property sale.

83. D: Conventional/conforming mortgages are loans that align with the loan limits established by government-sponsored enterprises such as Fannie Mae and Freddie Mac. These loans lack government insurance or guarantees but must meet specific criteria to be categorized as "conforming." Lenders can sell these conforming loans to Fannie Mae and Freddie Mac, enabling them to offer borrowers more advantageous terms.

84. B: Obtaining a preliminary title report serves the purpose of uncovering possible problems or shortcomings associated with a property's title. This report offers insights into the property's ownership lineage, outstanding liens, encumbrances, and any legal disputes or limitations that might impact its title. Its primary goal is to confirm the title's clarity and freedom from unresolved issues that could potentially influence the transaction or the rights of the new property owner.

85. B: The Consumer Financial Protection Bureau can summon a loan originator or other relevant individuals for examination when there are concerns about potential unlawful activities. This includes activities such as submitting false information on loan applications, misrepresenting borrower qualifications, or engaging in any form of loan fraud.

86. B: Federal Housing Administration (FHA) mortgages aim to increase homeownership opportunities for a diverse pool of borrowers, including those with limited savings and lower credit scores. These loans typically demand a smaller down payment in contrast to conventional mortgages and feature more-forgiving credit prerequisites, rendering them a suitable choice for first-time homebuyers and individuals with modest incomes.

87. A: The role of the Consumer Financial Protection Bureau (CFPB) includes the examination and resolution of complaints regarding consumer financial products and services. Its primary purpose is to safeguard consumers within the financial industry, ensuring they receive fair treatment from financial institutions and service providers.

88. B: Alt-A mortgages are a type of Non-qualified Mortgage (Non-QM). They are often considered a middle ground for borrowers who may not meet all criteria for a prime loan but still have reasonable credit. These loans add flexibility in terms of income verification, debt-to-income (DTI) ratios, and down payments compared to prime mortgages, while maintaining a lower risk profile compared to subprime loans.

89. B: "MIP" stands for "mortgage insurance premium." Some loans, like Federal Housing Administration (FHA) loans, require mortgage insurance to protect the lender if the borrower cannot pay. Borrowers include the MIP in their monthly mortgage payments, and the insurance helps the lender if the borrower defaults on the loan.

90. C: The Fair and Accurate Credit Transactions Act (FACTA) grants consumers the entitlement to request an annual free copy of their credit report from each of the three primary credit bureaus. This measure was introduced to advance openness and empower individuals to routinely review their credit details for inaccuracies or indications of identity theft.

91. C: The Consumer Financial Protection Bureau (CFPB) was created to protect consumers in the financial marketplace and has the authority to enforce regulations related to unfair, deceptive, or abusive acts. It is the main agency for overseeing and enforcing consumer financial protection laws and regulations.

92. B: An "assumable loan" is a loan that allows a buyer to take over the seller's existing mortgage with the same terms and interest rate. Assumable loans can be a valuable option for homebuyers in specific situations, providing potential cost savings, a simpler transaction process, and the opportunity to lock in a favorable interest rate. However, it is important to note that not all mortgages are assumable, and even when they are, the lender may require the new buyer to meet certain credit and financial qualifications.

93. B: The Consumer Financial Protection Bureau (CFPB) is the federal agency responsible for enforcing the Real Estate Settlement Procedures Act (RESPA) and its associated regulations, including Regulation X. The CFPB plays a crucial role in ensuring compliance with RESPA to protect consumers in real estate transactions. It oversees and enforces the rules governing mortgage servicing, disclosures, and various aspects of the settlement process, all aimed at promoting transparency, fairness, and consumer rights in the housing and mortgage industry.

94. C: When presenting or discussing loan conditions, it is acceptable to request details regarding the borrower's income origins to evaluate their capacity to repay the loan. This information aids lenders in ascertaining whether the borrower possesses a consistent income source capable of fulfilling their loan responsibilities.

95. A: The monthly payment is calculated using the following equation:

$$\text{Monthly payment} = \frac{P \times r}{1 - (1 + r)^{-n}}$$

Principal loan amount (P): $250,000

Monthly interest rate (r):

$$4.5\% \div 12 = 0.375\%$$

To get the decimal form of the interest rate, divide the percentage by 100%:

$$\frac{0.375\%}{100\%} = 0.00375$$

Loan term in months (n):

$$30 \times 12 = 360$$

Fill in the equation:

$$\text{Monthly payment} = \frac{\$250,000 \times 0.00375}{1 - (1 + 0.00375)^{-360}} = \$1,266.71$$

It is important to note that these estimates only include principal and interest. Other costs typically lumped into the monthly payment, including taxes and insurance, vary widely and are not included here.

96. A: In the event of a data breach that exposes borrowers' personal information, a mortgage company has an ethical and legal obligation to take prompt and responsible action. This allows affected individuals to take necessary steps to protect their identities and financial information while demonstrating the company's commitment to resolving the issue and preventing further harm.

97. B: The federal agency responsible for enforcing compliance with the Equal Credit Opportunity Act (ECOA) is the Consumer Financial Protection Bureau (CFPB). The CFPB ensures consumer protection in the financial market by overseeing financial institutions, enforcing fairness, addressing consumer grievances, enhancing transparency, and providing tools for making informed financial choices.

98. D: This scenario aligns with the definition of "taking a residential mortgage loan application" because it involves direct communication with the borrower to discuss and potentially reach a mutual understanding about the terms of a residential mortgage loan. It is important to note that this process is not limited to the physical receipt of an application form; it encompasses activities that facilitate the decision-making process related to loan terms, including direct interactions with borrowers regarding loan terms. The other choices (A, B, and C) involve handling applications or providing explanations but do not involve direct communication for the purpose of reaching an agreement on loan terms, as described in the definition.

99. C: Under the Truth in Lending Act (TILA), the Annual Percentage Rate (APR) includes both interest and fees, which gives borrowers a full view of the loan cost. This helps borrowers make informed choices when comparing loan offers. The total loan amount is just the principal, the interest rate does not cover all costs, and the APR is lender-based, not credit-based.

100. D: To calculate monthly income, use this equation:

$$\text{Monthly income} = \text{Rate per hour} \times \text{Hours per week} \times 52 \text{ weeks per year} \div 12 \text{ months per year}$$

$$\$32.50 \times 40 \times 52 \div 12 = \$5,633.33$$

101. C: To determine the monthly interest payment, multiple the loan amount by the annual interest rate in decimal form (the percentage divided by 100%), then divide by 12:

$$\text{Monthly payment} = \frac{\text{Loan amount} \times \text{Annual interest rate}}{12}$$

$$\frac{\$150,000 \times 0.05}{12} = \$625$$

102. C: Under the Real Estate Settlement Procedures Act (RESPA), lenders are required to disclose their affiliated business arrangements to borrowers. This includes any arrangements where the lender has a financial interest in a settlement service provider, such as a title company or an appraisal firm. RESPA aims to promote transparency in the real estate settlement process by ensuring that borrowers are aware of any potential conflicts of interest that could affect their transaction. Lenders are required to provide borrowers with a special information booklet and a written Affiliated Business Arrangement Disclosure when such arrangements exist.

103. A: Within the three-day right of recission interval, which is mandated by the Truth in Lending Act (TILA), the borrower retains the privilege to revoke the loan for any reason, free from any financial consequences. Its purpose is to offer borrowers a chance to reconsider their choice and ensure that they have a comprehensive understanding of the mortgage's terms and associated expenses. The lender is obliged to furnish the borrower with a notice outlining the right of rescission at the time of the loan closing.

104. C: Under the "Know Before You Owe" rules, lenders are required to provide borrowers with the Closing Disclosure at least three business days before the loan closing. This three-day waiting period is intended to give borrowers sufficient time to review the final loan terms and costs before they commit to the mortgage. If lenders fail to comply with this requirement, they face penalties and liability for damages.

The penalty for non-compliance include civil penalties imposed by regulatory authorities. Additionally, if the lender's failure to provide the Closing Disclosure on time results in financial harm to the borrower, the lender may be liable for damages, such as reimbursing the borrower for any costs incurred due to the delay.

105. B: Redlining is a specific and well-known discriminatory practice in lending and insurance that emerged in the United States in the 20th century. It originally involved literally drawing red lines on maps to designate certain neighborhoods, often those with predominantly minority populations, as high-risk areas. Financial institutions would then deny loans or insurance coverage to residents in these redlined neighborhoods based on their racial demographics or economic conditions. Redlining is widely recognized as a historical form of systemic discrimination, and it is important to distinguish it from broader terms like "discrimination" or "fair lending" because it specifically refers to this discriminatory practice.

106. B: The most appropriate action is to acknowledge the borrower's concern and explain the fee in detail. This allows the mortgage loan originator (MLO) to provide clarity and address any misunderstandings, ensuring that the borrower has a full understanding of the loan estimate and the associated fees. It also demonstrates professionalism and a commitment to resolving borrower concerns.

107. C: The primary focus of the Federal Trade Commission Red Flag rules is the detection and prevention of identity theft. These regulations necessitate specific businesses and entities, such as financial institutions and creditors, to create and execute identity theft prevention programs aimed at identifying "red flags."

108. B: The main focus of the Truth in Lending Act (TILA) is on consumer credit transactions. Mortgage loans require the provision of a Truth in Lending disclosure statement to ensure that borrowers are well-informed about their mortgage terms and costs.

109. B: Predatory lending involves unethical and exploitative tactics employed by lenders to coax borrowers into accepting high-cost loans characterized by unfavorable terms, often with exorbitant fees and interest rates. Such practices can expose borrowers to financial distress or even foreclosure. It is crucial to differentiate predatory lending from fair lending, as the former encompasses abusive practices that detrimentally affect borrowers, whereas the latter strives to guarantee unbiased access to credit, free from discrimination related to protected characteristics.

110. B: To find the monthly private mortgage insurance (PMI) cost, multiply the loan amount by the annual rate in decimal form (the annual rate divided by 100), then divide by 12.

$$\text{Monthly PMI cost} = \frac{\text{Loan amount} \times \text{Rate}}{12}$$

$$\frac{\$230,000 \times 0.0054}{12} = \$103.50$$

111. B: A kickback is an illegal practice where an individual or company receives a financial incentive or payment in exchange for referring clients to a specific business or service provider. This practice is generally considered unethical and illegal because it can lead to biased or unfair recommendations.

112. C: A power of attorney (POA) is a legal document that lets one person act on behalf of another. This document authorizes an individual, often called the "attorney-in-fact" or "agent," to make decisions, sign papers, and handle various tasks related to the deal. The POA is involved when the principal borrower can't be there in person for the transaction.

113. B: There is a mandatory 30-day waiting period before an individual can retake the SAFE MLO National Test after a failed attempt. However, it is essential to note that if an individual fails the test three times, the waiting period extends to 180 days. These waiting periods are in place to allow candidates adequate time for additional study and preparation between test attempts.

114. C: Table funding, where the lender directly provides funds at the loan closing, is done to streamline and expedite the process. It ensures a faster, more secure closing, reduces risk, and complies with regulations. This approach benefits both lenders and borrowers by simplifying the transaction and eliminating the need for fund coordination.

115. B: The Veterans Affairs (VA) mortgage program is specifically designed to assist eligible veterans and service members in obtaining home financing with favorable terms. This program offers benefits such as no down payment requirement and competitive interest rates, making homeownership more accessible to those who have served in the US military.

116. A: The Home Mortgage Disclosure Act (HMDA) mandates that lenders disclose detailed information regarding their mortgage lending operations to regulatory bodies, with the aim of fostering equitable lending practices and enhancing transparency within the mortgage industry.

117. C: Title insurance in a mortgage transaction primarily protects against undisclosed liens and title defects. When a property's title is transferred from one party to another, there is a risk of hidden issues such as unpaid liens, legal disputes over property ownership, or errors in public records. Title insurance ensures that the lender's investment is protected from these unforeseen problems, which could affect the borrower's ability to repay the mortgage loan. It provides financial coverage and legal support in case such issues arise, safeguarding the lender's interest in the property.

118. C: A title binder, often referred to simply as a binder, serves as a temporary insurance provision until the title search is finalized and the ultimate title insurance policy is issued. It functions as an interim safeguard typically extended by a title insurance company to shield the involved parties during the ongoing title search and examination process. While the binder is in effect, it guarantees a degree of insurance coverage for both the buyer and the lender, offering protection in case of unforeseen title issues or defects surfacing prior to the issuance of the ultimate title insurance policy. Following the completion of the title search and resolution of any identified problems, the final title insurance policy is issued, rendering the binder coverage unnecessary.

119. D: Subprime mortgages are mortgages linked to borrowers with lower credit scores or other risk factors that diminish their creditworthiness. Such loans typically carry elevated interest rates which serve as compensation to the lender for the increased risk of borrower default. Subprime mortgages may also feature adjustable-rate options, potentially yielding lower initial payments but posing higher risk in the event of rising interest rates. These loans are typically tailored to borrowers who may not qualify for prime or conventional mortgages due to their credit history or financial circumstances.

120. D: National origin is expressly forbidden as a basis for discrimination under the Equal Credit Opportunity Act (ECOA). Income (choice C) serves as an acceptable criterion for creditors to assess creditworthiness under the ECOA. Previous homeownership experience (choice A) and number of children (choice B) are not among the prohibited bases for discrimination under ECOA, but they are typically not used as direct factors for evaluating creditworthiness.

MLO Practice Tests #4 and #5

To take these additional MLO practice tests, visit our bonus page:
mometrix.com/bonus948/nmls

220

How to Overcome Test Anxiety

Just the thought of taking a test is enough to make most people a little nervous. A test is an important event that can have a long-term impact on your future, so it's important to take it seriously and it's natural to feel anxious about performing well. But just because anxiety is normal, that doesn't mean that it's helpful in test taking, or that you should simply accept it as part of your life. Anxiety can have a variety of effects. These effects can be mild, like making you feel slightly nervous, or severe, like blocking your ability to focus or remember even a simple detail.

If you experience test anxiety—whether severe or mild—it's important to know how to beat it. To discover this, first you need to understand what causes test anxiety.

Causes of Test Anxiety

While we often think of anxiety as an uncontrollable emotional state, it can actually be caused by simple, practical things. One of the most common causes of test anxiety is that a person does not feel adequately prepared for their test. This feeling can be the result of many different issues such as poor study habits or lack of organization, but the most common culprit is time management. Starting to study too late, failing to organize your study time to cover all of the material, or being distracted while you study will mean that you're not well prepared for the test. This may lead to cramming the night before, which will cause you to be physically and mentally exhausted for the test. Poor time management also contributes to feelings of stress, fear, and hopelessness as you realize you are not well prepared but don't know what to do about it.

Other times, test anxiety is not related to your preparation for the test but comes from unresolved fear. This may be a past failure on a test, or poor performance on tests in general. It may come from comparing yourself to others who seem to be performing better or from the stress of living up to expectations. Anxiety may be driven by fears of the future—how failure on this test would affect your educational and career goals. These fears are often completely irrational, but they can still negatively impact your test performance.

Elements of Test Anxiety

As mentioned earlier, test anxiety is considered to be an emotional state, but it has physical and mental components as well. Sometimes you may not even realize that you are suffering from test anxiety until you notice the physical symptoms. These can include trembling hands, rapid heartbeat, sweating, nausea, and tense muscles. Extreme anxiety may lead to fainting or vomiting. Obviously, any of these symptoms can have a negative impact on testing. It is important to recognize them as soon as they begin to occur so that you can address the problem before it damages your performance.

The mental components of test anxiety include trouble focusing and inability to remember learned information. During a test, your mind is on high alert, which can help you recall information and stay focused for an extended period of time. However, anxiety interferes with your mind's natural processes, causing you to blank out, even on the questions you know well. The strain of testing during anxiety makes it difficult to stay focused, especially on a test that may take several hours. Extreme anxiety can take a huge mental toll, making it difficult not only to recall test information but even to understand the test questions or pull your thoughts together.

221

Effects of Test Anxiety

Test anxiety is like a disease—if left untreated, it will get progressively worse. Anxiety leads to poor performance, and this reinforces the feelings of fear and failure, which in turn lead to poor performances on subsequent tests. It can grow from a mild nervousness to a crippling condition. If allowed to progress, test anxiety can have a big impact on your schooling, and consequently on your future.

Test anxiety can spread to other parts of your life. Anxiety on tests can become anxiety in any stressful situation, and blanking on a test can turn into panicking in a job situation. But fortunately, you don't have to let anxiety rule your testing and determine your grades. There are a number of relatively simple steps you can take to move past anxiety and function normally on a test and in the rest of life.

Physical Steps for Beating Test Anxiety

While test anxiety is a serious problem, the good news is that it can be overcome. It doesn't have to control your ability to think and remember information. While it may take time, you can begin taking steps today to beat anxiety.

Just as your first hint that you may be struggling with anxiety comes from the physical symptoms, the first step to treating it is also physical. Rest is crucial for having a clear, strong mind. If you are tired, it is much easier to give in to anxiety. But if you establish good sleep habits, your body and mind will be ready to perform optimally, without the strain of exhaustion. Additionally, sleeping well helps you to retain information better, so you're more likely to recall the answers when you see the test questions.

Getting good sleep means more than going to bed on time. It's important to allow your brain time to relax. Take study breaks from time to time so it doesn't get overworked, and don't study right before bed. Take time to rest your mind before trying to rest your body, or you may find it difficult to fall asleep.

Along with sleep, other aspects of physical health are important in preparing for a test. Good nutrition is vital for good brain function. Sugary foods and drinks may give a burst of energy but this burst is followed by a crash, both physically and emotionally. Instead, fuel your body with protein and vitamin-rich foods.

Also, drink plenty of water. Dehydration can lead to headaches and exhaustion, especially if your brain is already under stress from the rigors of the test. Particularly if your test is a long one, drink water during the breaks. And if possible, take an energy-boosting snack to eat between sections.

Along with sleep and diet, a third important part of physical health is exercise. Maintaining a steady workout schedule is helpful, but even taking 5-minute study breaks to walk can help get your blood pumping faster and clear your head. Exercise also releases endorphins, which contribute to a positive feeling and can help combat test anxiety.

When you nurture your physical health, you are also contributing to your mental health. If your body is healthy, your mind is much more likely to be healthy as well. So take time to rest, nourish your body with healthy food and water, and get moving as much as possible. Taking these physical steps will make you stronger and more able to take the mental steps necessary to overcome test anxiety.

Mental Steps for Beating Test Anxiety

Working on the mental side of test anxiety can be more challenging, but as with the physical side, there are clear steps you can take to overcome it. As mentioned earlier, test anxiety often stems from lack of preparation, so the obvious solution is to prepare for the test. Effective studying may be the most important weapon you have for beating test anxiety, but you can and should employ several other mental tools to combat fear.

First, boost your confidence by reminding yourself of past success—tests or projects that you aced. If you're putting as much effort into preparing for this test as you did for those, there's no reason you should expect to fail here. Work hard to prepare; then trust your preparation.

Second, surround yourself with encouraging people. It can be helpful to find a study group, but be sure that the people you're around will encourage a positive attitude. If you spend time with others who are anxious or cynical, this will only contribute to your own anxiety. Look for others who are motivated to study hard from a desire to succeed, not from a fear of failure.

Third, reward yourself. A test is physically and mentally tiring, even without anxiety, and it can be helpful to have something to look forward to. Plan an activity following the test, regardless of the outcome, such as going to a movie or getting ice cream.

When you are taking the test, if you find yourself beginning to feel anxious, remind yourself that you know the material. Visualize successfully completing the test. Then take a few deep, relaxing breaths and return to it. Work through the questions carefully but with confidence, knowing that you are capable of succeeding.

Developing a healthy mental approach to test taking will also aid in other areas of life. Test anxiety affects more than just the actual test—it can be damaging to your mental health and even contribute to depression. It's important to beat test anxiety before it becomes a problem for more than testing.

Study Strategy

Being prepared for the test is necessary to combat anxiety, but what does being prepared look like? You may study for hours on end and still not feel prepared. What you need is a strategy for test prep. The next few pages outline our recommended steps to help you plan out and conquer the challenge of preparation.

STEP 1: SCOPE OUT THE TEST

Learn everything you can about the format (multiple choice, essay, etc.) and what will be on the test. Gather any study materials, course outlines, or sample exams that may be available. Not only will this help you to prepare, but knowing what to expect can help to alleviate test anxiety.

STEP 2: MAP OUT THE MATERIAL

Look through the textbook or study guide and make note of how many chapters or sections it has. Then divide these over the time you have. For example, if a book has 15 chapters and you have five days to study, you need to cover three chapters each day. Even better, if you have the time, leave an extra day at the end for overall review after you have gone through the material in depth.

If time is limited, you may need to prioritize the material. Look through it and make note of which sections you think you already have a good grasp on, and which need review. While you are studying, skim quickly through the familiar sections and take more time on the challenging parts.

Write out your plan so you don't get lost as you go. Having a written plan also helps you feel more in control of the study, so anxiety is less likely to arise from feeling overwhelmed at the amount to cover.

STEP 3: GATHER YOUR TOOLS

Decide what study method works best for you. Do you prefer to highlight in the book as you study and then go back over the highlighted portions? Or do you type out notes of the important information? Or is it helpful to make flashcards that you can carry with you? Assemble the pens, index cards, highlighters, post-it notes, and any other materials you may need so you won't be distracted by getting up to find things while you study.

If you're having a hard time retaining the information or organizing your notes, experiment with different methods. For example, try color-coding by subject with colored pens, highlighters, or post-it notes. If you learn better by hearing, try recording yourself reading your notes so you can listen while in the car, working out, or simply sitting at your desk. Ask a friend to quiz you from your flashcards, or try teaching someone the material to solidify it in your mind.

STEP 4: CREATE YOUR ENVIRONMENT

It's important to avoid distractions while you study. This includes both the obvious distractions like visitors and the subtle distractions like an uncomfortable chair (or a too-comfortable couch that makes you want to fall asleep). Set up the best study environment possible: good lighting and a comfortable work area. If background music helps you focus, you may want to turn it on, but otherwise keep the room quiet. If you are using a computer to take notes, be sure you don't have any other windows open, especially applications like social media, games, or anything else that could distract you. Silence your phone and turn off notifications. Be sure to keep water close by so you stay hydrated while you study (but avoid unhealthy drinks and snacks).

Also, take into account the best time of day to study. Are you freshest first thing in the morning? Try to set aside some time then to work through the material. Is your mind clearer in the afternoon or evening? Schedule your study session then. Another method is to study at the same time of day that you will take the test, so that your brain gets used to working on the material at that time and will be ready to focus at test time.

STEP 5: STUDY!

Once you have done all the study preparation, it's time to settle into the actual studying. Sit down, take a few moments to settle your mind so you can focus, and begin to follow your study plan. Don't give in to distractions or let yourself procrastinate. This is your time to prepare so you'll be ready to fearlessly approach the test. Make the most of the time and stay focused.

Of course, you don't want to burn out. If you study too long you may find that you're not retaining the information very well. Take regular study breaks. For example, taking five minutes out of every hour to walk briskly, breathing deeply and swinging your arms, can help your mind stay fresh.

As you get to the end of each chapter or section, it's a good idea to do a quick review. Remind yourself of what you learned and work on any difficult parts. When you feel that you've mastered the material, move on to the next part. At the end of your study session, briefly skim through your notes again.

But while review is helpful, cramming last minute is NOT. If at all possible, work ahead so that you won't need to fit all your study into the last day. Cramming overloads your brain with more information than it can process and retain, and your tired mind may struggle to recall even previously learned information when it is overwhelmed with last-minute study. Also, the urgent nature of cramming and the stress placed on your brain contribute to anxiety. You'll be more likely to go to the test feeling unprepared and having trouble thinking clearly.

So don't cram, and don't stay up late before the test, even just to review your notes at a leisurely pace. Your brain needs rest more than it needs to go over the information again. In fact, plan to finish your studies by noon or early afternoon the day before the test. Give your brain the rest of the day to relax or focus on other things, and get a good night's sleep. Then you will be fresh for the test and better able to recall what you've studied.

STEP 6: TAKE A PRACTICE TEST

Many courses offer sample tests, either online or in the study materials. This is an excellent resource to check whether you have mastered the material, as well as to prepare for the test format and environment.

Check the test format ahead of time: the number of questions, the type (multiple choice, free response, etc.), and the time limit. Then create a plan for working through them. For example, if you have 30 minutes to take a 60-question test, your limit is 30 seconds per question. Spend less time on the questions you know well so that you can take more time on the difficult ones.

If you have time to take several practice tests, take the first one open book, with no time limit. Work through the questions at your own pace and make sure you fully understand them. Gradually work up to taking a test under test conditions: sit at a desk with all study materials put away and set a timer. Pace yourself to make sure you finish the test with time to spare and go back to check your answers if you have time.

After each test, check your answers. On the questions you missed, be sure you understand why you missed them. Did you misread the question (tests can use tricky wording)? Did you forget the information? Or was it something you hadn't learned? Go back and study any shaky areas that the practice tests reveal.

Taking these tests not only helps with your grade, but also aids in combating test anxiety. If you're already used to the test conditions, you're less likely to worry about it, and working through tests until you're scoring well gives you a confidence boost. Go through the practice tests until you feel comfortable, and then you can go into the test knowing that you're ready for it.

Test Tips

On test day, you should be confident, knowing that you've prepared well and are ready to answer the questions. But aside from preparation, there are several test day strategies you can employ to maximize your performance.

First, as stated before, get a good night's sleep the night before the test (and for several nights before that, if possible). Go into the test with a fresh, alert mind rather than staying up late to study.

Try not to change too much about your normal routine on the day of the test. It's important to eat a nutritious breakfast, but if you normally don't eat breakfast at all, consider eating just a protein bar. If you're a coffee drinker, go ahead and have your normal coffee. Just make sure you time it so that the caffeine doesn't wear off right in the middle of your test. Avoid sugary beverages, and drink enough water to stay hydrated but not so much that you need a restroom break 10 minutes into the test. If your test isn't first thing in the morning, consider going for a walk or doing a light workout before the test to get your blood flowing.

Allow yourself enough time to get ready, and leave for the test with plenty of time to spare so you won't have the anxiety of scrambling to arrive in time. Another reason to be early is to select a good seat. It's helpful to sit away from doors and windows, which can be distracting. Find a good seat, get out your supplies, and settle your mind before the test begins.

When the test begins, start by going over the instructions carefully, even if you already know what to expect. Make sure you avoid any careless mistakes by following the directions.

Then begin working through the questions, pacing yourself as you've practiced. If you're not sure on an answer, don't spend too much time on it, and don't let it shake your confidence. Either skip it and come back later, or eliminate as many wrong answers as possible and guess among the remaining ones. Don't dwell on these questions as you continue—put them out of your mind and focus on what lies ahead.

Be sure to read all of the answer choices, even if you're sure the first one is the right answer. Sometimes you'll find a better one if you keep reading. But don't second-guess yourself if you do immediately know the answer. Your gut instinct is usually right. Don't let test anxiety rob you of the information you know.

If you have time at the end of the test (and if the test format allows), go back and review your answers. Be cautious about changing any, since your first instinct tends to be correct, but make sure you didn't misread any of the questions or accidentally mark the wrong answer choice. Look over any you skipped and make an educated guess.

At the end, leave the test feeling confident. You've done your best, so don't waste time worrying about your performance or wishing you could change anything. Instead, celebrate the successful completion of this test. And finally, use this test to learn how to deal with anxiety even better next time.

Review Video: Test Anxiety
Visit mometrix.com/academy and enter code: 100340

Important Qualification

Not all anxiety is created equal. If your test anxiety is causing major issues in your life beyond the classroom or testing center, or if you are experiencing troubling physical symptoms related to your anxiety, it may be a sign of a serious physiological or psychological condition. If this sounds like your situation, we strongly encourage you to seek professional help.

Additional Bonus Material

Due to our efforts to try to keep this book to a manageable length, we've created a link that will give you access to all of your additional bonus material:

mometrix.com/bonus948/nmls

Made in United States
Orlando, FL
28 October 2024